THE BILLION DOLLAR APP

THE BILLION DOLLAR APP

ANUJ MAHAJAN

NDP

NEW DEGREE PRESS

COPYRIGHT © 2021 ANUJ MAHAJAN

THE BILLION DOLLAR APP

ISBN	978-1-63676-317-0	*Paperback*
	978-1-63676-316-3	*Kindle Ebook*
	978-1-63676-318-7	*Ebook*

To my Mom and Dad,
Family, friends, and mentors
Who've helped me write this book
Despite the difficulties of the pandemic.

CONTENTS

FOREWORD

There's a war going on in your smartphone.

It is a war not for land or oil, but for your attention and your money. Yes, we're talking about mobile apps, the programs that have become synonymous with our digital identities. And it seems they've taken over every aspect of our lives, from finances to dating to transportation to entertainment, and, well, you get the point.

Making an app these days isn't all that hard (given some technical chops or access to a competent developer). No, the real challenge now is getting relevant and staying relevant.

There are already millions of apps competing in this crowded market! And this simple fact begs the question: Why do a select few of them stand out?

That's why we've written this book: To find exactly what it is about apps such as WhatsApp, Instagram, and Duolingo that gets them millions of users, year after year. We deep-dive into the success stories of such billion-dollar apps (as well as many apps with billion-dollar potential) and find what separates them from the apps that have fallen off our radars. And then, we combine this anecdotal evidence with industry-leading research and insights from trusted field experts, renowned innovators, and best-selling psychologists.

Together with this elite company, we uncover the hidden side of the apps that have cemented themselves on our home screens and in our lives.

Note that our primary focus here is the user perspective. In other words: You'll read about it here, then open your phone and see, *Oh! That's why they did X and Y!* And so, while our book delves into topics like interface design, consumer behavior, and pricing models, we leave the technical engineering elements to the experts. We also try to keep it as mobile-app-specific as possible, meaning we don't harp too much on broader startup strategy and business development. (Though we have no shortage of recommendations for interested readers!) So, while a company like Yelp started as a website and then expanded to a mobile app, we'll be solely concerning ourselves with the merits of the latter.

Overall, our hope here is simple: To shed some light on the meteoric rise of mobile apps and help you see what's really going on in that little device in your pocket.

Let's dig in!

FOREWORD

There's a war going on in your smartphone.

It is a war not for land or oil, but for your attention and your money. Yes, we're talking about mobile apps, the programs that have become synonymous with our digital identities. And it seems they've taken over every aspect of our lives, from finances to dating to transportation to entertainment, and, well, you get the point.

Making an app these days isn't all that hard (given some technical chops or access to a competent developer). No, the real challenge now is getting relevant and staying relevant.

There are already millions of apps competing in this crowded market! And this simple fact begs the question: Why do a select few of them stand out?

That's why we've written this book: To find exactly what it is about apps such as WhatsApp, Instagram, and Duolingo that gets them millions of users, year after year. We deep-dive into the success stories of such billion-dollar apps (as well as many apps with billion-dollar potential) and find what separates them from the apps that have fallen off our radars. And then, we combine this anecdotal evidence with industry-leading research and insights from trusted field experts, renowned innovators, and best-selling psychologists.

Together with this elite company, we uncover the hidden side of the apps that have cemented themselves on our home screens and in our lives.

Note that our primary focus here is the user perspective. In other words: You'll read about it here, then open your phone and see, *Oh! That's why they did X and Y!* And so, while our book delves into topics like interface design, consumer behavior, and pricing models, we leave the technical engineering elements to the experts. We also try to keep it as mobile-app-specific as possible, meaning we don't harp too much on broader startup strategy and business development. (Though we have no shortage of recommendations for interested readers!) So, while a company like Yelp started as a website and then expanded to a mobile app, we'll be solely concerning ourselves with the merits of the latter.

Overall, our hope here is simple: To shed some light on the meteoric rise of mobile apps and help you see what's really going on in that little device in your pocket.

Let's dig in!

PART I

CHAPTER 1

A TIKTOK STORY |
THE POTENTIAL OF
MOBILE APPS

The year is 2020. The topic is mobile apps. And we're starting with an app that's burst onto the scene in unprecedented ways: TikTok.

Yes, *that* TikTok—the trendy viral video-sharing platform that's captivated Gen Z with its instant meme culture and quirky content. It's also the very same TikTok that's dominated international discourse thanks to privacy concerns, proposed bans, and lawsuits against the White House!

So, let's not underestimate it. After all, how many apps have lofted unknown rappers to the number one spot on *Billboard*'s Hot 100? How many apps have generated their own unique language of humor? How many apps have crashed onto the all-time download leaderboards?

Actually, let's answer that last one.[1]

Top 10 Apps by All-Time Download
Worldwide | 2010 - 2019F

Rank	Apps		Parent Company	HQ
1		Facebook	Facebook	United States
2		Facebook Messenger	Facebook	United States
3		WhatsApp Messenger	Facebook	United States
4		Instagram	Facebook	United States
5		Snapchat	Snap	United States
6		Skype	Microsoft	United States
7		TikTok	ByteDance	China
8		UC Browser	Alibaba Group	China
9		Youtube	Google	United States
10		Twitter	Twitter	United States

*Note: Combined iOS and Google Play data begins in January 2012.
Data through December 31, 2011 includes iOS data only;
2019F based on January to November data*

Yeah, TikTok is *that* popular. Two plus billion downloads, despite only hitting the scene in late 2016.[2] Today, its brand name is quickly entering the American lexicon alongside your Ubers and Skypes.

The gist of the platform is this: You create and watch short-form videos with audio, often incorporating dancing, lip-syncing, or silly sketch bits. Others can then react to or even build off your content, cultivating what the app calls an *exciting, spontaneous, and genuine* atmosphere.

---

1   "A Look Back at the Top Apps and Games of the Decade," AppAnnie, December 16, 2019.

2   Craig Chapple, TikTok Crosses 2 Billion Downloads After Best Quarter for Any App Ever," Sensor Tower, April 29, 2020.

We will get into the other pertinent details, but, for the time being, it really is that simple. And yet, in a few short years, it has launched its parent company ByteDance up to an approximate $140 billion net worth.[3] Big names like Instagram, Facebook, and YouTube are all working on competitive products to take a bite of this market share.

Somehow, someway, Zhang Yiming, the billionaire founder behind ByteDance and TikTok, has tapped into something that's resonated with users, at least for now. How did they emerge from a dense sea of aspiring apps? And what can they do to stay afloat?

STARTING WITH *THE GOOD*: HOW TIKTOK HAS FOUND SUCCESS?

On the surface, TikTok may look a lot like its video-centric predecessors. Remember Vine? That short video social platform from a few years back?

If you don't, it's because Vine notoriously burned out with a shortsighted business plan. TikTok, on the other hand, has gone the extra mile to win over users and secure profits. Here's how:

IT KNOWS HOW TO BRING EVERYONE TOGETHER

Based primarily in music, dance, and humor, TikTok crosses cultures and languages with an ease that most social apps

---

3   Echo Wang, Kane Wu, and Julie Zhu, "Exclusive: ByteDance Investors Value TikTok at $50 Billion in Takeover Bid - Sources," *Reuters*, July 29, 2020.

simply can't enjoy. And the developers have played into this sense of community, enabling a degree of interaction and content aggregation that Vine never did.

What you end up with are the app's Duet and React features, which let users engage in playful back-and-forths. These seemingly minor details go a long way in establishing your app's purpose (see Chapter 3).

IT MAKES THINGS PERSONAL. IN A GOOD WAY

TikTok's AI algorithms examine your content viewed and hashtags used to customize your feeds with tailor-made suggestions. Unlike other social media websites where you have to like and follow topics, TikTok does so in an expertly nonintrusive fashion. As *The New Yorker's* Jia Tolentino so eloquently puts it:[4]

> "Some social algorithms are like bossy waiters: they solicit your preferences and then recommend a menu. TikTok orders you dinner by watching you look at food."

The never-ending cycle of collecting user data and refining recommendation algorithms—that's ByteDance's bread and butter. And we'll dig into the main course in Chapter 6.

---

4   Jia Tolentino, "How TikTok Holds Our Attention," *The New Yorker*, September 23, 2019.

IT'S EASY AS PIE AND FULL OF FLAVOR

Finding snippets of your favorite songs takes just a few seconds. Recreating any dance challenge video is a breeze. The whole platform, for that matter, is incredibly intuitive, bottling down the complexities of video creation into a casual pastime. All *you* need to bring are killer dance moves.

That said, easy-to-use doesn't mean bare bones. TikTok is full of features that Vine lacked: Visual filters, sound effects, longer recording options, etc.... combined with the interface's simplicity, this versatility offers a transformative Interaction Design (IxD)—something we'll further explore in Chapter 5.

IT GETS ITS AUDIENCE. AND HOW TO SPEAK TO THEM

We already have highly political Twitter and fake news Facebook. We already have YouTube, dominated by established names and advertisers.

Now we have *simple, goofy, irreverent* TikTok, according to *TechCrunch*.[5] *The New York Times* calls it "the only truly pleasant social network in existence."[6] Free of news and full of supportive, jovial spirit, TikTok empathizes with the needs and wants of its overwhelming Gen Z audience (more on this in Chapter 4).

Not only does the app understand its users, but it also effectively communicates its value to them (see Chapter 10).

---

5   Sarah Perez, "It's time to pay serious attention to TikTok," *TechCrunch*, January 29, 2019.

6   Kevin Roose, "TikTok, a Chinese Video App, Brings Fun Back to Social Media," *The New York Times*, December 3, 2018.

For instance, famous TikTokers can and often make serious money by partnering with advertising companies. It's also recruited hip celebs from Cardi B to Jimmy Fallon to creatively use and promote the app.[7]

As mentioned, TikTok even helped previously unknown Lil Nas X reach number one on the *Billboard* Hot 100.[8] And that right there underlines the app's appeal: Anyone can get big here—even a kid in his living room.

IT BRINGS MONEY IN WITHOUT DRIVING USERS OUT

Estimates vary, but it's safe to say that TikTok generated upward of $50 million in revenue in 2019 Q4 alone.[9]

That's partially thanks to its in-app currency: Special coins with which users can buy digital gifts for their favorite creators (discussed further in Chapter 9).[10] More credit, though, probably lies with advertising. While TikTok initially avoided ads to be more user friendly, it now has a variety of ad formats that brands pay up to $150,000 per day.[11]

---

7   Michael Saponara, "Cardi B Challenges Offset to a Rap Battle, Loser Buys Christmas Decorations for Their Homes," *Billboard*, November 28, 2020; Todd Spangler, "TikTok App Nears 80 Million US Downloads, Lands Jimmy Fallon as Fan," *Variety*, November 20, 2018.

8   Todd Spangler, "TikTok App Nears 80 Million US Downloads," *Variety*.

9   Alex Wilhelm, "TikTok's revenue said to skyrocket over 300% in Q4," *TechCrunch*, January 3, 2020.

10 Arch, "How Do TikTok Gifts Work," Techjunkie, October 14, 2020.

11 Wiktoria Marszałek, "How To Use Short-Video App, Douyin, For Your China Marketing," Nanjing Marketing Group, June 13, 2018.

We'll circle back to monetizing in a way that complements the app experience in Chapter 7 (which, spoiler alert, starts by peering deeper into Vine's failures. Sorry, Vine.)

THE BIG PICTURE: THE APP INDUSTRY IS RIFE WITH OPPORTUNITY

As trivial as its content may be, TikTok works. It's built an impressive user base and revenue stream. And it's as representative as any current brand of the potential that apps presently hold.

If you can tap into cultural desires, fix a genuine problem, and create something of value…If you can design a seamless interface with a compelling monetization model…If you can nail the framework this book outlines, you stand to follow TikTok up the rankings.

And if you do, you'll find that a gold mine awaits. In fact, here's why so many developers are trying their luck with a virtual pickaxe:

1. LET'S REITERATE—THE APP INDUSTRY IS A GOLD MINE

We're currently north of 3.5 billion smartphone users. That's roughly 45 percent of our global population sitting one tap away from their respective app stores.[12] And truth be told, these numbers are likely to be even greater considering all the unaccounted revenue from third-party app stores in China.

---

12 "Worldometer—Real Time World Statistics," accessed November 4, 2020.

In 2019, apps were downloaded over 200 billion times, translating to over $80 billion in consumer spending—a number that will more than double by 2024:[13]

Global App Store and Google Play Spending 2019-2024

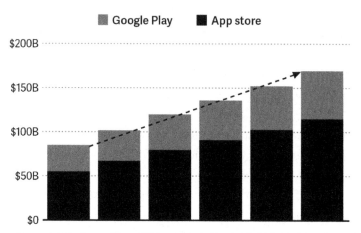

Does not refflect spending on third-party Android stores in China and elsewhere
Source: Sensor Tower Store Intelligence

And that's still only half the picture! Another $190 billion or so came from the advertisers' side in 2019 (early forecasts have this jumping past $250 billion soon after 2020).[14] Needless to say, the train is moving full steam ahead. The only better time to hop on would've been yesterday.

13   Lexi Sydow, "The State of Mobile in 2020: The Key Stats You Need to Know," AppAnnie, January 15, 2020; Randy Nelson, "5-Year Market Forecast: App Spending Will Double to $171 Billion by 2024 Despite COVID-19," Sensor Tower, April 1, 2020.

14   Lexi Sydow, "The State of Mobile in 2020," AppAnnie.

2. ALL SIGNS POINT TO MOBILE

In just ten years, apps have firmly integrated themselves into the rhythms of our day-to-day. So much so that mobile has finally—and historically!—beaten out television in terms of time consumption (at least in the US):[15]

TV and Mobile Devices: Average Time Spent in the US, 2014-2021
hrs:mins per day among population

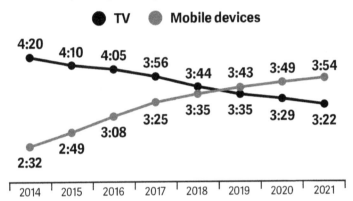

*Note: ages 18+; time spent with each medium includes all time spent with that medium, regardless of multitasking; for example, 1 hour of multitasking on desktop/laptop while watching TV is counted as 1 hour for TV and 1 hour for desktop/laptop; *excludes digital*
Source: eMarketer, April 2019

The TV will likely long remain a staple of consumerist culture, but it'll never compete with the convenience or multi-capability of smartphones.

---

15   Amy He, "US Adults Are Spending More Time on Mobile Than They Do Watching TV - EMarketer Trends, Forecasts & Statistics," eMarketer, Jun 4, 2019.

Consider that the average American uses almost forty mobile apps each month.[16] Sure, the TV can entertain, but can it help you pay your bills, track your diet, or read *The New Yorker*? Can it give you 24/7 connectivity to social messaging apps and location-based services no matter where you are?

No, only mobile apps hold that distinction. And they deliver at unprecedented speeds (often without needing an internet connection).

3. APPS INVITE MORE CONVERSATION

"When your business is missing a mobile application or even a website adapted for mobile, you are excluding a large group of potential customers."—Netguru's Android developer Mariusz Karwowski, in an interview with *Business News Daily*.[17]

Karwowski highlights one of the greatest advantages of mobile apps: Capturing new, different, or otherwise unattainable segments of the economy. TikTok is a prime example. Never has it been easier to mass connect with (and let's call it like it is, profit off) Gen Zers. Nor has it ever been easier to amass a global reach.

For now, suffice it to say, no matter the demographic, prospects will always prefer to shoot you a tweet, Facebook message, or Instagram DM over a phone call.

---

16 "The Average Smartphone User Accessed Close to 40 Apps per Month in 2017," AppAnnie, February 2, 2020.

17 Joshua Stowers, "A Guide to Developing a Mobile App for Business," *Business News Daily* (business.com), December 23, 2019.

4. AND THEY LET YOU KEEP THOSE CONVERSATIONS GOING

Apps aren't just great for reaching new users; they're also a powerful vehicle for developing existing relationships.

For these customers, there's no better way to offer premium support. If they have issues, you can bet they'll be more willing to open your app than to fill out some clunky online submission form or, god forbid, hop on a call. Again, it comes back to empathizing with their preferences.

On top of that, apps offer a more convenient line of reengaging your users with sales or marketing initiatives. Instead of hoping they come across your ads or open your direct mail, you can streamline some custom promotion right into their pockets. As it faces less distraction than your average web browser, mobile tends to deliver higher conversion rates.

Better messaging is a competitive advantage. Now, if only you could continue systematically building on this advantage.

5. USER DATA: THERE'S NO BETTER WAY TO GATHER OR IMPLEMENT IT

The longer we have them, the more our mobile devices reflect our identity. Banking info, social accounts, audio playlists— in a way, they're all part of what makes us unique.

The rich behavioral insights that apps obtain are both fascinating and, at times, alarming. We tackle the ethics and recent legal developments pertaining to personal info in Chapter 8.

But when not compromising our data, companies can use it to shape their apps in groundbreaking, user-serving ways. By collecting and measuring user analytics, developers can refine software performance and cultivate personalized experiences. And it's a win-win. Businesses can similarly fine-tune marketing efforts to guarantee greater monetary returns.

(Lots more coming on utilizing data to innovate and iterate in Chapter 11.)

6. MOBILE APPS CAN BE CAPTIVATING GOODIE BAGS
Loyalty programs, redeemable points, exclusive deals, etc.

To set up these incentives, more and more brands are turning to apps instead of those plastic loyalty cards that fill up everyone's wallet.

Unlike cards, apps can offer strategically timed promotions when users are near physical locations. And unlike cards, apps can shoot users visible notifications when such occasions arise.

Shoppers are rewarding these forward-thinking brands, with over 70 percent more likely to participate in a loyalty program if the gifts are easily redeemable from their smartphones.[18]

And while mobile loyalty programs aren't perfect (deals can be irrelevant; notifications can be annoying), they can be

---

18   "CodeBroker 2017 Shopper Loyalty Survey Results," Codebroker, accessed November 4, 2020.

instrumental for enticing repeat purchases. For evidence, just take a look at how seamlessly the Starbucks app sets up rewards and virtual payments.

7. AND THE MOST POTENT FORM OF MARKETING

For just a minute, let's put aside our users and focus on you: The app creator—the brand.

Even if you haven't opened your app since who-knows-when, your mere presence on someone's home screen is free exposure. Every time they see your logo, you build brand recognition and slowly chip away at their hesitancy. This is why *impressions* are such a valued marketing metric. They're a psychological investment for future sales.

Apps make particularly strong impressions because there's minimal distance between brand and user. People don't have to type in a URL. They don't have to drive by your store. They simply unlock their phones and see the brand image you put forth.

The look, the feel, the experience of your app—all of it directly impacts your reputation. And, ideally, you'll cultivate a unique brand image that's consistent across your mobile app, web presence, and physical stores (if any).

NOW, *THE BAD* AND *THE UGLY*: WHY TIKTOK MIGHT FAIL

So far, so good, right? Money's growing on trees, and the future is all roses.

And yet, we wouldn't have a whole book ahead of us if it were that simple. Navigating the intricate world of app development requires overcoming untold hurdles.

In fact, let's bring TikTok back into the mix. Even this great success story—this culture-shifting, smiley-face meme factory—has its laundry list of shortcomings.

We'll give it credit for largely dodging the bullet of bullying scandals that youth-targeted social apps often encounter. Don't you worry; We'll get to Yik Yak's spectacular flameout in Chapter 4. But TikTok has still had to face these unfortunate headlines:

IS TIKTOK A THREAT TO YOUNG USERS' PRIVACY?

One South China Morning Post (SCMP) article gained international traction for detailing the myriad ways that children were unwittingly leaking their personal info.[19] There's no magic filter to prevent names or addresses from being displayed on public videos, or to stop nefarious adults from sending these users solicitous messages.

Some even accuse the app of enabling a degree of sexual exploitation, particularly evident when older men perform duet videos of teenage girls.[20] You don't have to be well-versed in TikTok lingo to imagine that it gets creepy.

---

19 Karen Zhang, "Hong Kong Children Expose Their Identities, Thoughts and Flesh to Millions of Strangers on Popular iPhone App TikTok, Post Finds," *South China Morning Post*, May 19, 2018.

20 Marco Silva, "Video App TikTok Fails to Remove Online Predators," *BBC News*, April 5, 2019.

And TikTok itself isn't immune to privacy offenses. In 2019, the app incurred a $5.7 million fine from the Federal Trade Commission for its failure to enforce the lower age limit of thirteen years for user data collection.[21]

IS TIKTOK IN CAHOOTS WITH CHINA?

With Chinese roots, it's impossible not to worry whether all that user data is making its way into the wrong hands with more dangerous consequences than popularizing 'Old Town Road.'

It also begs the question of China's influence on the app. Which, TikTok maintains, is nonexistent, as the app's moderators are based externally.

That said, distrust of China has pushed countries such as Bangladesh, Indonesia, Armenia, and Pakistan to seek outright bans on the app.[22] In June 2020, India even banned TikTok and 223 other Chinese apps after a border clash with China.[23] Similar cyber-security concerns have been much publicized in the United States. The Trump administration signed executive orders to ban the app unless a *very*

---

21 "Video Social Networking App Musical.Ly Agrees to Settle FTC Allegations That It Violated Children's Privacy Law," Federal Trade Commission, February 27, 2019.

22 "Mustafa Jabbar: TikTok Shut down," *Dhaka Tribune*, February 18, 2019; Ayu Purwaningsih, "Indonesia Blocks 'pornographic' TikTok App," *DW Akademie*, July 5, 2020; "TikTok Fails Operating in Armenia," *Armenpress*, October 1, 2020; "Pakistan bans TikTok over 'immoral' content,'" *CNBC*, October 9, 2020.

23 Rishi Iyengar, "This Is What It's Like When a Country Actually Bans TikTok," *CNN*, August 13, 2020.

American company purchased it first. In response, TikTok execs went so far as to sue the Trump administration for unfair anti-China rhetoric.[24]

There have also been concerns that TikTok banned accounts of users who spoke out against China's mistreatment of Uighur Muslims.[25] *The Guardian* also notably published suspicions of censorship during Hong Kong's democratic rallies. As jarring footage of the protests circulated worldwide, a curious lack of related TikTok content pointed directly to China's involvement.[26]

IS TIKTOK PROMOTING #FAKENEWS?

Unsurprisingly, as this social media platform has gained traction, so too has it enabled sources of misinformation. And at the scale of one hundred million monthly active users, cracking down on this misinformation is like playing an unwinnable game of Whack-a-Mole.[27]

Even with rigid account-banning policies and a feature that lets users report content, misleading posts about the coronavirus or the elections can easily get millions of views in the

---

24 Ana Swanson and Mike Isaac, "Trump Says Microsoft Can Bid for TikTok," *The New York Times*, updated August 26, 2020; Echo Wang and Jonathan Stempel, "TikTok Sues Trump Administration over US Ban, Calls It an Election Ploy," *Reuters*, August 24, 2020.

25 Rory Cellan-Jones, "Tech Tent: TikTok and the Uighur Muslims," *BBC News*, November 29, 2019.

26 Alex Hern, "Revealed: how TikTok censors videos that do not please Beijing," *The Guardian*, September 25, 2019.

27 Alex Sherman, "TikTok Reveals US, Global User Growth Numbers for First Time," *CNBC*, August 24, 2020.

blink of an eye.[28] And if TikTok does act in time to remove a post or disable an account, they only add fuel to the fire of those posting conspiracy theories and hate speech. To them, TikTok becomes just another one of the evil corporations coming after their truth.

Plus, such action sends TikTok execs wandering down a murky rabbit hole of censorship ethics and corporate responsibility—a far cry from the app's lighthearted surface level.

HAS TIKTOK ALREADY REACHED ITS PEAK INTEREST?

We've praised the app for connecting with the youngest generation of smartphone users. But this could also be its downfall.

An inability to massively grow its audience beyond Gen Z may eventually spell disaster. If this generation of teens quickly grows out of it and the next generation jumps to the next fad, what then?

Particularly troubling is the app's poor long-term retention rates. Lots of people download the app to see what the buzz is about, but according to *The Verge*, very few stick around past the first month.[29]

---

28 Bobby Allyn, "TikTok Tightens Crackdown On QAnon, Will Ban Accounts That Promote Disinformation," *NPR*, October 18, 2020.

29 Casey Newton, "How TikTok Could Fail," *The Verge*, August 7, 2019.

WILL TIKTOK BE ABLE TO SUSTAINABLY CASH IN?

Things are looking steady for now, but TikTok is still very much a *wild west* in that it hasn't come close to capitalizing on its potential—particularly with regard to monetizing ad space and brand exposure.

This could be a glass-half-full: There's more room for growth! But there's also the glass-half-empty perspective: What if bringing more ads hurts the experience? What if the main avenue for profit is also the trigger that sends young users away? Can TikTok monetize in a way that preserves its *simple, goofy, irreverent* vibe?[30]

APPS CAN BE A GOLD MINE; THEY CAN ALSO BE A MINEFIELD

Which brings up this reality: As lucrative as the future of apps undoubtedly is, tapping into it is no cakewalk.

We've touched on some of the question marks that TikTok currently faces, but TikTok is already a sizable success. For aspiring app developers, there's a wide, seven-lane highway of roadblocks they might encounter. Before joining them, consider some facts:

1. THIS IS THE MOST COMPETITIVE GAME YOU CAN PLAY

In 2008, Apple's App Store had 500 apps.[31] Their early marketing tagline *There's an app for that!* probably better applies

---

30 Sarah Perez, TikTok, *TechCrunch*.
31 "The App Store Turns 10," Apple, July 5, 2018.

now that their app count is a shade above 1.7 million.[32] Over at Google, they've got over 3.2 million apps, adding some 3,500 on a daily basis.[33] And we're not even touching the app marketplaces at Amazon or Microsoft here.

That's your competition. And, unfortunately, it's a winner-take-all market: The top 200 apps account for 70 percent of all app usage, and the higher up you get, the more competitive the battlefield:[34]

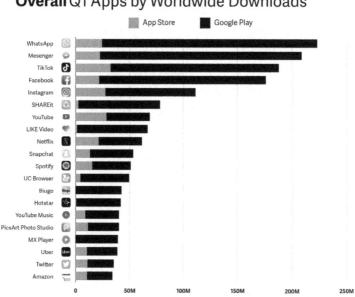

Overall Q1 Apps by Worldwide Downloads

32 Doug Gross, "Apple Trademarks 'There's an App for That,'" CNN, October 12, 2010; "Google Play vs. the IOS App Store | Store Stats for Mobile Apps," 42matters, updated November 4, 2020.

33 "Store Stats for Mobile Apps," 42matters.

34 "So Many Apps, So Much More Time for Entertainment," Nielsen, June 11, 2015; Jonathan Briskman, "Top Apps Worldwide for Q1 2019 by Downloads," Sensor Tower, May 15, 2019.

... "Competitive" is an understatement.

2. MOST APP DEVELOPERS ARE STUCK ON RAMEN AND CANNED SOUP

In 2014, Developer Economics released a report based on a study of over 10,000 app developers from all over the world. Its findings weren't particularly encouraging.

Somewhere in the ballpark of 60 percent of apps were under what they dubbed the *app poverty line*, which they set at $500 per month. The tier just above this line wasn't in such dire straits but taking them into account gives us an overwhelming 88 percent of apps that, at best, were barely scraping by.[35]

This research is dated, but it's far from irrelevant because as our app stores keep accumulating new services, the difficulty in breaking out of that 88 percent only continues to grow.

3. YOU CAN ALWAYS COUNT ON APPLE AND GOOGLE TO TAKE THEIR SHARE

Even if you do manage to reach that coveted 12 percent of respectably profitable apps, you won't be able to celebrate just yet. Thirty percent of your earnings (count 'em!) are now owed to Apple and Google as app store fees.[36] Now, we should clarify that this doesn't apply to real-world goods and

---

35   Sarah Perez, "The Majority of Today's App Businesses Are Not Sustainable," *TechCrunch*, July 21, 2014.

36   "Auto-Renewable Subscriptions - App Store," Apple Developer, accessed October 8, 2020; "Service Fees," Play Console Help, accessed October 8, 2020.

services bought online (i.e., Amazon deliverables, Lyft rides, Airbnb stays). But for the rest—Pandora's audio subscriptions, Nook's ebooks, Candy Crush's gold bars—Apple and Google are taking a meaty cut.

If this seems excessive to you, you're not alone. Companies like Spotify, Epic Games, and Netflix have all voiced their frustrations.[37] Apps have turned to various workarounds to make up the profits—from raising prices to handling payments to asking users to purchase via their website.

...AND THE LIST GOES ON AND ON

We've already mentioned the difficulty of capturing long-term attention and the concerns swirling around privacy. The challenges of communicating brand value. The efforts required to innovate. The uphill battle of standing out.

And have no doubt, we'll be mentioning them a whole lot more. For now, though:

LOOKING FORWARD: FALLING ON THE RIGHT SIDE OF HISTORY

With no hyperbole, we can say the app industry is the future of our culture. Ten years ago, Ubering to your Airbnb to prepare for a Tinder date at restaurants found on Yelp would've been gibberish. Now, it's Friday night.

---

37 Daisuke Wakabayashi, "Google Demands 30% Cut from App Developers in Its Play Store," *The New York Times*, updated October 9, 2020.

But apps are a tough industry to break into because there are a million ways to fail, and that may be underestimating it.

That's why we've started with TikTok—not because it's the blueprint to follow, but because its future still hangs in the balance. Currently, it's an app clearly on the upswing, but the real question is where it will be in 2025. Will it continue its grip on youth culture? Will we come to know it as *the* social video app, or will it be a nostalgic blip, replaced by the next big thing?

TikTok finds itself at a pivotal fork in the road. Over the coming pages, we'll tackle what constitutes a successful path on this road, we'll see some one-way tickets to the app graveyard, and most importantly, we'll come to understand the grand idea at the core of each winning app.

You won't have to wait long for that last one, though—it's the title of the following chapter.

CHAPTER 2

USER-CENTRIC MONETIZATION | THE CURE FOR APP FAILURE

———

It's a loaded term—user-centric monetization. But before we dive into what it is, let's clarify what it isn't.

Now, we've already seen that creating a profitable app is no easy feat. More often than not, we see developers get swept off their feet in the razzle-dazzle of app creation and eventually crashing down to Earth with one of these common pitfalls.

That's not to belittle the nature of these mistakes. Even the biggest giants of Silicon Valley fall prey to them. Companies like Google and Apple can absorb the shock of failure and move on but for the rest of us, avoiding these errors is a matter of survival.

WHERE APPS GO WRONG: SHORTSIGHTED VENTURES WITH DEAD-END CONSEQUENCES

1. CREATING SOLUTIONS WITHOUT SOLVING PROBLEMS

We love innovation! But not solely for the sake of innovation.

Unfortunately, many apps are solutions to problems their users simply aren't facing. In the words of Paul Graham, notable author, programmer, and Y Combinator co-founder:[38]

"Why is it so important to work on a problem you have? Among other things, it ensures the problem really exists. It sounds obvious to say you should only work on problems that exist. And yet by far, the most common mistake startups make is to solve problems no one has."

Which goes to say: Creative ideas are a dime a dozen. What's more important is (a) identifying an existing pain point that (b) your target audience faces often or intensely (or both), and then (c) creating a user-friendly solution that's (d) superior to the best available alternative.

Of course, this A-B-C-D is much easier said than done. When tasked with producing value, some companies instead throw their hands in the air and give us comically useless apps like:

- iBeer—A $3 app that lets you simulate drinking beer by tipping your phone like a mug.[39]

---

38 Paul Graham, "How to Get Startup Ideas," PaulGraham.com, November 2012.

39 Jim Reed, "BBC - Newsbeat - Technology - Virtual Beer War Hits the iPhone," BBC, October 17, 2008.

- I Am Rich—A simple page reading:

*"I am rich
I deserv [sic] it
I am good,
healthy and successful"*

That's it. That was the whole app. All for a spectacular cost of $999![40]

Sure, we can laugh at these gimmicks—the proverbial essential oils of the app industry. But we also see this shortcoming significantly plague some big-name apps too.

Mini case study

Consider Evernote, for instance. The virtual note keeping, content archiving app is still extremely popular, with hundreds of millions of global users. But, at times, it seems it's reached success in spite of itself.

The past few years have seen Evernote commit several cardinal sins of app development, namely putting too much on its plate. Instead of perfecting the most valued parts of their app, Evernote's developers set their sights on other initiatives: a marketplace app, then a social food app.[41]

---

40 IBT Staff Reporter, "Top 20 Most Expensive IPad Apps," *International Business Times (IBTimes)*, July 1, 2011.

41 Kyle Russell, "Evernote Market Has Sold $12M In Products Since Launch," *TechCrunch*, October 2, 2014; Eli Etzioni, "App of the Week: Evernote Food Helps You Remember the Meals That Made an Impression," *GeekWire*, July 23, 2015.

In a vacuum, neither was a bad idea, but neither was particularly necessary either. The bulk of their target audience wasn't looking for an Evernote marketplace or virtual cookbook, and both projects were soon abandoned.[42] And just imagine: All that wasted effort could have been dedicated toward strengthening existing app functions (and thus the value of their paid plans).

Credit to Evernote for surviving these strikeouts, but it took a massive loss by steering away from its purpose and focusing on irrelevant solutions—more on this in Chapter 3.

2. LOSING SIGHT OF WHAT REALLY MATTERS

An app's success depends on two streams of thought:

a. **Getting inside users' brains**—Who are they, and what do they need? Which pain points do they want to avoid? Which benefits do they wish to gain?

b. **Standing out from the crowd**—What are competitors offering that you aren't? What can *you* offer that *they* don't? What angle can your marketing embrace for differentiation's sake?

The problem is that many companies fail to cover these bases. One study found that 42 percent of companies don't consult with target buyers or collect any feedback.[43]

---

42   Nick Statt, "Evernote Is Shutting down Its Lifestyle Product Store," *The Verge*, February 1, 2016; Jon Russell, "Evernote Is Killing Off Its Dedicated Food App," *TechCrunch*, August 27, 2015.

43   Marcus Andrews, "42% of Companies Don't Listen to Their Customers. Yikes. [New Service Data]," HubSpot, updated June 05, 2019.

These companies want to ride the next fad or copy competitors without first gaining a deeper understanding of their markets. They spend millions on product development with nothing but a vague hope that users will embrace their offerings. But then, when push comes to shove, it turns out their apps aren't unique or compelling enough to entice users.

What companies really need before developing anything is a thorough understanding of their market at large. Who is the target audience? What are their pain points? What does the competitor landscape look like? Is your product better than the alternative? As we'll see in Chapter 4, talking directly to users with the goal of answering these questions is an absolute must to create something of value.

Mini case study

A poor read of the market and/or audience is how you end up launching products at the wrong time. And we saw this very prominently with Google's attempt at social media in the form of Google+.

If you're struggling to remember what Google+ looked like, that's exactly the point. Over the past decade, Google squandered its prime positioning in our digital consciousness to tap into the social media boom.

So how did far-reaching almighty Google fall short? Because:

    a. Google+ failed to solve any unique user pain points.

    b. It did not set itself apart from existing solutions.

In fact, it's abundantly clear that Google's primary motivation was to take a shot at Facebook's dominance in the social media space. The product ended up reflecting that desperation. Google+ didn't offer anything users couldn't get from Facebook, and, frankly speaking, the Facebook platform was superior in practically every way.

Limited features, an unintuitive mobile experience, poor marketing.... Even Google's enormous preexisting user base wasn't enough to overcome these flaws.[44]

Over the years, we've actually seen a number of Google's social ventures fall short: Google Plus, Wave, Orkut, Buzz. Unlike with daily utility apps—your Maps and Docs and Gmails—Google never quite managed to put their finger on the pulse of social media.

3. PROCEEDING WITHOUT A FORWARD-THINKING BUSINESS PLAN

At the end of the day, your app needs to make money. But believe it or not, that's where many companies fall short.

They come in with a solid vision for the app they want to launch but, unfortunately, don't have a monetization plan. Or if they do, they fail to update that strategy as the market changes and business scales upward. In other words, they get stuck in the old ways of doing things, and while they're stuck, new players easily come in and lap up the market.

---

44 JP Mangalindan, "Why Google's Social Network Was a Spectacular Failure," *Yahoo! Finance*, October 9, 2018.

It's understandable why such companies might prioritize software development way above monetization but doing so often ends up hurting the value of their awesome product.

In this respect, you can't emulate the handful of companies that boomed without turning a profit. Sure, Uber, Facebook, and Snapchat spent years prioritizing user growth over revenue, but they're the lucky exceptions. Take their victories with a grain of salt.

For the rest of us, we need to monetize effectively from day one. Now, in no way does this mean selling our souls for ads or paywalls. User experience and monetization can (and must!) happily coexist. As we'll see shortly, getting this balance down is both an art and a science.

Mini case study

At first, Apple's iTunes business model revolutionized the music industry. It paved a legal path for internet-based audio consumption: 99 cents per track, worth its cost for convenience and iPod connectivity.

But iTunes was only the first domino of this music revolution. And its downfall came swiftly thanks in part to the innovation of Spotify's streaming model.

No longer did paying per download make any justifiable sense. As a result, iTunes fizzled out and made way for Apple

---

Music, which currently enjoys a sizable sixty million plus audience.[45]

However, had Apple read the tea leaves and foreshadowed the rise of music streaming, it could be up with Spotify's 320 million plus users instead.[46]

4. LACKING A COMPREHENSIVE MARKETING PLAN

Apps are a uniquely personal medium. They give companies a direct line to the user—an extraordinary opportunity if capitalized.

The best apps utilize this two-way channel to make each user feel special with personalization and timely support. In return for feeling heard, users reward their apps with favorable feedback, consistent engagement, and, of course, money. Throughout these chapters, we'll further explore this sort of *ongoing dialogue*.

But apps can't thrive solely off the users they already have. They need strong external marketing, as well. From core messaging to app store promotion—we'll touch on all of it in chapter 10. For now, let's just say that without a marketing plan, your ship will sink just as Everpix did.

45   Stuart Dredge, "How Many Users Do Spotify, Apple Music and Streaming Services Have?" Music Ally, updated July 9, 2020.

46   "Company Info," Spotify, accessed November 12, 2020.

Mini case study

Handy photo-organizing service Everpix took off in 2012. Within two years, the app company was out of business.[47]

The problem, ironically, was too much emphasis on quality. And, by all accounts, the developers delivered because reviews of the app were top-notch.

But they also succumbed to the fatal flaw of believing this was enough. "The app will sell itself," somebody probably claimed in a board meeting. To make their long story short: It didn't.

The Everpix team obsessed over the tiniest software details but didn't invest in a sales strategy, which goes to show the best apps aren't necessarily the *best* apps. Oftentimes, they're just the smartest salesmen with an above-average product.

5. CREATING A WEAK CORE PRODUCT

This issue comes up when companies get overly consumed with the *idea* of their app.

They might throw around fancy buzzwords—blockchain this, augmented reality that—without honing down a straight-headed service. But fancy tech doesn't equate to practical problem-solving.

---

47 Colleen Taylor, "Everpix, The Cloud-Based Photo Startup, Is Shutting Down," *TechCrunch*, November 5, 2013.

The same can be said for excessive design. Sure, you want to grab attention, but it's always preferable to be industry- and audience-appropriate than overly flashy.

Or maybe these companies will come up with something that sounds too good to be true because it is too good to be true. Where the solution, in theory, ends up much nicer than the application in practice.

The point being, no matter how impressive your technology is, how attractive your platform looks, or how catchy the messaging sounds, you can only masquerade a weak core product for so long before the ruse is exposed.

Mini Case Study: COVIDSafe

This Australian-based app works to fight the spread of Covid-19 by tracking contact between individuals. Which definitely sounds great, until you realize that in order for the app to function effectively, it requires the following:[48]

- **Users to download the app.** That's already a big ask—of the first 926 positive cases announced following COVID-Safe's launch, only forty (approximately 4 percent) had the app.[49]

---

48 "COVIDSafe App," Australian Government Department of Health, updated October 28, 2020.

49 Ben Grubb, "Coronavirus Australia: COVIDSafe Hasn't Detected One COVID-19 Case despite 6 Million Downloads," *The Sydney Morning Herald*, June 28, 2020.

- **And register their details.** It asked for their mobile phone number, name, age range, and postcode—another wall for users to climb.
- **And keep their Bluetooth on.** This drains the phone's battery.
- **Users to be fully honest about self-reporting.** Which, even if you take for granted, doesn't guarantee much because you need....
- **Infected users to test positive.** This means all those asymptomatic carriers are still unaccounted.

If that's not enough to make you wonder, *what's the point?*—we've got some bad news for you. Because on top of all that, the app barely even works as is! There have been numerous reports of unreliable results (particularly on iOS devices), interference with other Bluetooth-using apps, and we're not even getting into the bevy of privacy concerns from all the personal information sharing.[50]

On paper, the app looks great. It helps solve a hot-button issue while giving the panicked public some much-needed comfort. It looks so good, in fact, that the Australian government threw $2 million into it and then defended it after it became clear that COVIDSafe was not the reliable virus detector originally promised. Some officials even pitted the blame of the app's shortcomings on Apple and Google instead of

---

50 Martin LaMonica, "How Safe Is COVIDSafe? What You Should Know about the App's Issues, and Bluetooth-Related Risks," *The Conversation US*, May 7, 2020.

admitting the simple truth: That they may have invested in an ineffective core product.[51]

WHERE APPS GO RIGHT: MONETIZING WITH USERS IN MIND

Let's flip over to an optimistic dial. Sure, success in this industry isn't easy, but there *is* room for new apps to become mainstays of our lives. As modern times create more problems, we'll continue to seek fresh solutions. If you don't provide them, a competitor will.

Now, the best mobile apps aren't just lucky that their solutions rose to prominence. There's a reason why Spotify has conquered music streaming. Why Tinder raked in over a billion dollars in 2019. Why Duolingo acquired over 300 million users worldwide.[52]

We'll analyze each of these cases later. But broadly speaking, app companies have two ways to prevail in their respective industry battlefields:

1. **Lowering prices.** Either by reducing costs or optimizing operational efficiency (i.e., eliminating value chain waste). The problem with mass cost reductions, though, is that they open the door to profit-killing price wars. Just ask

---

51 Ben Grubb, "Coronavirus Australia," The Sydney Morning Herald; Stilgherrian, "COVIDSafe's Problems Aren't Google or Apple's Fault despite Government Claims," *ZDNet*, July 21, 2020.

52 Frederic Lardinois, "Duolingo Hires Its First Chief Marketing Officer as Active User Numbers Stagnate, but Revenue Grows," *TechCrunch*, August 1, 2018.

Uber and Lyft about their drastic price cuts in San Francisco a few years back.[53]

2. **Creating more value.** This can take the form of *new* value—performing a novel task (remember the Pokémon Go phenomenon?). Or this can be *improved* value—performing the same activity in a better way (think Instagram stories beating Snapchat's or, of course, TikTok over Vine).

No matter if it's new or improved, each following chapter is a piece of the *creating more value* puzzle. And at the center lies one concept that ties it all together.

LET'S NOW ASK: WHAT DOES CREATING VALUE LOOK LIKE?

If you run in design circles, you've likely heard of user-centric design. If not, it's exactly what it sounds like: A philosophy in which the needs of users direct product design. The goal is an end result that's as beneficial and accessible as possible to the user.[54]

We'd like to branch off ever-so-slightly and explore a related concept: *user-centric monetization.*

With *monetization*, we have the process by which companies generate repeatable, measurable business. Then, the *user-centric* part delivers the irreplaceable value that fosters long-term loyalty. The key, then, is making them work together.

53 Brian Solomon, "Is Uber Trying to Kill Lyft with a Price War?" *Forbes*, January 25, 2016.

54 "What Is User-Centered Design?" Interaction Design Foundation, accessed November 5, 2020.

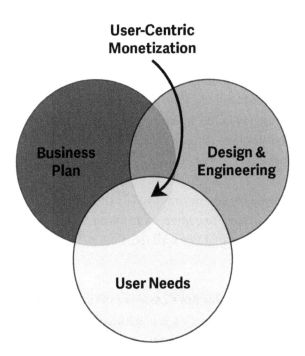

Most billion-dollar apps have found the middle of this Venn diagram by building monetization right into the core product—not on the periphery. These companies have mastered the customer/company give-and-take: For them to pay, you have to provide continuous value.

This requires a monetization model that looks beyond money to in-app engagement, customer satisfaction, and prospect acquisition. This means genuinely serving users, not tricking them with locked-in contracts, convoluted opt-outs, or exploited data.

In fact, what this really means is demonstrating certain essential qualities.

THE NINE PRINCIPLES OF USER-CENTRIC MONETIZATION

The past decade-plus of mobile app development is starting to speak for itself.

What follows reflects hundreds of app industry success stories (as well as a handful of notable flameouts). From Instagram to Candy Crush, Domino's to TurboTax, we've scoured through them and brought their real-world stories to the table.

Couple that with sprinklings of the latest expert research: From Clayton Christensen's milkshake-based jobs theory to Dan Ariely's psychological price framing to Google's moonshot innovation.

As we combed through it all, nine distinct themes emerged. Nine characteristics of our upper-echelon apps. Nine principles of user-centric monetization:

1. **Purpose** | *The Art of Problem-Finding. As this chapter has stressed, you need to find and define the problem you're tackling before jumping into the solution.*
2. **Empathy** | *It's Personal and It's Business. You can't create an app for everyone. Nor can you succeed without taking smart approaches to understanding your users.*
3. **Interaction Design** | *Give Power to the People. Even the smallest changes to an interface can have huge ripple effects on usability, revenue, and more.*
4. **Personalization** | *Be Unique...For Everyone. A million customers will use an app in a million different ways. You want to make each user feel like one in a million.*

5. **Monetization | *Strategies for Striking Gold.*** *There are dozens of ways to make money from a mobile app. Choosing the right one makes all the difference.*
6. **Data Privacy | *In Apps We Trust.*** *With data privacy as today's hot-button issue, building rapport and expressing reliability have never been more important.*
7. **Pricing | *All Numbers Don't Come Equal.*** *User behavior isn't nearly as rational as we might think; sometimes, clever pricing is all you need to drive sales.*
8. **Messaging | *Find Your Voice; Speak Their Language.*** *With increasingly intense competition, great software isn't enough; you also have to learn to sell it effectively.*
9. **Innovation | *Try, Test, Adapt, Repeat.*** *App development isn't a one-time event. It's a continuous process of experimenting, adjusting, and, yes, failing.*

These are the puzzle pieces with which we're working. By the end of this book, we'll put them all together to gain a clear picture of user-centric monetization.

We'll see how they lie at the heart of user experience, engagement, and competitive differentiation. And we'll demonstrate their instrumental role in attaining billion-dollar app excellence.

It's certainly a lofty journey we're setting for ourselves. So, as we dive into the principles, let's start the first one off with something simple. How about with a tall glass of juice?

PART II

CHAPTER 3

PURPOSE | THE ART OF PROBLEM-FINDING

———

"The Purpose of a Business is to Create a Customer"

PETER DRUCKER, AUTHOR AND MANAGEMENT GURU

In April 2017, a promising Silicon Valley company imploded and became an instant internet meme.

For over a year prior, Doug Evans had promised a revolutionary juicer that would forever change juice consumption. The product was the *Juicero Press*, a WiFi-connected, tech-savvy machine that created high-quality juice from proprietary packets of precut fruits and veggies. As these packets were sold exclusively by Juicero, the idea was to save people the hassle of buying, cleaning, cutting, and squeezing their own produce.[55]

———

55 "Juicero: Juicing Boss Defends $400 Machine," *BBC News*, April 21, 2017.

Evans had previously served as the CEO of Organic Avenue, a retail chain that sold pricey juice and salad lunches. The company went bankrupt in 2012 after people hopped off the juice-cleansing diet fad. And after that, he served as an advisor and investor in the food and wellness industry, but he'd never before run a tech company.[56]

That didn't stop him from making lofty claims. He declared that his juicer had a force of four tons—"enough to lift two Teslas"—and even compared himself to Steve Jobs.[57] Yes, *the* Steve Jobs. Evans insisted he would provide everyone with personal juice presses in the same way Jobs did with personal computers.[58]

And he sold it well: Evans' masterful storytelling won over the likes of Google Ventures, Campbell Soup, Kleiner Perkins, and other millionaire investors who poured over $120 million into his startup.[59] This got tech blogs buzzing. They dubbed his product the *Keurig for juice*.[60] He even managed to get a shoutout from Katy Perry on Instagram.[61]

---

56 Katherine Rosman, "How Organic Avenue Lost All Its Juice," *The New York Times*, November 4, 2015; "Doug Evans," People, Crunchbase, accessed October 13, 2020.

57 Ellen Huet and Olivia Zaleski, "Silicon Valley's $400 Juicer May Be Feeling the Squeeze," *Bloomberg*, April 19, 2017.

58 Eric Johnson, "Full Transcript: Juicero CEO Doug Evans on Too Embarrassed to Ask," *Vox*, last modified September 12, 2016.

59 "Juicero—Funding, Financials, Valuation & Investors," Crunchbase, accessed October 13, 2020.

60 Huet and Zaleski, "$400 Juicer," *Bloomberg*.

61 Katy Perry (@katyperry), "Was a good 🐈at my recovery party for @katyperrycollections having my carrot juice aka Beta Glow from @juicero with my bud and founder @dougevans 🍾🍾🍾HIGHLY recommend...," Instagram, April 18, 2017.

However, when Juicero finally hit the market, things quickly started to sour. For starters, the press itself was considerably expensive. It started selling at $399, a price already reduced from an initially whopping $699. And the subscription price for single-serving fruit/veggie packets was set at $8 a pop.[62]

Things went further south when a Bloomberg investigation revealed that you didn't actually need the $400 juice press at all. Instead, you could simply hand-squeeze the company's proprietary packets to make juice that was nearly indistinguishable in quantity or quality. In many cases, hand-squeezing turned out to be faster.[63] This left many people, investors included, scratching their heads and wondering what the whole point really was.

So, to wrap it up:

- Juicero was more expensive than a normal juicer.
- It didn't offer any noticeable advantages over hand-squeezing.
- The pouches were only sold to those who owned the machine.
- And these pouches suffered from a short shelf-life.

To most spectators, Juicero seemed like armed robbery in broad daylight.

---

62 "Juicero," *BBC News.*
63 Huet and Zaleski, "$400 Juicer," *Bloomberg.*

BEFORE ANYTHING ELSE, MAKE SURE YOU'RE DEALING WITH REAL PROBLEMS

Caught in all the hype, Evans overlooked a simple truth: People would rather go through the slight inconvenience of manual juicing than pay hundreds of dollars for his product. It was such a grave miscalculation that Juicero completely folded soon after launch.

But Evans isn't the first to make such a mistake. And he surely won't be the last.

We commonly see the founders of successful companies misunderstand their own customers. Google, for instance, failed to convince us that Google Glass, their internet-connected smart glasses, wouldn't be creepy or invasive.

Segway, quite notably, was supposed to revolutionize personal transportation. But users weren't willing to spend $5,000 on a device that needed to be charged and carried upstairs, especially with walking and public transport as the alternatives.

And how about Amazon's attempt at smartphones? Its Fire Phone was hoping to break into a market dominated by Apple, Samsung, and Google. Except users weren't so eager to click *Buy* when their needs were so much better met by more established providers.

These companies failed to identify user needs and thus ended up creating solutions without a relevant purpose. Which brings us to a point that cannot be emphasized enough. Great solutions to irrelevant problems will fail. Thus, validating your app's problem statement must happen before you start working on anything else.

There is a reason why this is our first principle of user-centric monetization. In fact, the reason is two-fold:

- **A defined problem.** Einstein himself once said, "If I had an hour to solve a problem, I'd spend fifty-five minutes thinking about the problem and five minutes thinking about solutions."[64] Too often, creators are quick to embark on the roller coaster of *saving the planet*—coding a platform, structuring a business model, or even launching an actual app. They become enamored with their exciting light bulb idea but neglect to ask users about the benefits they wish to receive. Remember, you're building this thing to support users' values, not your own.
- **A sanity check.** Juicero is a prime example of how easy it is to get stuck in an echo chamber where the viability of a dead-end product seems reasonable. Instead, you want to inspect your idea from a variety of perspectives to uncover insights and opinions you would have missed otherwise. So that if your idea is actually shortsighted, you'll find out before putting crazy amounts of time and resources into it.

In other words, the first step toward creating an app that solves a real problem for users is making sure the app will solve a real problem for users.

---

64 "Quote by Albert Einstein: 'If I Had an Hour to Solve a Problem I'd Spend 5...,'" Goodreads, accessed October 13, 2020.

It appears this is where Juicero fell short. Take a look at how eventual CEO Jeff Duns promoted his company in a Medium post:[65]

"Our connected press itself is critical to delivering a consistent, high quality, and food safe product because it provides:

1. The first closed-loop food safety system that allows us to remotely disable produce packs if there is, for example, a spinach recall. In these scenarios, we're able to protect our consumers in real-time.

2. Consistent pressing of our produce packs calibrated by flavor to deliver the best combination of taste and nutrition every time.

3. Connected data so we can manage a very tight supply chain because our product is live, raw produce, and has a limited lifespan of about eight days.

The value of Juicero is more than a glass of cold-pressed juice. Much more."

Do regular people care about remote protection, produce calibrating, or connected juicer data? Maybe. But it's safe to say very few users would drop hundreds of dollars for these features.

That's not to mention that elsewhere in the post, Dunn uses the phrase "raw, plant-based nutrition" twice to describe his

---

65   Jeff Dunn, "A Note from Juicero's New CEO," Medium, April 20, 2017.

primary product, which is simply juice. Such language indicates that either Juicero's team neglected to speak with their target users, or they strictly consulted with those sharing similar high-tech Silicon Valley values.

All in all, not speaking with prospective users led to a poor problem statement, which manifested in a product that lacked purpose. But had they dug deeper with these users, Juicero's viability (or lack thereof) may have been apparent much earlier on. And it may have saved the company a world of trouble and unfortunate memes.

LOOKING FORWARD: PROBLEM-FINDING ISN'T A GUESSING GAME

Naturally, your idea won't appeal to everyone. This is to be expected, and you shouldn't be discouraged by it.

In fact, an app idea that appeals to everyone is not only too broad and difficult to implement, but it's also way more likely to fail. Instead of trying to do everything for everyone, use these early idea validation conversations to find a niche. By focusing on a specific user problem, you narrow down your scope and better position your product to provide genuine value and, ultimately, to justify its price tag.

This means the first step is to gather as much data as possible to identify the problem you're trying to solve. And that's your goal here: To arrive at a user problem, not the solution. By meticulously defining this problem, you'll later be able to direct your efforts and resources more productively.

HOW DO YOU KNOW YOU HAVE A GOOD PROBLEM?
Chief Designer Sarah Gibbons of Nielsen Norman Group, a leading design and consulting firm, defines a user need statement or user problem statement as:[66]

An actionable problem statement used to summarize who a particular user is, the user's need, and why the need is important to that user. It defines what you want to solve before you move on to generating potential solutions in order to 1) condense your perspective on the problem and 2) provide a metric for success to be used throughout the design thinking process.

The first step in creating a user problem statement tends to be interviewing potential users Eric Koester, a serial entrepreneur and Professor of Entrepreneurship at Georgetown University, recommends the following steps to validate your ideas:[67]

1. Talk with at least sixty to one hundred real people who are facing the problem that you are trying to solve. The more customer interviews you do, the more people you talk to, the deeper the insights you'll find.
2. Engage with all kinds of users. Go beyond your obvious prospects to obtain more surprising insights. It is important to leave behind any presumptions you may have about your potential audience when you start interviewing users.

---

66 Sarah Gibbons, "User Need Statements," Nielsen Norman Group, March 24, 2019.
67 Eric Koester, "The Startup Holy Grail: Product-Market Fit (Startup Factory Live Stream)," Facebook, March 12, 2020.

3. Share a theory or a rough mock of your solution with these customers and see if you can get their buy-in. If there is some resistance, understand what's holding them back.

4. It is important to stay objective: Let people express their opinions without responding defensively. If your hunch fails at this step, see if you can pivot to a different solution and start from step one.

That's the *how* but we also need to make sure you're collecting the right *what*. To ensure you arrive at a well-defined user problem statement, keep in mind the following general framework:

"**As a** [user], **I want to** [desire or goal] **so that I** [reason or outcome]."

In the above statement, the *user* is a segment of the audience for which you want to create a solution. *Desire or goal* refers to the result if the user's problem gets resolved. And *reason or outcome* is what the user will gain when the problem resolves.

For example, if your user is a fitness enthusiast, they might want to eat healthy meals every day to feel good about themselves.

Here, we're not talking about specific features that will help the user eat healthy meals and accomplish this goal. Rather, we're arriving at a broad yet tangible statement that any entrepreneur can work toward solving. After many interviews, you'll find patterns emerge out of the problems your people face.

As we learned from Juicero, the *desire or goal* should be that of your audience, not that of you and your team. Keep in mind: Even though users may tell you what they want, they might not always know what they need. It is your job to understand the real need of your user.

A famous quote attributed to Henry Ford says, "If I asked people what they wanted, they would have said faster horses."

In the next chapter, we'll see some strategies for creating the user need statements that result in automobiles, not faster horses.

So, let's reiterate: You need to understand the problem before you go searching for the solution. And we'll get to the solution; in fact, that's what most of these chapters are all about. But without a relevant problem, they're all as meaningless as Juicero proved to be.

Now, identifying that problem isn't a matter of checking some boxes and answering some cookie-cutter questions. As we're about to see, it's a matter of empathizing with your users on a deep, emotional level.

CHAPTER 4

EMPATHY | IT'S PERSONAL AND IT'S BUSINESS

"A satisfied customer is the best business strategy of all."

MICHAEL LEBOEUF, AUTHOR

Have you heard about the fabled empty seat at Amazon exec meetings? Apparently, Bezos and Co. always have one as a reminder of their ultimate stakeholder: The customer.

However much you subscribe to such symbolism is up to you. But you can't ignore the underlying message: Decisions made at the top have to prioritize user needs. That's how successful products are built.

WHICH IS WHY BUILDING EMPATHY WITH YOUR USERS IS SO VITAL

As this book will hammer home time and again, the best apps create experiences that directly solve users' problems, hence the *user-centric* part of user-centric monetization. Still, in order to address these pain points, you need "the capacity to step into other people's shoes, to understand their lives, and start to solve problems from their perspectives."[68] That's how the champions at global Design firm IDEO define Empathy.

As intuitive as this all sounds, it's actually where product teams often fall short. They instead push out features that appear valuable from their point of view, not from the users'. That's how you end up with a catastrophe like Yik Yak.

Remember Yik Yak? It was an anonymous messaging app that burst onto the high school/college scene in 2014. It functioned as a sort of anonymous Twitter feed, except posts were exclusive to people within a five-mile radius of you. A year after launch, it was already burning bright, with its market value peaking at $400 million. By 2017, the company had vanished just as spectacularly as it had arrived.[69]

So, what went wrong?

1. **They created a fundamentally unsafe space**. A forum that's both local and anonymous is just begging for rampant cyberbullying. Snowballing incidents led victims,

---

68 "Design Kit," Design Kit, accessed October 12, 2020.

69 Nick Statt, "Yik Yak, Once Valued at $400 Million, Shuts down and Sells off Engineers for $1 Million," *The Verge*, April 28, 2017.

parents, feminist groups, you name it, to protest and request schools to block the app.

2. **They tried revealing the man behind the curtain.** Removing users' anonymity makes sense in theory. Anonymity enables virtual harassment, so introducing accountability should curb it. But the implementation was subpar, and users abandoned the app in droves.

3. **Nothing could reduce the threat of proximity.** One of Yik Yak's initial selling points became its great downfall. Because if you were the victim of an attack, you knew with absolute certainty that the perpetrator was physically close. Why would anyone keep using an app that fosters such anxiety?

As cool and trendy as it was, Yik Yak failed to alleviate its users' very real worries. And these weren't some small concerns about features or preferences; these were matters of personal safety. They were more than enough to throw the app into a vicious cycle of bad press and plummeting usage.

Yik Yak found out the hard way: Empathy demands more than eye-catching aesthetics. And while a top-notch design is certainly important (as we'll discuss in Chapter 5), empathy runs deeper than that.

SO HOW DO WE ACHIEVE EMPATHY? BY STARTING WITH SOME USER RESEARCH

It may sound counterintuitive—connecting on human emotion via data.

But in truth, data is our clearest window into users' motivations, pain points, and circumstances. It removes some of our inherent biases and sheds an honest light on others' experiences.

For our purposes, customer research is either:

Quantitative. This tells us the big picture *what* behind customer behavior, often through surveys, polls, experiments, and assessments of existing metrics. Or ...

Qualitative. Which gives us the more detailed *why* of user trends. This encompasses those deep-dive interviews with open-ended questions mentioned in the previous chapter, field studies of users in their natural environments, and focus groups of representative population samples.

Blending a variety of these methods eventually paints a picture of undeniable user facts.

Take the hospitality industry: It's no stretch to say that most people who use rental marketplaces like Airbnb are seeking more authentic experiences or are simply more frugal. Whereas guests at Hilton hotels are more likely to be business travelers looking for consistent comfort.

You can bet that both these brands dug much deeper into their data to identify their ideal prospects and, in turn, developed a platform that empathizes with their needs and wants. Not simply out of the kindness of their hearts, mind you, but because empathy is a powerful business tool.

In listening and empathizing with your users, you really want to be able to answer these questions:

- What relevant problems and frustrations are users facing right now?
- How do they currently solve these problems without your solution?
- What are the alternative offerings, and whom might your competition be?
- What will your solution do to solve these problems?

HOW TO GET TO THE HEART OF YOUR USER BASE

"You've got to start with the customer experience and work back toward the technology—not the other way around."

STEVE JOBS

Generally speaking, there are two main strategies for painting a portrait of your users. The first starts with deep diving into who the typical customers are—what are their personas? The second goes from the other end of the tunnel, asking what result the customer actually needs to be completed.

We see tech companies use either one to make their user portraits as realistic as possible and thus fill Jeff Bezos' empty seat, so to speak.

1. IDENTIFY THEIR PERSONAS

With the personas approach, you're using extensive research to create detailed fictional characters that reflect your real users' behaviors. You then use your understanding of these behaviors to guide your product development.

Like all fictional characters, the best personas have extensive backstories—not only outlining their demographics but also their core wants, needs, and pains. The more accurately you can pinpoint these distinct values, the greater your ability to satisfy them.

As an example, consider these three user personas for Instagram:

Influencer Iva: Iva is a twenty-something beauty guru. She creates content that shares her passion for makeup, showcases her skills, and establishes her as an expert. She's also working to monetize by recommending brands to her loyal followers.

Entrepreneur Elliot: Elliot owns a mattress store. He's analytical, savvy, and always looking to increase in-store sales. What he needs are insights into who goes online to check out his business. That way, he can create targeted ads that give him the most bang for his buck.

Friendly Fiona: Fiona is a college student. She'd love to keep in touch with her high school friends now that they've all moved to different cities. School keeps her busy, though, so she doesn't always have time to send a text or shoot a call.

It's not hard to imagine these different types of Instagram users, is it? And if you're Instagram, you somehow have to cater to each one with utmost care.

In actuality, Instagram execs likely put together much more intricate personas than these brief blurbs (and you can bet they have more than three). Now, how do they ensure their customer prototypes are accurate? By answering a long list of illuminating questions, such as:

- Exactly what do your different users want or not want? And why?
- How can your app play into these desires? And how can it alleviate potential roadblocks?
- What tone, voice, or style resonates with these audiences?
- What type of content or media do they engage with?
- Which channels of marketing and advertising do they respect?

The better insights you have about your audience, the closer you get to realistic (nonidealistic) personas that provide context for future decisions—decisions that appeal to everyone.

After all, that's the purpose here: Capturing all pockets of your audience and serving their true needs, regardless of their interests in cosmetic tutorials or mattress sales, or casual correspondences.

That's why answering these questions is so critical. Otherwise, you can easily fall victim to the common pitfalls of tunnel vision, either by obsessing over a single segment, by imagining a nonexistent user type or worse, by designing based on your own desires.

Below is a sample template you can use to create your own user personas.

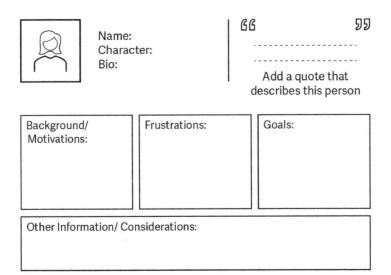

Name: Character: Bio:	66　　　99 - Add a quote that describes this person

Background/ Motivations:	Frustrations:	Goals:

Other Information/ Considerations:

Case study: Buzz, Jill, and the winning formula of Best Buy's personas

Once upon a time, retail stores filled their shelves with products for every average Joe. But that time is long gone. Now, industry behemoths like Amazon and Walmart offer competitive advantages in price, convenience, delivery, assortment, and quality. As for the brick-and-mortar sector, it's now reduced to survival of the fittest.

And yet, Best Buy is thriving. Thanks to decades of in-depth segmentation studies, the electronic retailer has cultivated its corporate strategy and marketing tactics toward its highest value customers. In other words, Best Buy has nailed its user personas. So, let's meet some of them:

You have Buzz, the young professional who's always interested in the newest gadget or latest video game. Then there's

Jill, the busy suburban mom who doesn't really know much about this tech stuff. You've got Barry, the affluent tech-aficionado who's willing to drop thousands on top-of-the-line products. And we'll cap it off with Ray, the responsible dad who doesn't need all the thrills, just a quality laptop at a reasonable rate.[70]

To clarify, we didn't make these names up. These are *actual* persona categories that Best Buy has established and tries to cater to. And they do so with unbeatable custom experiences.

For starters, Best Buy trains in-store associates to answer any question Buzz, Jill, Barry, or Ray may ask. But more to the point, the stores themselves are built differently based on the kind of clientele they tend to receive.

Think about that! At one location, Barry may find a high-end home theatre department equipped with leather couches and flat screens playing movies. At another, Buzz can saddle into the gaming lounge to test out various consoles. And in a town full of Jills, the local Best Buy likely has an extended home appliance section and maybe even a rec room for child-friendly electronic toys.

This is their main competitive advantage. Not just knowing their customers but providing them with exciting, hands-on, personalized experiences. Even rivals who sell the same exact products (remember Circuit City?) can't match this combination of utility and fun.

---

70 Kristi Arellano, "Best Buy's Plan: Cater to 'Buzz,' 'Jill,'" *The Denver Post*, updated May 8, 2016.

Best Buy capitalized on the in-person excitement of tech—a pocket of opportunity that online shopping can't touch. Stores that first adopted these location-specific models saw sales growth of 9 percent over those that didn't.[71] And this brings us full circle. Leveraging need-based data can unlock next-level segmentation and keep your business humming in a world of Amazons and Walmarts.

The benefits

- **Balance.** As seen with Insta, fully considering distinct users' needs ensures each of them feels prioritized.
- **Alignment.** As perfected by Best Buy, ensuring a cohesive vision of product purpose and business direction across your teams.
- **Empathy.** We may have started with stats and numbers, but we ended up with a very real face on our users.

The limitations

- **Gatekeeping.** If not carefully created, user personas can accidentally exclude certain segments (think: those with a disability, from different cultures, etc.)
- **Misapplication.** Sure, demographics play a role. But don't be one of those companies that focuses so heavily on prospects' backgrounds that you lose sight of their deeper goals and problems.
- **Biases—implicit or explicit.** Can be difficult to avoid, even with the best personas. So be wary: The more

---

71 Ben Rogers, "Customer Segmentation to Increase Revenue: 3 Real Examples," Qualtrics, August 27, 2018.

pronounced your biases are, the more far-reaching their ripple effects.

2. DETERMINE THE *JOBS TO BE DONE*

Our discussion of personas heavily revolved around figuring out *who* our customers are. What do they care about, and what do they want to avoid? And, ultimately, what drives them to our product or service?

This next framework takes a different road to answer these questions by asking: What exact functions does a user need to be done?

Well, let's start by thinking about why we create resumes.

Employees use them as personal marketing materials to highlight skills and demonstrate proficiencies. Companies then evaluate these qualifications, ultimately hiring the person most suited to solve existing pain points or advance future initiatives.

With this in mind, let's ask: What does a milkshake's resume look like? What job can a milkshake do?

This seemingly absurd idea was explored by Harvard Business School's Clayton Christensen in his book *Competing Against Luck*. Christensen previously authored *The Innovator's Dilemma*, which *The Economist* called one of the most influential books ever written.[72] But while *The Innovator's*

---

72 "Business Books—Aiming High | Books & Arts," *The Economist*, June 30, 2011.

Dilemma covers big companies' failure to innovate, *Competing Against Luck* is all about what helps grow successfully.

In it, Christensen seeks to answer, *What causes a customer to purchase and use a particular product or service?* As an answer, he promotes a theory called *Jobs to be Done*, which suggests we don't purchase products. Instead, we hire them to do specific things for us. "What causes us to buy products and services is the stuff that happens to us all day, every day. We all have jobs we need to do that arise in our day-to-day lives, and when we do, we hire products or services to get these jobs done," he explains.[73]

To prove his theory, Christensen shares his fascinating experience with milkshakes.

QUICK CASE STUDY: MCDONALD'S DO-IT-ALL MILKSHAKES
Many years ago, McDonald's sought to increase their milkshake sales. So, they invited their quintessential customers to participate in focus groups to find what would make the milkshakes more delicious and more worthy of being purchased.

McDonald's received very clear feedback and responded by making the milkshakes chunkier, chewier, and cheaper. Yet, despite all of this, the sales impact was negligible.

So, Christensen and his team approached the problem from a different perspective. They began by asking a simple

---

73 Clayton Christensen et al., *Competing Against Luck: The Story of Innovation and Customer Choice.* New York: Harper Business, 2016.

yet profound question: "What job causes people to hire a milkshake?"[74]

After carefully observing and collecting data on customers who came to McDonald's all day long, Christensen and co. realized that almost half of the customers were buying milkshakes on their way to work. Here was their big "A-ha!" moment.

Christensen explains that "what these milkshake buyers had in common had nothing to do with their individual demographics. Rather, they all shared a common job they needed to get done in the morning: 'Help me stay awake and occupied while I make my morning commute more fun.'"

This is the key insight that led Christensen to his Jobs-to-be-Done Theory. These commuters knew they'd be hungry soon and were looking to hire something that could do their job for them—that is, keep their stomachs full. And the typical solutions all have their flaws: Bananas are too quickly eaten, donuts are too messy, bagels often require both hands.

But milkshakes are perfect. They're viscous enough to last for a significant portion of a morning drive and easily held with one hand or in a cup holder. McDonald's even worked to improve their milkshake's Job-to-be-Done," making it even thicker, adding fruit chunks for textural variety, moving the dispensing machines up front, and providing easy-swipe cards for rushing commuters.

---

74 Ibid.

Plus, their market competition expanded well beyond Burger King's milkshakes to merchants of coffee, bagels, donuts, fruit, granola bars, and even candy bars.

But this still didn't get McDonald's the success they wanted.

So, Christensen's team examined other customers who were *hiring* milkshakes throughout the day. And another main segment emerged: Parents tired of saying no to their kids all day long who still wanted to be the good guy. A smaller milkshake for kids quickly served that purpose and, this time, the milkshakes did not need to be so viscous.

For the kid's milkshake, Christensen explains the Job-to-be-Done: "In that moment, the milkshake isn't competing against a banana or a Snickers bar, like the morning milkshake is. It's competing against stopping at the toy store or my finding time for a game of catch later on."

Thus, McDonald's used the same product to create two unique experiences. They observed the situation holistically, from a social, cultural, and emotional lens, and truly understood the job that needed to be done.[75]

Below is a template you can use to create your product's Jobs-to-be-Done.

---

75   Ibid.

Situation	Motivation/ Struggles	Desired Outcome
JTBD 1: When I ...	I want to ...	So that ...
JTBD 2: When I ...	I want to ...	So that ...
JTBD 3: When I ...	I want to ...	So that ...

So why do people hire mobile apps?

Think back to Instagram. Previously, we looked at the app's purpose from the prism/angle of its user types and found, unsurprisingly, that it's way more than a mere photo-sharing program.

Now, let's shift gears to the *jobs* that Instagram fulfills:

- **Image cultivation.** Instagram doesn't just record for posterity's sake like an old photo album might. Rather, it allows for real-time exhibition of one's identity—from thoughts and desires to hobbies and relationships. This is an avenue for capturing and displaying everything you want people to know about you.
- **Relationship management.** You can keep tabs on the people you know as well as the public figures you wouldn't otherwise have access to. And if you wish, you can directly message them as well.

- **Entertainment.** Quite simply, scrolling through Instagram is fun. On top of friends and celebs, there are countless hobby and interest-driven accounts. And it's an easy (if not addicting) outlet to turn to when you have a few minutes to kill or just want to give your brain a rest.

Posting photos may be what Instagram technically does, but these are the purposes it fulfills—the problems it answers. Much like you could boil down Airbnb's *jobs* to affordable rentals, available bookings, and authentic experiences. Or Uber's down to fast transport, convenient drop-off/pick-up, and dependable payment.

We're simplifying a bit, sure, but the point is that people need a milkshake for the host of jobs it represents.

The benefits

- **Dimensions.** Understand the many hidden reasons users may *hire* your app.
- **Competitive edge.** Think bigger and start regarding your indirect competitors (i.e., Uber competes with Lyft but also public transport and city bikes).
- **Innovation**...that actually benefits your goals. You don't need to build a Swiss army knife to cut butter; sometimes, all you need is to make a thicker milkshake.
- **And Empathy.** Teams often want quick fixes that fail to thoroughly think through a user problem. Here, we seek above all else to comprehend the social, emotional, and functional dynamics of each job.

The limitations

- **Practicality.** It's the challenge of implementation. Many companies find Jobs-to-be-Done Theory simply to be an easy meeting catchphrase that's difficult to translate into actionable steps.
- **Infrastructure.** Similarly, not all teams have the tools, philosophies, or resources to make it work; sometimes, it's not as simple as making a thicker milkshake.
- **Scope.** It could push product teams to focus narrowly on functional aspects alone.

PERSONAS VS. JOBS-TO-BE-DONE—WHICH WORKS BETTER?

Naturally, the answer isn't going to be black-and-white. If our exploration of Instagram's personas and jobs done is any indication, the two frameworks are sides of the same coin.

In fact, using them in tandem is the best way to curb each one's shortcomings. Jobs-to-be-Done is excellent for identifying the end goal, while personas help us consider users along their journeys.

Take a look at the diagram below to see one way of getting the best of both approaches:

Persona A:	JBTD 1:
	JBTD 2:
	JBTD 3:
Persona B:	
	JBTD 1:
	JBTD 2:
Persona C:	
	JBTD 1:
	JBTD 2:

Each persona can have multiple Jobs-to-be-Done. And distinct Jobs may satisfy multiple personas.

It's a mix-and-matching game with no rules except one: Empathy. Finding what users need from you and not stopping until you provide it.

That's how you find the problems that actually matter. And that's how you put yourself in a position to find solutions that deliver genuine value.

The next challenge? Building an app that walks the walk.

CHAPTER 5

INTERACTION DESIGN | GIVE POWER TO THE PEOPLE

———

"Good design is actually a lot harder to notice than poor design, in part because good designs fit our needs so well that the design is invisible."

DONALD A. NORMAN, *DESIGN OF EVERYDAY THINGS*

It's 2017, we're looking at Snapchat, and they're in trouble.

For starters, their biggest rival, Instagram, has started copying features like stories, face filters, and disappearing messages to great success. In fact, there are more people using Instagram's Story feature than there are total active users on all of Snapchat. Stories become so popular that Instagram's parent company Facebook decides to extend the feature onto its own platform and into WhatsApp.[76]

---

76 Alex Heath, "Timeline of Facebook Copying Snapchat in Instagram, Messenger, Other Apps," *Business Insider*, May 27, 2017.

What's even worse, Spectacles, Snapchat's foray into hardware camera glasses, is a massive failure. Sixty million's worth of Snap Spectacles now lie rotting away in some warehouse.[77]

And that's not all of Snapchat's problems. Recently, it introduced a revenue-oriented redesign that increases visibility for advertisers and paid publishers. The response? Swift wrath of the consumer—thousands of negative reviews, some three million active users lost, and over a million signatures petitioning Snapchat to roll back the update.[78]

According to numerous sources, Snapchat's stock even lost upward of $1.3 billion in stock value after influencer Kylie Jenner publicly tweeted disappointment with the app.[79]

So, what gives? Why such intense backlash to a small design change? Why not simply adjust, as users often do for other apps? And most importantly, what can we learn from it?

The answer lies in interaction design (IxD).

WHAT EXACTLY IS INTERACTION DESIGN?

To truly understand it, let's go back to ancient China.

---

77 Max A. Cherney, "Snap Earnings: Spectacles Were Big Money Losers, but More Are Coming," MarketWatch, May 1, 2018.

78 Paresh Dave, and Munsif Vengattil, "CORRECTED-Snap Loses Users for the First Time, Beats on Revenue," *Reuters*, updated August 7, 2018; Nic Rumsey, "Petition · Snap Inc.: Remove the New Snapchat Update," Change.Org, accessed October 12, 2020.

79 Kaya Yurieff, "Snapchat Stock Loses $1.3 Billion after Kylie Jenner Tweet," CNN, February 23, 2018.

Their 6,000-year-old philosophy of feng shui is the original form of interaction design optimization. Its purpose, essentially, is to organize spaces and objects in such a way that most enhances the flow of energy (qi).[80]

Translated literally as *wind-water*, feng shui is said to draw upon the natural order of the world in guiding manmade practices such as architecture and interior design to a greater harmony. According to feng shui, there is an optimal way to position buildings within a city, as well as furniture in relation to the doors and windows of a bedroom.[81]

While feng shui may be pseudoscientific, a more modern and scientific twist on the idea applies to the arrangement of an app's interface, and how it makes you feel. You want to be able to move around it with that same harmonious flow.

Now fast forward some 5,975 years where we find Don Norman at Apple coining "User Experience," an umbrella term that "encompasses all aspects of the end-user's interaction with the company, its services, and its products."[82]

Norman deliberately made UX a broad term that merges engineering, marketing, customer service, industrial design, and interface design. We'll be touching on some of these key facets of UX in later chapters (i.e., Personalization, Privacy,

---

80 Guo Pu (276-324), "The Zangshu, or Book of Burial," Translated by Stephen L Field, PhD, accessed October 12, 2020.

81 Anjie Cho, "The Basic Principles of Feng Shui," The Spruce, September 17, 2020.

82 Don Norman, and Jakob Nielsen, "The Definition of User Experience (UX)," Nielsen Norman Group, accessed October 7, 2020.

Messaging), but for now, we're giving the discussion a laser focus on a key subset of UX and one of Apple's greatest strengths: Interaction Design.

At the center of good UX, and specifically good IxD, lies a purpose similar to that of feng shui—namely, a design that prioritizes users' needs and wants. Over the years, all of Apple's innovative products have this notion at its core.

Sure, the iPhone may not be the first touchscreen phone, but the user-centric interface is certainly far superior to early alternatives like the HTC Touch Pro or Nokia N95.[83] Once the smartphone era takes off, apps grow more and more popular, and user experience takes on a whole new level of importance.

For readers interested in a broader deep dive into the role of UX, check out *Design of Everyday Things* by Don Norman and *Don't Make Me Think, Revisited* by Steven Krug.

GREAT MOBILE IXD REFLECTS A DEEP EMPATHY WITH USERS

Back to present day: Imagine a duck in a pond. On the surface, our duckling may appear to be swimming with grace and ease, but beneath the surface, it's paddling its legs frantically to propel forward.

No matter how frantically our app works behind the scenes, we need to keep a still surface appearance.

---

83 Rory Cellan-Jones, "Apple iPhone Faces Serious Rivals," BBC News, June 28, 2007.

This is by no means an easy task; hundreds of tiny, crucial decisions have to be made about each aspect of the design. How many navigation screens should we have? Do we want to save users' credit card details? If so, should we prompt them before or after the purchase? What about if they change the language to German. Will the text still be legible?

And so on. You get the point. Or, if you designed something that looks like this website, you missed the point entirely:

*(It's a real site! Go check it out at https://www.
theworldsworstwebsiteever.com. It is owned by Explorations
Media Group, LLC, a web design company in Kentucky).*[84]

This eyesore is a great example of what we *don't* want to do: Distract and overwhelm our users. On the contrary, we want to make their journey from A to B as streamlined as possible.

---

84 Explorations Media Group LLC, "The World's Worst Website Ever!" accessed October 12, 2020.

Finally, it's worth touching on the grander significance of IxD. Because it's not just *what users see*, it's the physical point of contact between our brand values and their consumer needs. And, as Snapchat can attest, that bridge hangs on by a thread.

So, we can agree that smart IxD is vital. Here's what it looks like:

1. EMPOWERING PEOPLE TO BE IN CONTROL

The best apps give users the freedom to make mistakes and undo unwanted actions. Convenient, intuitive design elements let them explore their options without any second thoughts.

For instance, the messenger platform WhatsApp allows you to delete sent messages. By holding down the chat in question to delete your text, a menu pops up to let you delete your message a) for yourself, or b) for the receiver, provided they have not read it yet.[85]

Or how about dating app Bumble, which lets you unmatch—and report, if needed—users whom you're having second thoughts about.[86] To take some of the stress out of dating, it gives you the power to nip those all-too-common uncomfortable situations right in the bud.

---

85 WhatsApp Messenger, v. 2.20.201.23 (WhatsApp Inc.), Android 4.1 and up, updated October 27, 2020.

86 "Bumble—Dating, Make New Friends & Business," v. 5.193.1 (Bumble Holding Limited), Android 5.0 and up, updated October 27, 2020.

In fact, if you do unmatch someone, Bumble follows up with a tender "Everything Okay?" message. In response, you can anonymously report any inappropriate behavior whatsoever, giving you just another small sense of a safety net that the dating world often lacks.

Customizable settings. Do users want to receive push notifications? What permissions do they want to give? For all such questions, let *users* be the judge.

Just look at how many different options you get from renowned language-learning app Duolingo:[87]

Notifications		
Practice reminder	📱	✉
Reminder time		12:00 PM
Weekly progress		✉
New follower	📱	✉
Friend Activity	📱	✉
Leaderboards	📱	
Product updates + learning tips	📱	✉
Marketing messages	📱	✉
Streak Freeze Used	📱	✉
Streak Saver	📱	

---

87 Duolingo—Language Lessons, v. 6.90.0 (Duolingo, Inc), iOS 12.0 or later, updated October 26, 2020.

For most choices, you get to decide which notifications come through phone or email (or both or neither!).

It's also worth noting that Duolingo takes particular care in making sure these notifications aren't annoying to users. For instance, if you don't respond to those practice reminders, Duolingo has the sense to stop bugging you (they even send you a somewhat dejected "we'll stop sending these reminders" message).

Simple error messages. This goes back to making site navigation as smooth as possible.

To err is human. So, our explanations of what to do when things go wrong should be human, too.

For instance, when you're sending some cash through the money transfer app Venmo, a pop-up emerges if you try to complete the payment without writing in a brief blurb. You don't get taken to a new page. Your transaction isn't cancelled—you just get this quick, simple message of "Note cannot be empty" and can immediately return to make the fix. It's painless and straightforward, right in line with Venmo's whole brand identity. [88]

---

88 Venmo, v. 8.8.0 (PayPal Inc.), Android 5.0 and up, updated October 13, 2020.

2. MAKING IT AS USER-FRIENDLY AS POSSIBLE

Keeping feng shui in mind, you want each aspect of your app to sync up with your users' natural tendencies and subconscious expectations.

Consider the primary elements at play here: physical touch, visual aesthetic, and cognitive interpretation. The best apps feel natural at each point of this perceptive spectrum.

Personalized suggestions. What better way to appeal to your user than speaking directly to his or her individual needs?

Targeted recommendations make customers feel heard, as though your services are specifically tailored to them.

Amazon, of course, does a great job of this on their app's home screen. Front and center, they show both recently viewed items and inspired suggestions to help cultivate our shopping behavior.

Netflix follows a similar pattern by presenting movies and series by relevant category. If you've ever used the streaming service, you're plenty familiar with all the "Because you watched *The Office*" recommendations they also throw at you.

(Much more on the role of personalization in the following chapter).

Easy tapping. Not all sections of a screen are equal. Just ask Steven Hoober, the author of *Designing Mobile Interfaces* and a leading researcher of how people really use touchscreen phones and tablets.[89]

He explains that mobile users don't read mobile screens in a top-to-bottom, horizontal 'F' pattern—named for the natural direction we hand-write the letter. F patterns are common for reading websites, but mobile content is often interacted with from the inside out. [90]

Here's a diagram of what he means:[91]

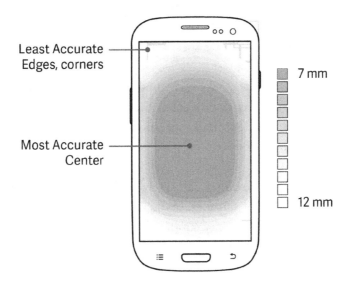

_____

89 Steven Hoober, Eric Berkman, *Designing Mobile Interfaces: Patterns for Interaction Design*, O'Reilly Media, November 1, 2011.

90 Steven Hoober, "1, 2, 3 For Better Mobile Design—4ourth Mobile," February 2, 2020.

91 Steven Hoober, *Designing Mobile Interfaces*.

Hoober's findings show that our tapping tendencies are most accurate in the central *green* area of the phone. Here, our hand-eye coordination is more comfortable with smaller touch targets than with those around the edges.

This is a pretty strong indicator that the bulk of our attention naturally goes toward this center. Meaning that this is the sweet spot where apps should place their primary content:[92]

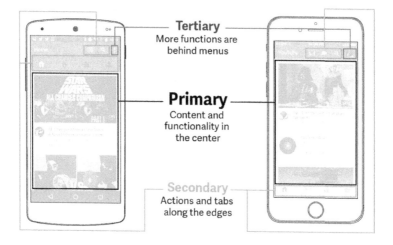

Tertiary
More functions are behind menus

Primary
Content and functionality in the center

Secondary
Actions and tabs along the edges

It may seem counterintuitive from Hoober's findings. Why put smaller icons in precisely the areas where they're harder to reach? That's because there's another variable: Prioritization. Those secondary and tertiary buttons are the whipped cream and cherries on top. They can sit in the corners of the app, but we want the sundae itself front and center, where it's most accessible.

---

92   Ibid.

Aesthetic appearance. This is what really takes your users from "Yeah, it works" to "Wow, I love this!" Plus, the look you give your app reinforces the vibe you want your brand to convey.

Consider this a prime opportunity to boost user experience and brand reputation in one fell swoop. Here's Duolingo's sleek interface design:[93]

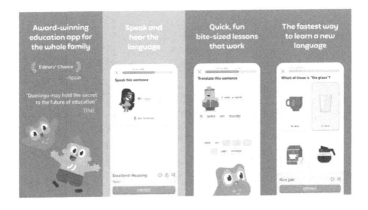

It simultaneously feels casual and cutting edge. Bursting with playful graphics, yet not overwhelmingly so. Overall, it's a uniquely warm look for a language learning app.

Accessibility. You hear this term tossed around in meetings and pitches all the time, but it's more than a buzzword. Just ask Domino's.

In October of 2019, the global pizza chain was sued by a blind man claiming that their website lacked proper

---

93 Duolingo—Language Lessons, Duolingo Inc.

accommodations for the disabled (i.e., not having screen-reading functionality). Domino's appealed the suit to the Supreme Court but was rejected, in what signified a noteworthy win for accessibility advocates.[94]

But accessibility isn't just about legal compliance; it's about satisfying a moral commitment to help people with their needs. After all, if we lay our business mindedness aside for a minute, it's really a matter of principle. Even the most menial apps are just solutions to problems, so let's make sure as many people as possible can access that solution.

Back to the business side of things: Accessibility is a means of maximizing your potential user base. By adding simple features, large text options, for instance, you're opening the door to an otherwise lost demographic of users. And, frankly speaking, you'd be adding a nice badge of user-friendliness to your brand resume.

3. MINIMIZING COGNITIVE LOAD

What exactly does minimizing cognitive load mean? Aforementioned author and programmer Steve Krug explains it quite simply:

"As a user, I should never have to devote a millisecond of thought to whether things are clickable or not."[95]

---

94 Tucker Higgins, "Supreme Court Hands Victory to Blind Man Who Sued Domino's over Site Accessibility," CNBC, October 7, 2019

95 Steve Krug, *Don't Make Me Think: A Common Sense Approach to Web Usability*, Pearson Education, 2009.

Once again, we're coming back to that same core message. Interaction design should be as effortless as possible. We want to do all the work for them, and here's how:

No-brainer decisions. Remember, an abundance of choice often results in no choice at all.

A 2000 study showed as much by comparing shoppers' reactions to two display tables with jam: One with twenty-four varieties and one with only six. The twenty-four varieties attracted more buyer attention, but when it came to pulling the trigger and making a purchase, the assortment of six outsold its counterpart *by a factor of nearly ten.*[96]

The more information we're presented with, the more we subconsciously seek to block the excess noise and look elsewhere. So, help users avoid the stress of decision paralysis. The most popular food ordering apps often do so by integrating *Picked for you* or *Featured* sections that look something like this:

---

96 Sheena S. Iyengar and Mark R. Lepper, "When choice is demotivating: Can one desire too much of a good thing?" *Journal of Personality and Social Psychology*, 79(6), 995–1006.

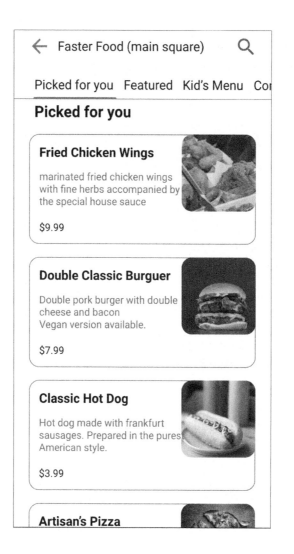

← Faster Food (main square)   Q

Picked for you   Featured   Kid's Menu   Cor

Picked for you

Fried Chicken Wings

marinated fried chicken wings
with fine herbs accompanied by
the special house sauce

$9.99

Double Classic Burguer

Double pork burger with double
cheese and bacon
Vegan version available.

$7.99

Classic Hot Dog

Hot dog made with frankfurt
sausages. Prepared in the pures
American style.

$3.99

Artisan's Pizza

These apps initially showcase a handful of items so that users aren't immediately flooded with an endless menu. Such customized picked-for-you sections work by embracing minimalism and gently nudging users toward an easy purchase.

User needs—Anticipated. This is yet another way to personalize the experience and shorten the distance from opening the app and achieving the desired goal.

For example, let's take Yelp (which, if you've never used it to find the perfect date spot, is a platform for comparing customer reviews of businesses, often restaurants). Instead of leading users to a generic homepage and letting them sort through thousands of listings on their own, Yelp starts people off with a short, intuitive navigation menu with its most popular options. Delivery, takeout, and reservations are all right there, in a prime location at the front and center of the page.[97]

Beside them are a few of Yelp's other most sought-after services—think *Keys & Locksmiths* or *Home Cleaners*—but the more niche businesses are bunched together under the *more* umbrella option. So, we end up with a nice balance of anticipating users' most common needs and keeping the choices to an easily digestible amount.

Ridesharing app Lyft goes a step further by letting you save your most frequent destinations. This appears right when you open the app, so you're instantly just a click away from home or work without having to type anything in.[98]

---

97   Yelp: Find Food, Delivery & Services Nearby, v. 12.72.0 (Yelp Inc.), iOS 12.0 and watchOS 6.0 or later, updated October 19, 2020.

98   Lyft—Rideshare, Bikes, Scooters & Transit, v. 6.55.3 (Lyft Inc.), iOS 11.0 or later, updated October 26, 2020.

It's a minor detail, sure, but it makes our experience with the app a fraction of a percentage more efficient.

And that's really what we're gunning for here: A bunch of tiny, marginal improvements that eventually add up and leave a lasting impact. In a similar vein…

Minimal user input. A crucial consideration when your app is dealing with a complex, frustrating activity, like taxes.

For all the headaches of filing taxes, TurboTax has long made a name for itself as a software that simplifies things. And their app does much of the same.[99]

Instead of throwing a stack of paperwork at you, they go through the arduous process of taxes small step by small step; the entire process is organized into manageable umbrella sections with bite-sized subsections.

And when you *do* come across those intimidating, tedious tasks, TurboTax streamlines and automates them as much as possible. Uploading documents, verifying data, calculating refunds—all a click or a snap away.

The result is a program that has miraculously taken the overwhelm out of one of our most notoriously overwhelming chores.

Simple learning curve. Recall feng shui; the interplay of visual and textual elements should naturally guide your users toward their desired X and Y. Nobody came to your app to solve a puzzle.

Instead, infuse your design with clarity and breed familiarity where possible. You want them to feel at home, right? So, don't overdo it by reinventing the wheel; rather, speak to their intuition with the colors, phrases, and symbols you use. Green can still mean *go*, and red can still mean *stop*.

---

99 TurboTax Tax Return App—Max Refund Guaranteed, v. 6.12.0 (Intuit Inc.), iOS 6.0 and up, updated October 9, 2020.

Yes, you do want to be original, but pick and choose your spots. An upstart music service isn't going to win anyone over by introducing a nontriangular *play* button.

And once you do establish this simple learning curve, the key is maintaining it throughout the app. When you introduce new functionalities or updates, users shouldn't be faced with a guessing game; they should *get it.*

In many ways, you want your interface to be easily predictable. If it isn't…well, just ask Snaphat.

4. PROVIDING INSTANT FEEDBACK

Users want to know that their actions aren't in vain. That pressed buttons work, and that they won't have to sit around all day waiting for loading pages.

Quick response times. This one's pretty obvious: Nobody wants to wait a second longer than they need to. And if you miss that second, they'll be gone.

When it comes to loading times, it helps to think of your user as a passenger waiting to board a bus… Except they're considerably less patient, and there are a million faster buses available just around the corner.

Needless to say, offer the fastest bus.

Visual cues. Let's say a request *does* prompt a load time— that's fine, but don't leave your users hanging. Give them some indication that "Hey, we're working on it. Just one second!"

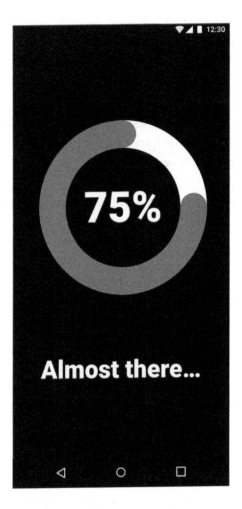

Something as minor as a loading wheel, a progress bar, or a change in color when pressing a button goes a long way in earning users' goodwill. Even this minimal "Almost there…" screen is better than complete radio silence.

SO WHY DID SNAPCHAT'S REDESIGN FAIL?

On a micro-level, two main reasons:

First, they inexplicably crammed individual messages and friends' stories onto one page. Suddenly, nothing separated snaps made *for you* from snaps put out for the masses, despite the differences between these two formats.

Then, a second wave of restructuring broke the barrier between friends' stories and brands' stories. The goal was to drive revenue by offering these professionals more prominent exposure, but users couldn't look past this mixing of personal and advertising content.

But that's not *really* why Snapchat's redesign suffered. The problem was that the new interface was wholly unfamiliar. It was unnecessarily convoluted and considerably less intuitive than the previous version.

Perhaps worst of all, it was a clear cash grab. Snapchat's execs seem to have made these decisions with their profit margins top of mind—not their users' best interests. A further case in point: All their tinkering led many confused users to lose their coveted Snap streaks (fun little icons indicating consecutive days that two friends keep up their back-and-forth).[100]

In other words, they tried to monetize without prioritizing the *user-centric* component. Hence the importance of

---

100 Maya Kosoff, "'It Was Cataclysmic': Can Snapchat Survive Its Redesign?" *Vanity Fair*, May 10, 2018.

making nuanced, thoughtful, people-friendly IxD decisions, even when making minuscule changes, the impact on users and businesses can be tremendous.

Here's how some of the best mobile app teams have gotten their IxD right:

1. THINKING BIG PICTURE: DESIGN AS A BUSINESS STRATEGY

Spotify, the audio streaming giant, had a problem. Its five navigation buttons—*Home, Browse, Search, Radio*, and *Your Library*—cluttered the main page. Therefore, in late 2018, they consolidated the options for Premium subscribers down to just three buttons—*Home, Search*, and *Your Library*—from which users could more intuitively get around.[101]

The reactions to the tweak were positive, but Spotify wasn't done there. In 2019, they redesigned *Your Library* to easily switch between two main category tabs: *Music* and *Podcasts*. Under *Music*, you now find Playlists, Artists, and Albums, while under *Podcasts*, you have three parallel options: Episodes, Downloads, and Shows.

In a public statement, Spotify explained that "the new design gives you more control over your podcast listening

---

101 "What's New with Spotify Premium," Spotify Newsroom, October 18, 2018.

experience, and quickly helps you discover new shows and episodes."[102]

That all may be good and true, but these changes really come down to two overlapping goals: Winning over subscribers and competing with Apple. And while Apple may currently dominate the podcast space, Spotify has shelled out upward of $400 million to acquire podcast production companies like Gimlet Media, Parcast, and The Ringer.[103]

So, to bring it full circle: Spotify has incorporated a whole world of podcasts in their efforts to win the audio streaming war. And despite all this, they've still managed to sort *music* and *podcasts* into six total menu options that feel less cluttered than the original five!

AND THINKING SMALL PICTURE: AI AND COMPLEXITY REDUCTION

Banking mobile apps, in particular, are facing a growing concern: Too many features, too much complication. And as the features grow, the average user is bound to feel overwhelmed.

Part of the problem is that banks initially planned for mobile to support online banking, not replace it. Apps were meant for basic transactions like balance inquiries and account transfers, but their unparalleled convenience left users wanting more. With banking, though, it's hard to add more

---

102 "Spotify's 'Your Library' Refresh: What You Need to Know," Spotify Newsroom, June 13, 2019.

103 Zack O'Malley Greenburg, "Spotify's Purchase of The Ringer Won't Be Cheap, But the Payoff Could Be Huge," *Forbes*, February 7, 2020.

features without tipping the balance and muddling the app in confusion.

Here's where Bank of America has found the sweet spot. Their do-it-all virtual assistant Erica now helps well over seven million users navigate the feature-loaded app.[104]

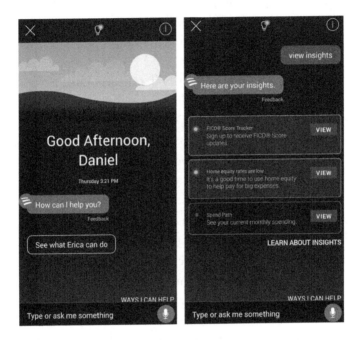

Erica makes it easy on many levels: If you ask her, Erica will pull up your account balances, give you a snapshot of your spending habits, remind you of upcoming bills, monitor any

104 Will Hernandez, "Cure for Banking App Fatigue: Make Things Simpler." *American Banker,* August 01, 2019; Bank of America Mobile Banking, v. 20.09 (Bank of America Corporation), iOS 11.0 and watchOS 3.0 or later, updated October 5, 2020.

refunds or duplicate charges, and even track changes to your credit score.

Without Erica's help, "[the app] can be overwhelming," admits Christian Kitchell, BoA's AI Solutions and Erica Executive. "You don't always know where to look."[105] But with the assistant, you can easily reach your destination without an inkling of stress. It's just one way that BoA has introduced simplicity into a process that normally lacks it, much like the folks at TurboTax did.

FINAL THOUGHTS ON THE BALANCING ACT OF INTERACTION DESIGN

A design study run by Google and AnswerLab concluded that "mobile users are very goal-oriented. They expect to be able to get what they need, immediately, and on their own terms."[106]

Allow us to add a slight addendum to this quote: And it's the job of our apps' interfaces to lead users to those goals in a timely and satisfactory manner. All while keeping in mind Don Norman's idea of blending design seamlessly into the experience, almost unnoticed.

Managing all this can seem like a nightmare. The app needs to be aesthetically pleasing yet subtle. Extensively functional yet quick and intuitive. Unique yet familiar. It sounds like a paradoxical challenge with no middle ground.

---

105 Will Hernandez, "Cure for Banking App Fatigue," *American Banker.*
106 Jenny Gove, "What Makes a Good Mobile Site? | Web Fundamentals," Google Developers, accessed October 28, 2020.

But there is a middle ground. It's difficult and delicate, yes, but far from impossible: For every failed Snapchat redesign, there's a Spotify navigation menu success story right across from it. And as we're about to see, a big part of nailing this balancing act is designing the optimal app experience for each individual user.

CHAPTER 6

PERSONALIZATION | BE UNIQUE... FOR EVERYONE

———

"Remember that a person's name is, to that person, the sweetest and most important sound in any language."

DALE CARNEGIE, *HOW TO WIN FRIENDS*

AND INFLUENCE PEOPLE

In the summer of 2018, a devastating earthquake hit the Indonesian island of Lombok, killing hundreds.[107] Naturally, people logged onto Facebook to send well-wishes to the many displaced, missing, and otherwise affected by the incident.

Only, their experience wasn't quite what they were expecting.

---

107 Nicole Chavez and Mochammad Andri, "Indonesia Tsunami and Earthquake Death Toll Tops 400, Hundreds More Injured," CNN, updated September 30, 2018.

You see, the Indonesian word for *to survive* and *safe* is *selamat*. Unfortunately, *selamat* also means *congratulations*. So, when users commented on their concerns, Facebook interpreted the latter definition and sent a festive balloon gliding up their screens:[108]

Not exactly a smooth move by Facebook. And the world let them have it, with Indonesian news outlets and John Oliver alike digging into their egregious error.[109]

But looking past this massive *oops* moment, it's worth digging into Facebook's intentions here: Not only optimizing the app experience for its international audience but also installing graphics that respond to user activity. In a correctly

---

108 Herman Saksono (@hermansaksono), "'Congrats" in Indonesian Is "Selamat." Selamat Also Means "to Survive." After the 6.9 Magnitude Earthquake in Lombok, Facebook Users Wrote "I Hope People Will Survive." Then Facebook Highlighted the Word "Selamat" and Throw Some Balloons and Confetti," Twitter, August 5, 2018.

109 John Oliver, "Facebook: Last Week Tonight with John Oliver (HBO)," uploaded on September 23, 2018. YouTube Video, 00:02:30.

translated vacuum, this is exactly the kind of business strategy that keeps users coming back.

It didn't pay off here, sure, but Facebook has continuously thrived by tapping into the well of personalization.

BECOMING MORE THAN *JUST ANOTHER APP*

A standard app experience is kind of like one of those random holiday gift exchanges, like *White Elephant* or *Yankee Swap*. Basically, since the gifts purchased might end up in anyone's hands, you try to offer something that can appeal to anyone.

The apps we're talking about, though, work to emulate your loved ones, who send you handwritten cards and presents inspired by years-long inside jokes. They're trying to deliver *gifts* that are tailored to your unique needs and wants. Or, at the very least, that's how they want you to feel.

This is what we call app personalization.

Why is personalization so important that Facebook would dedicate effort to Indonesian translations? Because user attention is such a limited resource.

In fact, studies have found that we give most of our digital attention to just a handful of apps:[110]

---

110 Comscore Mobile Metrix, Share of Time Spent on Apps by Rank, Custom Defined List, Age 18+, June 2017, US.

Smartphone users spend half their time on their #1 most used app, while tablet users spend almost 2/3ʳᵈˢ of their time on it

Share of Individual Users' Time Spent on Apps by Rank
Source: comScore Mobile Metrix (Custom), U.S., Age, June 2017

Avg. # of Different Apps Used per Month

25   14

Smartphone   Tablet

Rank	Smartphone	Tablet
1	49%	65%
2	18%	17%
3	10%	7%
4	6%	4%
5	4%	2%
6	3%	1%
7	2%	1%
8	2%	1%
9	1%	0%
10	1%	0%
11	4%	1%

Breaking into that upper echelon is almost impossible without personalization. It's how you grab attention, maintain relevance, and surpass profit targets. In fact, research has shown personalization to reduce user acquisition costs by up to 50 percent, lift revenue by 5 to 15 percent, and improve marketing returns by 10 to 20 percent.[111]

The point being we, as consumers, greatly appreciate personalization. And according to studies done by the University of Texas, the reason for this is twofold:

For starters, it satisfies our need for control. Of course, it's not control in the traditional sense of choice making, but we still

---

111   Brian Gregg et al., "Marketing's Holy Grail: Digital Personalization at Scale," McKinsey, November 18, 2016.

get the illusion of shaping things to our liking. By impacting the app, we uniquely control how it meets our expectations.

The second is its negation of information overload.[112] No user wants a bombardment of infinite choices or full content libraries; we need some relevant direction. As we're about to see, such catered filtration plays a big role in meeting users' exceedingly high demands.

PERSONALIZATION ACROSS THE THREE STAGES OF APP USAGE

Think of your users as party guests. Your job as host is to persuasively invite them, provide a memorable experience, and then follow-up thoughtfully.

At each stage, the more personalized your message, the more likely they are to respond favorably. Even on the handheld scope of an app, everyone loves a little bit of VIP treatment. And since you probably can't pick users up in a limo, do whatever else possible to make them feel special.

Note that this isn't a gimmick or a last minute cherry on top. Personalization should be a foundational element in your design that shines for users at every stage.

---

112 Laura Frances Bright, "Consumer Control and Customization in Online Environments: An Investigation into the Psychology of Consumer Choice and Its Impact on Media Enjoyment, Attitude, and Behavioral Intention," UT Electronic Theses and Dissertations, Texas ScholarWorks (TSW), December 2012.

STAGE 1—ONBOARDING: THE UNFORGETTABLE INVITATION

We all know how important first impressions are. They're why business cards are still a billion dollar industry.

According to Leanplum, a leading customer engagement platform, the average app loses over 90 percent of users through the first ninety days after install.[113] Think of your app's onboarding process as its own *business card*. You will never have as much of their attention as you do right now, while interest and excitement are still bubbling. So, leverage it to prove your long-term worth.

Users stick with those apps because they immediately deliver benefits. There's no time suck or steep learning curve.

But there's no single recipe for success; onboarding varies company to company, industry to industry. What's important, no matter what, though, is keeping the process easy and engaging throughout.

Let's take a look at how some billion-dollar apps approach it:

1. **Find what they're seeking**—People can have many distinct purposes for downloading your app. It's up to *you* to guide each of them through all your offerings to that specific purpose.

---

113 "With Declining App Usage, Mobile Engagement Matters," Leanplum, February 3, 2019.

You see this commonly with content apps (like Twitter, You-Tube, Quora, and Medium), which ask newcomers to follow a few topics to tailor their experiences, like so:

Tag Town

Topics of your interest

Tag Town is a place for you! Choose the topics of your interest to make the most of your experience!

#Happiness #Culture #Art

#Music #Drawing #Food

#Literature #Astrology

#Lifehacks #Nature

#Sports #Health #Beauty

#Finance #Funfacts

#Fitness #Movies

NEXT ›

Then, as more interests are selected, these content apps follow up with relevant suggestions.

Below we see a different example common with fitness apps. In order to recommend appropriate exercises, they ask essential questions that capture user intent from the get-go.

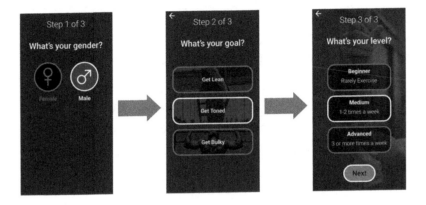

Notice that it's also good practice to display the number of onboarding steps. In doing so, otherwise discouraged users can see the light at the end of the tunnel.

2. **Help them explore**—This is your best chance to show users what you're all about. To get the ball rolling and solidify the value you offer.

Health app Lifesum shows one way to do it, utilizing charming visuals and text snippets to explain everything directly:[114]

---

114 Lifesum: Diet & Macro Tracker, v. 11.2.1 (Lifesum AB), iOS 11.2 and watchOS 3.0 or later, updated October 19, 2020.

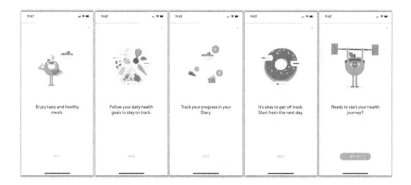

The game Two Dots goes one step further, actually involving the user in their interactive tour:[115]

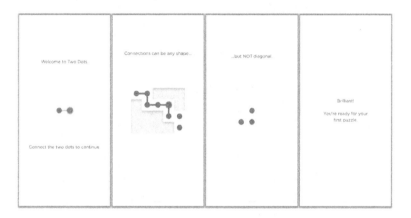

This minimalistic, easy-to-follow design teaches the rules in a matter of seconds. Sometimes, less really is more.

---

115 Two Dots, v. 6.10.1 (PlayDots Inc.), Android 4.1 and up, updated October 26, 2020.

Through all this app exploration, the fewer roadblocks, the better. In fact, it may be wise to add a *skip* function to let users move ahead if they wish:

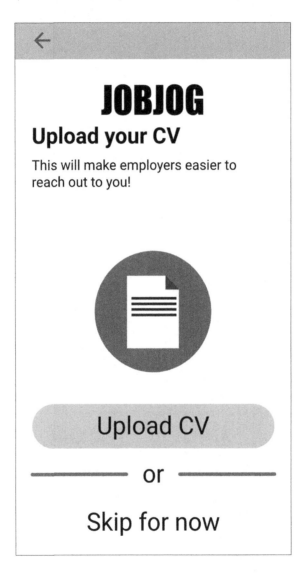

3. **Direct their journeys**—Here comes the meat of the app. Once users are in, how do you ensure they know how to get around? How do they play their first song or post their first photo or buy their first item?

If you don't show them what lies in the various corners of your app, they may not find it at all.

One way to steer users in the right direction is with pop-up tooltips:

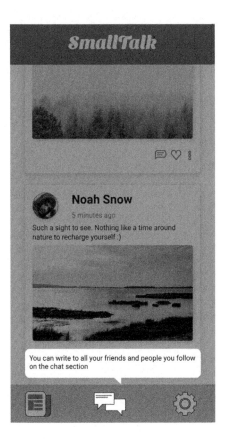

These messages conveniently do all the explaining as you go through the app.

You can also prompt users with calls to action like Lifesum does with its progress tasks:[116]

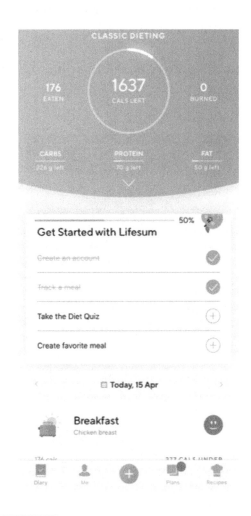

---

116 Lifesum, Lifesum AB.

And when users *do* successfully complete a task, it doesn't hurt to validate their progress. We can look at Two Dots again, as they congratulate us with a "Brilliant!" message after completing their simplest puzzle:[117]

It's a tiny detail, but that's exactly the kind of affirmation that people subconsciously covet.

4. Facilitate their choices

We'll talk more about distinct monetization models in the next chapter and various app pricing strategies in Chapter 9, but for now, suffice it to say: Not all users are equal, so not all plans have to be equal.

Our most popular content platforms know this well, and so they personalize their subscription tiers accordingly:[118]

---

117 TwoDots, PlayDots Inc.
118 YouTube, v. Varies with device (Google LLC), updated October 28, 2020.

YouTube Premium

Enjoy a YouTube Premium membership for the whole family.

> **TRY IT FREE**

Family • 1-month free trial • Then $17.99/month • Add up to 5 family members (ages 13+) in your household.
Recurring billing • Cancel anytime

Individual • 1-month free trial • Then $11.99/month **TRY IT FREE**

Student • 1-month free trial • Then $6.99/month **☑ TRY IT FREE**
Eligible students only.
Annual verification required.

Home   Explore   Subscriptions   Inbox   Library

YouTube and the YouTube Logo are registered trademarks of Google LLC, used with permission.

Here, we see YouTube Premium offer diversified plans to attract a wider audience. Students on a budget? Check. Families looking for a convenient package deal? Check. Individuals riding solo? Also check, with the still reasonable regular price.

It's not a huge discount, monetarily speaking, but it also carried the benefit of making those students and families feel taken care of during signup. And if they feel taken care of, they are more likely to stay with YouTube in the long term.

So, you've gotten the hang of personalized onboarding. Well done! You can get users to use your app... Once. But then the challenge really begins.

Your next task: Convince users to return for a second time, and a third, and so on...

STAGE 2—SMART RECOMMENDATIONS: THE PARTY ITSELF

By this point, you've got insights into what your users initially want. Now, it's time to find the thing they want *next*.

Enter: Recommendations. We see them everywhere, using past activity to propose the next item to buy or the next content to consume.

The technicalities of their algorithms are beyond the scope of this book. But what we will explore are the three main approaches to personalized app recommendations and what they mean for your users:

1. **Collaborative.** The basis of our first type of recommendation is on similarities between users' interests.[119] If Jack and Jill display similar music tastes, the system will recommend one of Jill's favorites to Jack and vice versa.

The core assumption is that users who have previously displayed similar interests will do so again in the future. That is, these users are more likely to agree than two randomly selected people.

The benefit of this approach is that it strictly relies on past user behavior. There is no need for extensive information about the items to be recommended (i.e., genre, release year, mood, etc.), as we'll see in other recommendation systems. And, generally speaking, the collaborative algorithm is more conducive to discover newer, more serendipitous interests.

Unfortunately, the system also suffers from a *cold start problem*, in which upstarts face great difficulty in gaining traction.[120] In other words, neither Jack nor Jill is particularly likely to see a brand new song.

Otherwise, it can be quite effective. Amazon's ever-present recommendations (for example, "Customers who bought this item also bought...") are a prime example of how collaborative filtering can entice further engagement.

Netflix's *Trending Now* and *Top 10* lists do much of the same by aptly capturing the popularity of the moment. Remember

---

119 Dietmar Jannach et al., *Recommender Systems: An Introduction*, Cambridge: Cambridge University Press, 2010.
120 Ibid.

the *Tiger King* documentary? If you had Netflix in March of 2020, you couldn't have avoided it if you tried. Because as Joe Exotic captivated more viewers, Netflix recommended the documentary more aggressively.

2. **Content.** This approach goes at it from the other end, based on the similarities of items consumed.[121]

So, if you listened to two Taylor Swift songs yesterday, you're more likely to receive a third today. And over at Pandora, they've turned audio filtering into an exact science. Their Music Genome Project is a meticulous initiative led by professional musicians to identify some 400 core characteristics of songs.[122] This precise categorization currently generates 100 percent of the app's daily recommendations for its sixty million plus users.[123]

Now that's taking the content recommendations about as far as they go, but we also see them quite often on a lesser scale. For instance, if you open your Google Play Store or Apple App Store right now, you'll undoubtedly encounter some suggestions "based on your recent activity." These stores' algorithms somehow qualify each of their apps, gaining a comprehensive picture of your preferences the more you use them.

---

121 Ibid.

122 "Pandora Radio—Listen to Free Internet Radio, Find New Music," Pandora, accessed October 28, 2020.

123 "2019 Form 10-K Annual Report" (PDF), SiriusXM Holdings, Retrieved July 21, 2020.

And it makes sense intuitively: A subscriber to *The New York Times* Crossword Puzzle app is more likely to be interested in playing Sudoku.

The downside, though, is that for these recommendations to work well, they require a pretty advanced classification system. The characteristics of these classifications are often created manually, meaning they are expensive and error-prone.[124] And, unfortunately, most apps don't have the resources to run something like Pandora's Music Genome Project.

Thankfully, though, forming a recommendation strategy isn't an *either/or* game:

3. **Hybrid.** As is often the case with app development, the best solution is the nuanced one. Personalizing with both collaboration and content in mind brings out the best of both worlds.

It'll look different for every app and industry, but this dynamic approach tends to be strongest. And if you go over to Netflix, you'll see a particularly salient example of this.

In addition to the collaborative features just mentioned, Netflix further personalizes things by keeping tabs on the content you've liked. This way, it can suggest shows and movies based on similar users' activity *or* based on shared characteristics with this liked content. This is how Netflix avoids falling into that cold-start problem for new content discovery.

---

124 Dietmar Jannach, Recommender Systems.

The result is a presentation that feels so natural we never think to question it.

For more on how such recommendation algorithms work, direct your curiosity toward *Recommendation Engines (The MIT Press Essential Knowledge series)* and *Recommender Systems: An Introduction*.[125]

STAGE 3—DELIVERY: THE THANK-YOU NOTE

You've made a strong first impression, and you've given users what they wanted. Now comes the *after* part of personalization, once users have left your app.

Part of this deals with evaluation. How well did your recommendations work? Another part ponders the next steps. How do you bring these people back? And finally, we have the matter of improvement. What practical changes will further these goals?

1. **Gather user feedback.** How do you improve your recommendations? First, try asking.

Ask if they enjoyed the last item they ordered. Ask them to rate the last show they watched. And if the response is negative, ask why. None of your speculations can match the truth you get straight from the horse's mouth.

---

125 Michael Schrage, *Recommendation Engines*, The MIT Press, September 20, 2020; Dietmar Jannach, Recommender Systems.

Obtaining more and more feedback, you'll see certain preferences emerge. And with them, you can refine your recommendations accordingly.

2. **Find the middle ground with notifications.** As users, we all have a love-hate relationship with notifications. Making sure your app falls into the *love* category is a delicate balancing act. You don't want to annoy your audience with too many pings, nor do you want to fall out of mind with too few.

The best apps out there find this sweet spot and take pains to create the type of notifications that spur excitement and action—that hook, rather than repel.

For instance, companies like Macy's and Starbucks use GPS technology to send nearby customers relevant in-app offers.[126] Likewise, Netflix reminds users of recent in-app activity in the form of "Pick up where you left off" or "New Arrivals."

Neither update is annoying or invasive; just a quick "hey, by the way..." tap on the shoulder to keep up engagement.

3. **Opt for deep links where possible.** How many times have you encountered web links that don't play nice with mobile apps? You click on them, and they send you to a web browser instead of the installed app, resulting in a lower-quality experience. And maybe a small headache.

---

126 Julien Boudet et al., "The Future of Personalization—and How to Get Ready for It," McKinsey, June 18, 2019.

That's why we have *deep links*, which direct you straight to a specific page in an app. So, if your friend shoots you a message with a hotel room posting, clicking that link will open that listing on the hotel app instead of a buggy browser page. This process typically looks something like this:

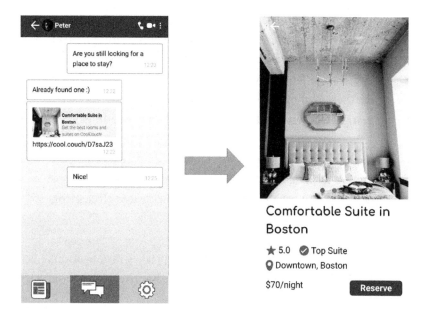

These personalized deep links may be subtle, but they're a beloved tool of marketers everywhere working on retargeting campaigns.

4. **And most importantly…test, test, and test again**. Whether you're onboarding new prospects, recommending hot-button items, or sending perfectly balanced marketing notifications, you want to monitor and analyze your audience's behavior throughout.

This could entail techniques ranging from surveys to A/B tests, all with the purpose of zeroing in on the perfect user experience. The power of repeatedly using data to innovate cannot be understated. We even dedicate Chapter 11 to it.

A WORD OF CAUTION AND A WORD OF INSPIRATION

Let's not forget, as instrumental as personalization is, even a company of Facebook's magnitude can easily succumb to basic errors. And they're not alone. Pinterest once notably sent their own mistaken "You're getting married!" messages to single women curating photos for dream weddings.[127]

The faults don't stop with inaccuracy. Many apps also have troubles with a lack of diversity in their recommendations: Their suggestions fall into loops that quickly lose all elements of intrigue.

And perhaps most concerning are the privacy ramifications of user data collection. This is yet another tricky tightrope to tiptoe, but more on that in Chapter 8.

That said, personalization is worth the effort it demands. Implemented correctly, it becomes a key cog in differentiating from the competition, bringing higher returns on marketing investments, and providing subscribers with optimum value.

---

127 Alison Griswold, "Pinterest Congratulates All the Single Women on Their Weddings," September 04, 2014.

That right there is the win-win of effective personalization. Users receive their desired benefits (and then some!) while apps win them over and cement their brand loyalty.

And now that you've captured your audience's attention, it's time to talk about generating some revenue.

CHAPTER 7

MONETIZATION |
STRATEGIES FOR
STRIKING GOLD

———

"A goal without a plan is just a wish."

ANTOINE DE SAINT-EXUPÉRY, FRENCH
WRITER, AVIATOR, AND POET

Here's a loaded question: Why do businesses fail?

The answer, of course, isn't simple. Nor can it be found without meticulously considering different companies, their users, and their respective industries in depth. With that in mind, let's explore one of the most famous flameouts of the 2010s: Vine.

By tapping into 2013's emerging GIF culture, the short video sharing platform quickly exploded in popularity. And yet, Vine proved to be a fleeting shooting star; it couldn't get past its hype to become a mainstay of digital communication.

Even though the app itself was extremely user-centric, with its straightforward interface and emphasis on creativity, Vine's developers severely neglected the monetization component. There was no plan for generating sustainable income, and they failed to revamp the app to meet advertisers' needs (i.e., by not allowing longer video lengths). Without a unified business plan, Vine entirely missed out on the world of branded marketing and celebrity posts that we now see Instagram profit from doing.[128]

Which brings us to this: Much like any business, an app's longevity hinges on its monetization strategy.

We still maintain that designing an experience that users fall in love with is the most important part of app creation. But without nailing the next step, you won't be at it for long.

Because app monetization is the process by which you leverage your user base into profit. If user experience is your heart, monetization is the lifeblood that keeps it pumping.

As we'll discuss below, this strategy can come in a variety of forms: a one-time payment, a subscription, or perhaps a profitable partnership with some third party (i.e., a sponsor). But no matter where the money comes from, the core idea is simple. You provide value in exchange for adequate compensation.

---

128 Casey Newton, "Why Vine Died," *The Verge*, October 28, 2016.

STEP ONE: HAVE A PLAN. STEP TWO: ADJUST WHEN NECESSARY

To get the most of a monetization strategy, though, companies don't just map it out on day one and blindly stick to it. Rather, we often see them undergo continuous experimentation as they build a multifaceted model that serves them best.

Take YouTube: Before YouTube became YouTube, it was a video dating site with the slogan *Tune In Hook Up* that couldn't get much traction.[129] So, the founders drastically pivoted to create the platform we now know, and then they incorporated that willingness to pivot into their monetization journey.

Over the past fifteen years, YouTube has adopted a number of distinct approaches to making money. It began with clickable semi-transparent ads on videos, which gave way to the more effective full-screen video ads.

To further expand its scope, YouTube went ahead and developed its flagship Partner Program, which enables content creators (YouTubers) to directly profit off the ads in their videos. The more these YouTubers create, the more they earn, and the greater a cut YouTube receives—a true win-win.[130]

Then we started seeing various subscription services, including a music app (to compete with Spotify) and a premium ad-free version (YouTube Premium, previously YouTube Red) that now offers movie/TV streaming (to compete with

---

129 Paige Leskin, "YouTube History: How the Video-Sharing Website Became So Popular," *Business Insider*, May 30, 2020.
130 Ibid.

Netflix). For the latter, they even collaborated with premium content providers such as NBC, ABC, and CBS.[131]

The point being, it seems like whenever a new market opportunity arises, YouTube is quick to jump in and take a bite out of it. They keep their eggs spread out in different monetization baskets, and whenever an egg hatches, they're there to capitalize on it.

Now, sure, most apps don't get the chance to partner with NBC. Nor do they have the safety net of Google's funding behind them. We'd be remiss if we didn't at least acknowledge that no, YouTube isn't your average, run-of-the-mill mobile app.

But let's put that disclaimer aside for a minute to see what we can learn from YouTube's overarching approach to monetization. Because what YouTube could do isn't as important as what they made sure not to do: Namely, pigeonhole themselves into an inescapable corner.

Which brings us back to Vine. The main reason they couldn't parlay their impressive engagement numbers into long-term revenue is that their hard-capped six-second video length drove advertisers elsewhere. The team at Vine didn't adapt quickly enough, so by the time they finally extended their video lengths, the money had already gone to Instagram, who had long allowed longer clips.[132] In other words, Vine

---

131 Dave Lee, "YouTube Takes on Cable with New TV Service," *BBC News*, updated March 1, 2017.

132 Casey, "Why Vine Died," *The Verge*.

unnecessarily pigeonholed itself and left the door open for someone else to offer what they offer—only better.

We saw a similar story play out in the music app industry in 2010. The company Rdio came along with a phenomenal audio player, but they charged a small fee for their mobile and web platforms. So, when Spotify presented their superior marketing and appetizing *free* option, Rdio stood no chance.[133] By relying on users paying at the start, they pigeonholed themselves and undermined their growth potential. Could Rdio have survived if they'd followed Spotify's lead and abandoned this initial monetization model? Perhaps, but like with Vine, the Rdio team wasn't flexible quickly enough; they put all their eggs in one basket and weren't prepared with possible contingency plans.

Now back to YouTube—there's a reason YouTube *could* stay flexible and freely pivot between strategies. Because no matter what they were doing on the monetization end, their platform was always optimized for growth. So even if one monetization failed, they had other baskets to put their eggs.

Unlike Rdio, YouTube preached user accessibility from day one. And they kept preaching it as the product grew and grew. The content was and continues to be freely available to everyone. Viewers have never faced any significant obstacles—no necessary fees, no aggressive paywalls, just an occasional ad for all the content in the world. And, for that matter, YouTube also removed obstacles for advertisers and content partners.

133 Casey Newton, "Why Rdio Died," *The Verge*, November 17, 2015.

In fact, they've even invested over $100 million in original content creation.[134]

Now just imagine if Vine had managed to do the same.

WHAT MONETIZATION ACTUALLY LOOKS LIKE

In practical terms, app monetization wears many unique hats—so many, that it's often difficult to decide which one fits best. Here, we'll touch on nine of the most common models:

1. Paid Apps
2. Subscriptions
3. Freemium
4. In-App Purchases
5. Advertising
6. Sponsorships
7. Affiliate marketing
8. Transaction Fees
9. Data monetization

Now, you don't need to have deep pockets like YouTube to make these strategies work; you just need to adopt the ones that best support and supplement your product. To avoid the pigeonhole shortcoming, think of them as possible tools hanging from your belt—each with its own pros and cons for you to weigh and consider.

---

134 Sarah Perez, "YouTube to Invest $100M in Kids' Content That Showcases Character Strengths, like Compassion and Curiosity," *TechCrunch*, February 5, 2020.

1. PAID APPS

Plain and simple: Unlimited access for a one-time fee.

You commonly see this approach from utility apps (i.e., TouchRetouch photo editor), mobile games (i.e., Monument Valley), or niche apps (i.e., SkyView® Explore the Universe constellation finder).[135] Here's an example of what a paid app looks like in the Google Play Store:

---

135 TouchRetouch, v. 4.4.12 (ADVA Soft), Android 5.0 and up, updated September 17, 2020; Monument Valley, v. 2.7.17 (ustwo games), Android 4.1 and up, updated January 23, 2020; SkyView® Explore the Universe, v. 3.6.3 (Terminal Eleven), Android 5.0 and up, updated December 3, 2019.

While these upfront payments were originally the standard, developers have veered away due to now-obvious drawbacks. For instance, paid apps will repel some users, no matter what. They're off the table. And as for the ones who do pony up, they can only be monetized once. In other words, these apps depend on a consistent flow of new users for their revenue.

Plus, they have to compete with cheaper alternatives that come up. The industry's barrier to entry is low, and users will always prefer the lowest bidder. With that in mind, it's no surprise that less than 5 percent of all apps on Google Play and App Store are paid apps.[136]

2. SUBSCRIPTIONS

Slightly less plain but still fairly simple; users get access in exchange for recurring payments. Typically, on a monthly or yearly basis, these fees may unlock content libraries, exclusive services, and coveted upgrades.

According to Sensor Tower, US buyers shelled out some $3.8 billion on the hundred most popular nongame subscription apps in 2018. In 2019, that jumped more than 20 percent up to $4.6 billion. It's a safe bet to assume we'll continue to see the arrow pointing up through 2020—especially considering all the big-name apps currently offering month-to-month plans (Tinder, Pandora, YouTube, HBO Now, Bumble, Hulu, and even LinkedIn headline the list).[137]

---

136 "Google Play vs. the IOS App Store | Store Stats for Mobile Apps," 42matters, October 7, 2020.

137 Katie Williams, "US Subscription App Revenue Grew 21% in 2019 to $4.6 Billion," Sensor Tower, January 23, 2020.

The advantages here are pretty convincing: Unlike paid apps, subscriptions bring in steady revenue from the same buyers, thus mitigating feast-or-famine uncertainty. And if users keep investing in the service, they'll keep engaging to reap the paid-for benefits.

There are also fewer obstacles for users as the payment itself doesn't happen until *after* downloading the app. With some apps, users can even play around with a free version before deciding on a subscription... but we'll get there.

All of this works great as long as you, the creator, ensure your product is worth it. Updates, improvements, unceasing quality, high-end support—you have to put in the time, effort, and resources to cement users' renewing commitment.

Your friendly app stores, by the way, incentivize app creators to promote subscription services. How? Well, remember from Chapter 1 that Apple and Google have a blank 30 percent cut over any money users spend within the app, including monthly subscriptions? The app stores lower their cut to 15 percent for all subscribers retained over a twelve-month period.[138]

3. FREEMIUM

Here's where things get spicy: When you start offering different versions of your service.

---

138 "Auto-Renewable Subscriptions," Apple Developer (App Store), accessed October 8, 2020; "Service Fees," Play Console Help (Google Play), accessed October 8, 2020.

As the name suggests, this consists of a limited *free* version and a paid, feature-heavy *premium* plan. This approach has gained rapid traction over the past few years and with good reason—not only does it harness all the advantages of the subscription model, but it also invokes that mesmerizing word…

Free.

We'll dive into it in Chapter 9 but consider this experiment on the power of *free!* from Dan Ariely's book *Predictably Irrational.*

Participants are given a choice between paying fifteen cents for Lindt's famous truffles or one cent for Hershey's Kisses. Understandably, 70 percent opt for the superior chocolate. But when the researchers reduce both prices by one cent and the Kisses become *free!* that 70 percent swings to Hershey's side, despite the same fourteen cent price disparity.[139]

In short, the difference between fifteen cents and one cent is less pronounced than the difference between one cent and zero cents.

And that's how freemium models win, by capturing this enticing *free!* factor, even if the ultimate goal is converting their users.

---

139   Dan Ariely, *Predictably Irrational, Revised and Expanded Edition: The Hidden Forces That Shape Our Decisions,* HarperCollins, June 6, 2009.

Of course, a majority of users won't ever be converted. *Harvard Business Review's* Vineet Kumar even estimates that, on average, only 2 to 5 percent of Freemium apps' users are paying. But he also points out that this isn't a bad thing:

"It's important to recognize the full value of your free users, which takes two forms: Some of them become subscribers, and some draw in new members who become subscribers. A free user is typically worth 15 percent to 25 percent as much as a premium subscriber."[140]

Free users generate traffic. And the higher your traffic is, the lower you can allow your conversion rate to be. If 5 percent of one million users convert, you'll make substantially more than if that number is 50 percent of 10,000 users.

The difficulty with freemium, though, is striking a balance with your offerings. You need to offer substantial enough value to bring in free users and keep them engaged, but not so much value that your paid subscriptions aren't enticing.

4. IN-APP PURCHASES (IAPS)

If you're a retailer, selling new products is much easier after people step inside your store, right?

The same can be said for apps. With IAPs, we add another layer to the freemium model in which additional items are sold from within the mobile app. A subtler conversion tool,

---

140 Vineet Kumar, "Making 'Freemium' Work," *Harvard Business Review*, accessed October 8, 2020.

it's more likely to appeal both to die-hards and noncommittal users.

If you've ever played *Pokémon GO* or the colorful tile-matching game *Candy Crush*, you're well versed in the world of in-app purchases. Around 80 percent of mobile games implement some form of virtual currency or power-ups.[141] And if you ever wondered how *Clash of Clans* could afford a Super Bowl ad starring Liam Neeson, it's in large part thanks to the rise of in-app purchases.

And the rest of the industry is quickly catching up; an estimated 50 percent of nongame apps have adopted IAPs.[142]

These IAPs come in all shapes and sizes, but let's organize them under two distinct umbrellas:

The nonconsumables: These are the one-off buys. For instance, if you're unlocking a new level in a game, you pay once and move onward. Free stargazing app Star Walk 2 even put a one-time price on permanent ad-removal.[143]

The issue with nonconsumables is similar to that of paid apps: Developers need a constant influx of new users to prevent cash flow from drying up. Or they need to keep creating new IAPs that'll attract current users.

---

141 Matt Miller, "Monetization Insights from App Professionals," AppAnnie, accessed October 8, 2020.

142 Ibid.

143 Star Walk 2—Night Sky Map, v. 2.11.2 (Vito Technology Inc.), iOS 10.0 and watch OS 2.0 or later, updated September 29, 2020.

Nonconsumables aren't bad tools for monetization, but they can't be relied upon solely.

The consumables: These are the timeless moneymakers. In *Candy Crush*, these are the gold bars that you can use for infinite upgrades. On the dating app Bumble, it's the Spotlight option that boosts your dating profile to the top of the queue as many times as you want. On the mobile marketplace OfferUp, these are the one- or three-day product advertisements you purchase. Unlike nonconsumables, these OfferUp ads can be purchased as many times as you want for as many items you sell.

Much like subscriptions, consumable IAPs allow developers to monetize off new and existing users again and again. The pressure of constant innovation goes away, and you're able to penetrate your market while perfecting your existing product.

One notable disadvantage, as we have previously discussed, is that Google and Apple charge a 30 percent fee on all these transactions. That's a sizable piece of the pie, but the whole pie still brings in tens of billions of dollars annually.

5. ADVERTISING

Kumar gave us two benefits of free users, but there's a monumental third: Ad revenue.

For each ad you display, you stand to profit off each view, each click, and even each action. In 2019 alone, brands paid over $190 billion for the privilege of this exposure.[144]

Why exactly is ad spend projected to skyrocket into the stratosphere? Because it's a straightforward, versatile strategy for merchants and developers alike. The former can accurately target audiences in an enticing manner, while the latter can rake in revenue in a clean, user-friendly way.

...Oh, and it lets apps proudly wear that badge of *free!*

And sure, we all know ads can be nuisances. But not if you know how to separate the headaches from the cash cows. For starters, take stock of the four primary types of ads at your disposal:

Banner and Text Ads

In 2014, a little game called *Flappy Bird* took the world by storm. The challenge—guiding a pixelated bird through endless Mario-style pipes—was so addicting that Dong Nguyen pulled it offline within weeks.[145]

...But not before bringing in $50k per day with banner ads.[146]

---

144 "The State of Mobile in 2020: The Key Stats You Need to Know," AppAnnie, accessed October 26, 2020.

145 David Kushner, "The Flight of the Birdman: Flappy Bird Creator Dong Nguyen Speaks Out," *Rolling Stone*, March 11, 2014.

146 Ellis Hamburger, "Indie Smash Hit 'Flappy Bird' Racks up $50K per Day in Ad Revenue," *The Verge*, February 5, 2014.

Like virtual billboards, banners are commonly used because they're so easy to throw in without harming the app experience. They sit quietly on one end of the page and don't force any interaction.

But that is also its big negative. Many marketers criticize these ads because users learn to ignore them in a phenomenon dubbed *banner blindness*.[147] The result is low engagement, around 60 percent of which comes from accidental

147 Kara Pernice, "Banner Blindness Revisited: Users Dodge Ads on Mobile and Desktop," NN/g, April 22, 2018.

clicks.[148] These *fat finger* errors only frustrate users and deliver poor prospects.

Larger companies still like to use banners, more for brand awareness than direct conversions. And upstart apps like Flappy Bird often oblige for the quick revenue bump.

But in today's app store, we're getting a bit more creative:

Interstitial Advertising

"Full-screen ads that appear at natural transition points in the user flow of an app."[149]

That's how Google defines these pop-up ads that take advantage of in-app pauses. So, when you reach a new level or turn to the next page, interstitial ads work their magic:

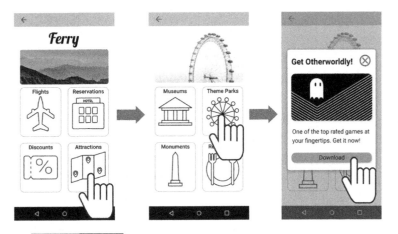

---

148 Ben Frederick, "60% of All Mobile Banner Ad Clicks Are Accidents," *MediaPost*, February 4, 2016.

149 "In-App Advertising Formats," MoPub, accessed October 26, 2020.

These ads are effective because, unlike banners, you can't ignore them. This means more opportunity for impressive visuals, higher click-through rates (CTR), and increased conversions.

...That's if you do them well. Plenty of apps drive users away by getting greedy and inserting interstitials left and right. But nobody's going to stick around if ads come up after every other action. Or if they appear at highly inconvenient moments.

Worse yet are the deceivers. Those promotional boxes that hide their X-out buttons. This doesn't just send the user over the edge; it tarnishes the company being advertised and causes way more damage than the extra few seconds of exposure are worth.

Google even has some Play Store guidelines that penalize apps that utilize exploitative tactics.[150]

Video Ads and Rich Media Content

This is where the creativity turns up a gear. Promotional clips and interactive content tend to raise engagement and CTR. One of their main draws is feeling more like entertainment than marketing.

We see a particularly effective offshoot in many games, where simply watching a promotional video gives the viewer tangible rewards. An overwhelming number of users respond

---

150 Ibid

favorably to these ads as they offer a choice *and* provide immediate incentives.

The brands aren't complaining either, as they enjoy a more attentive and agreeable audience. And neither are apps, which see total video ad spend in the annual ballpark of $20 billion in 2020.[151]

As for the cons, they're similar to that of interstitials: developers need to be careful to keep these ads from being excessive or disruptive. We've all rolled our eyes at those unskippable videos with loud auto-playing audio—an unnecessary waste of a high-potential medium.

Native Advertising

These are the clever ads that blend right into your app. You typically come across them on your Facebook and Instagram—apps with content-heavy feeds.

Because they fit so naturally, they impact usability least of all. And they're considerably more likely to garner attention since they don't look like advertisements; they look like the rest of the app!

151 Rahul Chadha, "Mobile Video Advertising 2019," eMarketer, January 7, 2019.

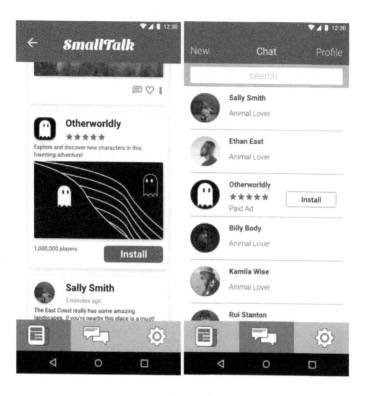

Unlike the eyesore banner we saw in Flappy Bird, these native ads don't instill any ad overwhelm. And here's the crazy thing: Even though users *know* these are ads, they often don't care! One Stanford study found that though people recognized native posts as ads, native ads are still more likely to be clicked.[152]

The one potential drawback is that these inserts can sometimes appear deceptive, as though they're trying to trick unsuspecting readers into clicking. But according to the

---

152 Sachin Waikar, "Disguised 'Native' Ads Don't Fool Us Anymore," Stanford Graduate School of Business, January 8, 2018.

researchers at eMarketer, this hasn't presented a major issue; they estimate that over 60 percent of display advertising, to the modest tune of $33 plus billion, is now native.[153]

6. SPONSORSHIPS

Advertising's cousin, sponsorship, distinguishes itself by being more pertinent to its user base. Typically, you see sponsorships framed as ongoing partnerships where the purpose isn't direct solicitation. Instead, they're allies—part of the team and part of the experience. On top of recognition, they cultivate a specific brand value.

Much like with ads, sponsors purchase virtual and physical real estate to promote their businesses. This can come in several forms—visual placement, audio mention, merchandise—and often takes on a collaborative feel.

As an example, we saw some particularly creative teamwork from Snapchat and Domino's back in 2018. What Snapchat did was they set up a special augmented reality (AR) lens within their app. So, when users scrolled through camera filters that day, one of them would pop up a Domino's pizza on screen. Users could directly interact with this appetizing graphic and even buy a pizza right there within Snapchat! But even without any purchases, this innovative feature let Domino's make memorable, winning impressions on tens of millions of users.[154]

---

153 Nicole Perrin, "US Native Advertising 2019 - EMarketer Trends, Forecasts & Statistics," eMarketer, March 20, 2019.

154 "Snapchat Ads for Business | Mobile Advertising," Snap Inc., accessed October 8, 2020.

One aspect to consider while seeking sponsorships is which businesses are worth teaming up with. Sure, getting revenue is nice, but you don't want to undermine your brand in the process. Your sponsors reflect on your organization, so they need to make sense for your audience.

7. AFFILIATE MARKETING

Unlike advertising or sponsorship, affiliate marketing is all about performance. Therefore, in order for you, the referrer, to get paid, your affiliate partner needs to get the agreed-upon results.

These results can come in the form of users referred or click rates, but typically the goal is revenue produced for the affiliate. When they profit, you receive a predetermined percentage, unlike with display advertisers, which just pay for the spot.

This means there's an incentive to work with your affiliate and ensure these promotional efforts are effective. Their success results in your financial gain and, as just mentioned, a stronger market reputation.

For instance, finance management apps often have affiliate pages that promise heightened exposure—which relevant businesses like credit cards and auto insurers are always seeking. If you've ever used the Mint app to track your personal finances, you've seen this. They very openly put their banking partners front and center.[155]

---

155 Mint: Personal Finance & Money, v. 7.20.0 (Mint Software, Inc.), iOS 11.0 and watchOS 5.1 or later, updated October 21, 2020.

So, these lucky businesses boost their outreach, and in return, Mint gets a cut of the revenue it generates while fostering credible corporate associations. Everybody wins as long as Mint brings in the revenue. That's the asterisk of affiliate marketing. The deals have to be enticing, and the app needs to have a large enough audience. We mention Mint because they check both boxes, but for many apps, this path isn't so lucrative.

And as with sponsorships, it is worth keeping in mind the reputation of the businesses you choose to promote as affiliate partners.

8. TRANSACTION FEES
"Just Venmo me."

It's quickly entered the millennial lexicon of "FaceTime me" and "Let's Uber there." And it still almost seems too good to be true—a free money-transfer app with no catches and no hidden fees.

Naturally, you may have wondered: How in the world does Venmo make money? The short answer: Transaction fees.

When apps act as the middleman, they levy charges for facilitating exchanges, often a fixed percentage or preset amount. In the case of Venmo, you can use it for years without spending a single penny. Regular transfers between peers or into your debit account are on the house. Part of why it's become so ubiquitous is because it only charges three specific transactions.

First are credit card payments, of which Venmo takes 3 percent. But you can justify this as a convenience fee for facilitating your credit spending.

Second are instant transfers, which let you bypass the one to three business day wait time and send cash straight to your bank account. Venmo charges a 1 percent fee for transfers (with a minimum fee of $0.25 and a maximum fee of $10), but again, it's reasonable given the convenience factor.[156]

Last, we have merchant fees. Thanks to the infrastructure of its parent company PayPal, Venmo has teamed up with over two million merchants.[157] These businesses pay a small price for each sale conducted through the app, and they do so happily, as Venmo gives them access to over forty million users. Users aren't charged for these expenditures.[158]

As you can see, the transaction fee model lends itself to win-win scenarios if done right. Plus, it's easy to scale and lets you keep your interface user-friendly (notice that Venmo doesn't have any flashy ads or blaring videos).

That said, most apps don't have the financial safety net or preexisting customer base of PayPal behind them. And that leads to one potential drawback. Setting such low and sparse transaction fees as Venmo has requires a certain flexibility and reach.

---

156 "Resources—Our Fees," Venmo, accessed October 8, 2020.
157 "Venmo Now Accepted at More Than Two Million US Merchants," *Business Wire*, October 17, 2017.
158 Donna Fuscaldo, "PayPal All in with Venmo In 2020," *Forbes*, January 30, 2020.

9. DATA MONETIZATION

One hundred-eighty trillion gigabytes of online data.

That's the astronomical figure expected for 2025.[159] Between websites, social media, online tests, and dating apps, all that data translates into a bona fide goldmine, in more ways than one.

Insights into user behavior have enabled online and offline businesses to make billion-dollar improvements. It's why companies like Facebook give such weight to analytics: to guide product innovation and audience targeting. In other words, data helps brands refine practices and sell products.

And we should also mention that data monetization plays nicely with scalability. The more you scale, the more daily or monthly active users you have, the higher your data revenue can get.

Facebook has also shown us another way to monetize user data: selling it to third parties. If done with users' consent, it can be a solid profit avenue that actually improves the recipient's product. This is how Instagram posts targeted ads, and how Yelp decides which relevant restaurants to feature. But, of course, this is where we come across ethical concerns.

Privacy, legality, and transparency are some of the big buzzwords plaguing data monetization today. Considering the laundry list of data-breach incidents over the past few years,

---

159 Tom Coughlin, "175 Zettabytes By 2025," *Forbes*, November 27, 2018.

encryption practices and GDPR compliance are as vital as ever. More on this, though, in Chapter 8.

FINAL WORD: SO, WHICH MODEL SHOULD YOU CHOOSE?

Well, there's no right or wrong answer. One strategy may spell instant success for one app but crickets for another.

More often than not, a successful solution will combine a number of these approaches in varying degrees. And, as You-Tube has so artfully demonstrated over the years, the extent to which you should rely on one approach or another will change with the times.

In fact, dare we say, you might use a different technique altogether. Companies are always redefining the ways they make money. It's their unceasing innovation that came up with video ads, AR lenses, and in-app currencies. When it comes to monetary creativity, the sky's the limit. With more advanced analytics becoming widely available, monetization truly has become both an art and a science.

As for how to make the art and science of monetization work in your favor, we turn to the critical topic of trust. Without it, you can't hope to sell your product, particularly in these data-sensitive times.

So, let's turn the page and talk about how to build it.

CHAPTER 8

DATA PRIVACY | IN APPS WE TRUST

———

"Trust takes years to build, seconds to break, and forever to repair."

UNKNOWN

You've likely heard the saying: If something online is free, *you* are the product. In other words, the cost of using *free* digital services is your personal data.

And while this tagline may be catchy, it's also quite true.

Just ask Facebook and Google! They've made billions selling filing cabinets of information about you. Age, location, photos, calendar, friends, family, sexual orientation, political leanings, and other likes and dislikes—all of it tracked and stored.

Over the past few years, though, these all-powerful tech giants have witnessed their users' trust erode thanks to numerous data leaks and privacy scandals, most notably with Facebook. A 2018 *New York Times* article found that British political consultancy firm Cambridge Analytica harvested and exploited the data of over eighty-seven million Facebook users to influence the 2016 presidential campaign in favor of the Trump campaign.[160]

Unfortunately, Facebook isn't our only culprit. In 2016, Uber released a dubious update enabling the company to collect users' location data post-trip, even with the app shut off.[161] The feature was quickly removed a year later.[162]

And then there's FaceApp, A Russian-based photo filter program that uploaded users' content and data to Google Cloud and Amazon Web Services.[163] Or how about weather forecasting apps like The Weather Channel, WeatherBug, and Accuweather, which collected and sold detailed location data to dozens of companies for targeted advertising purposes?[164] Even *Pokémon GO* got in on the action, as parent company Niantic previously required wide-sweeping access to users' Google accounts.[165] It seems we can't even trust Pokémon gaming apps to leave our data alone!

---

160 Matthew Rosenberg, Nicholas Confessore, and Carole Cadwalladr, "How Trump Consultants Exploited the Facebook Data of Millions," *The New York Times*, March 17, 2018.

161 Kate Conger, "Uber Begins Background Collection of Rider Location Data," *TechCrunch*, November 28, 2016.

162 Laurel Wamsley, "Uber Ends Its Controversial Post-Ride Tracking of Users' Location," *NPR (The Two-Way Blog)*, August 29, 2017.

163 Matthew Panzarino, "AI Photo Editor FaceApp Goes Viral Again on IOS, Raises Questions about Photo Library Access," *TechCrunch*, July 16, 2019.

164 Jason Koebler, "Stop Using Third-Party Weather Apps," *Vice*, January 4, 2019.

165 Adam Reeve (@adamreeve), "Pokémon Go Is a Huge Security Risk," Tumblr, July 8, 2016.

That said, as consumers, we can take solace in knowing that the pendulum is starting to swing the other way on these nefarious data farmers. Privacy breaches are now being met with swift consequences. And for evidence, we can again look at Facebook.

Following the Cambridge Analytica scandal, the Federal Trade Commission (FTC) hit Zuckerberg's social media company with unprecedented penalties, including five billion in fines and top to bottom operational changes.[166] The latter of these included new privacy standards, transparency requirements, third party sharing restrictions, corporate reshuffling, and FTC monitoring procedures.

Suffice it to say: Betraying user privacy is no joke. Particularly with the General Data Protection Regulation (GDPR) now enforcing stricter compliance worldwide.[167]

This is, of course, great news for concerned consumers. But for apps, even the tiniest lapse in security can now spell a death sentence: Considering that app abandonment is at an all-time high, a red flag as glaring as a security fault is sure to send users away in droves.

All of which goes to show that our greatest challenge in developing a successful app is actually building trust.

---

166 "FTC Imposes $5 Billion Penalty and Sweeping New Privacy Restrictions on Facebook," Federal Trade Commission, July 24, 2019.

167 "General Data Protection Regulation (GDPR) Compliance Guidelines," GDPR, accessed October 2, 2020.

WHAT IS TRUST AND WHY DOES IT MATTER TO APPS

Simply defined, trust is an instance in which one party places confidence in the actions of another. Of course, that barely covers the bases. So, let's turn to Dan Ariely, renowned Ted-Talker and best-selling author on behavioral psychology, to extend our concept a bit further:[168]

> "Trust…is a common good. It is everywhere, and it's an important lubricant for modern society."

When you use Uber, you trust that the driver will show up at point A and drive you safely to point B. Likewise, the driver trusts that you won't pose any harm or hindrance. Even with Uber's rating system, emergency help options, and background checks, an underlying element of trust must exist.

Such trust is an integral part of our day-to-day transactions—from going to the barber or buying groceries to driving on the road or working in an office. But with mobile apps and technology in general, the recent scandals have put that trust in jeopardy.

In 2015, before those major data breaches came to light, Pew Research found that among smartphone users, "six-in-ten downloaders had chosen not to install an app when they discovered how much personal information the app required

---

168 Dan Ariely, "Why Trust Is So Important and How We Can Get More of It?" TEDxJaffa, uploaded on October 20, 2017. YouTube video, 00:01:35.

in order to use it. Separately, 43 percent have uninstalled an app for the same reason after initially downloading it."[169]

6-in-10 Smartphone App Users Have Chosen Not to Install an App Because of Concerns About Personal Information

% of app downloaders who chose to do each of the following after discovering how much personal information the app required

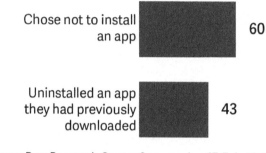

Chose not to install an app   **60**

Uninstalled an app they had previously downloaded   **43**

Source: Pew Research Center Surveys, Jan.27-Feb. 16, 2015. N=461 adults ages 18 and up. The margin of error for all adults in +/- 5.8 percentage points.
PEW RESEARCH CENTER

Therein lies the complicated dilemma for apps: Asking for data repels users, but access to this data is often necessary for these apps to work.

This is simply the nature of mobile devices. We love them for their unparalleled convenience, for neatly packaging life's

---

169 Monica Anderson, "Mobile Apps, Privacy and Permissions: 5 Key Takeaways," Pew Research Center, November 10, 2015.

most essential tasks right inside our pockets. But no matter what you're using it for, phone, camera, music, banking, ride-sharing, social media, or what have you, these tasks require a level of access.

And now, these channels of access are finally being held to close scrutiny, which means that it's as important as ever to establish trust with your users from the initial interaction. After all, the app world isn't kind on second chances at a first impression.

For any app to succeed, trust needs to be strategically created and maintained. To do so, billion-dollar apps rely on the following elements:

1. INTEGRITY

Collecting user data can certainly help make more money, but what separates great companies from the rest is collecting this data in the right way. The intentions and methods behind your app matter.

Generally, you want to make your choices about them, the users, not about you. Here's what's worth keeping in mind:

Don't sell out to advertisers. People can tolerate ads if they are relevant or unobtrusive, but too many will make your app look like a low-effort cash grab. The same goes for sharing your users' data with advertisers without their consent. For your users' sake, carefully monitor the quality and quantity of ad content as well as perform due diligence on your advertising partners.

Keep notifications useful. Similar to ads, notifications can be a double-edged sword. If done right, they'll keep bringing users back, but if overdone, you'll only end up frustrating your users.

Be honest about subscription services. Stories abound of apps deceiving customers into making unwanted payments. You've likely seen them: Free trials that mysteriously expire, confusing payment interfaces, overly aggressive subscription pop-ups, and so on. Is that the kind of app you want to put out there?

Give users control over their data. GDPR laws have already put this ball in motion, requiring companies to uphold certain standards like:[170]

a. Right to access data—If users ask for it, companies are legally obligated to disclose their data and explain how it was being used.
b. Right to be forgotten—Otherwise known as the Right to Erasure, this article stipulates that companies (and third-party extensions) must fulfill all requests for removal of personal information (whether that data is controlled directly or through a tool used within the app, like Google Analytics).
c. Notification of breach—If data is compromised, the onus is on the company to be forthright about this news to its entire user base.

---

170 "General Data Protection Regulation (GDPR) – Official Legal Text," gdpr-info.eu, accessed October 2, 2020.

2. COMPETENCE

Let's start with a simple rule of thumb: Good design fosters trust. An app with a coherent style and intuitive interface will help users feel comfortable, while unprofessional design and muddled navigation will do the opposite. Attending to the smallest of details will signal to your users that you genuinely care about their needs and wants.

As an extension of this rule, smooth performance also matters. Apps that are constantly freezing, crashing, or bugging out will disrupt users' experience and send them straight for your *uninstall* button. And while no app is 100 percent perfect, product teams that listen to user complaints and respond with regular updates are sure to build greater trust with their users.

If you play your cards right, upholding these values can even earn you featured distinction in Google's Play Store or Apple's App Store. They often reward competent apps with front-page credibility and the perks that come with it—views, downloads, and, yes, revenue.

3. TRANSPARENCY

A calculator app that asks to make and manage calls? Yeah, no, thank you.

Often, though, the question of granting permissions isn't so cut and dry. Some users are comfortable with their Google assistant reading texts and tracking locations; others find it creepy. The line between invasiveness and helpfulness is more of a murky grey area, with trust as the key to ending up on the right side of it.

But here we're presented with another dilemma: People won't use your app if they don't trust you. But to build trust, you need them to use the app.

How can we break through this vicious cycle and get users to buy in? The answer lies in transparency. A tricky prospect for sure, but one that the best apps have taken great pains to get right. And here are their main ingredients for success:

Show your hand first. How can you foster trust if users don't even know who you are? Putting together a detailed *About* section is a great way to open up about your professional backgrounds, company goals, and higher value points. Use this opportunity to humanize your app; a contact form or valid email address for feedback also goes a long way.

With that out of the way, make your privacy policy more accessible. Feature it on a prominent screen (i.e., the sign-up page) and, where possible, do away with that virtually illegible legal jargon.

Check out how Norton presents it on their mobile antivirus app:[171]

---

171 LifeLock for Norton 360, v. 1.23 (NortonMobile, 2020), Android 6.0 or later.

These terms and conditions are far from the typical eyesores, wouldn't you say?

Only ask for necessary permissions upfront. You wouldn't ask someone to marry you after the first date, would you? Likewise, refrain from asking for permissions before you need them. You don't want to overwhelm the user with requests.

Of course, some apps need certain access right away in order to perform their basic functions. For instance, Snapchat, Instagram, and Pinterest have a pop-up message asking for access to your device's camera, much like this:

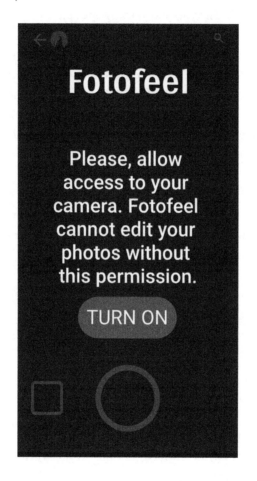

But camera access isn't the only permission these apps ask for from you. Depending on what you're up to, they may need you to let them record audio, for instance.

If that's the case, though, these apps hold off on asking for those permissions until absolutely necessary. This way, they don't burden you with a bunch of privacy messages right off the bat. Instead, they give themselves the chance to cultivate more trust while you're still using the app.

Be clear about your requests. First off, candidly indicate which information you need to collect. And then, link that data to concrete benefits (i.e., a ridesharing app needs location access to pick users up faster). This is how we answer the "Why do you need this?" question and alleviate concerns over invasions of privacy.

Continue this transparency by clarifying where that information goes from here—namely, how users can manage, delete, update, and export it. The more open you are, the less skepticism you invite.

Furthermore, presentation also plays a role here. You can throw intimidating blocks of text at your users, or you can opt for concise, simple language alongside illustrations or even explanatory videos.

Consider, for example, the challenge faced by the app Robinhood. As a stock-trading fintech company, they need to obtain extremely sensitive information in order to work. But how eager are you to share your social security number with some new app?

If you log on, though, you'll see that Robinhood does an outstanding job of explaining themselves. For each step, they provide succinct, reasonable justifications—i.e., citing the

US Patriot Act for legally mandated SSN collection. This text works alongside a smooth, minimalist design to bolster subtly yet effectively.

Allow users to change their minds. Continuous consent is key. If people know they can change their minds later about receiving notifications or granting in-app permissions, they're much more likely to sign up from the get-go.

Likewise, data collection should always be an opt-in selection. Apps often need certain browsing data to provide relevant recommendations (think: Amazon, Netflix), but going behind users' backs with automatic opt-in settings will rub them the wrong way. Instead, explain the value of your data collection and win your users over for good.

Inform them of any third-party data sharing. In the spirit of full transparency, let users know who you're working with.

Now, you don't need to flash your data-sharing practices in neon lights every time someone opens the app. But your privacy policy should at least be forthright about the various affiliates, research institutions, or government organizations you're partnered with so that users know what they're consenting to.

Also—and this should go without saying—do your homework and make sure these external entities are themselves GDPR compliant, with a strong reputation and commitment to best privacy practices.

4. RELIABILITY

Only once you *do* get access to users' data does the true battle begin. And whether or not you win this battle may be the difference between sustained success and having your brand dragged through the mud.

Secure your app with encryption. Shield the transfer of data between you and your users with hard-to-penetrate encryption algorithms.

This is where we turn to the rigorous communication protections of HTTPS (Hypertext Transfer Protocol Secure) and SSL (Secure Sockets Layer) or the more updated TSL (Transport Layer Security). SSL/TSL certificates are small data files that lock up essential company info behind cryptographic keys.

Now, we won't get too deep into the nitty-gritty, but take a page out of WhatsApp's book and make sure your channels are properly secured with these certificates. Back in 2016, the chatting platform installed end-to-end encryption for all communications between its 1.5 billion active users.[172]

And take a look at the security measures taken by popular banking apps. Bank of America and Acorns, for instance, are heavy on verifying sign-ins and timing out unresponsive page visitors.

---

172 Mike Issac, "WhatsApp Introduces End-to-End Encryption," *The New York Times*, April 5, 2016.

Be diligent in dealing with privacy matters. With big name companies recently toppling like dominoes to data breaches, it's no wonder that the general public is more and more hesitant to share sensitive data. Nor is it surprising that they're reluctant to deal with companies that carry substandard security reputations.

At the very least, you can avoid such a fate by investing the proper effort and resources into your security strategy. For instance, consider giving users options for reinforcing the protections on their data (i.e., multi-factor authentication).

Perhaps most important is what you do if issues pop up. It's always best to stay ahead of them and assuage users' fears by promptly communicating and resolving the hiccups. To do so effectively, you may need to implement new surveillance software and develop company-wide data breach policies.

This all may sound a bit overwhelming, but if you're going to take data security seriously, you need to actually take it seriously. Here's the thing, though—if you've done your due diligence, don't be shy about it! Give your users the peace of mind that you're protecting their personal info and fully complying with the GDPR. Use this to your advantage—to strengthen your brand.

ULTIMATELY, YOU WANT YOUR USERS FEELING SAFE AND IN CONTROL

This means taking a good, hard look at your data-gathering processes and designing appropriate components for acquiring user consent. And while the moral lines here may still be blurry, our laws and culture are heavily trending toward empowering users, not companies. So, make sure your policies act accordingly.

As a final word, designer Cennydd Bowles sums it up perfectly:

"You may end up with less rich customer insights than you had before. Some KPIs may slump. But for companies that have direct customer relationships, it's all manageable, and on the upside, you not only reduce your compliance risk but benefit from the increased trust your customers will show in you and the online world in general."[173]

Without this *increased trust*, it's hard to do much of anything with your user base. But with it, now we can really talk more about the ultimate show of trust: The purchase.

---

173 Cennydd Bowles, "A Techie's Rough Guide to GDPR," Cennydd Bowles, last modified October 12, 2018.

CHAPTER 9

PRICING | ALL NUMBERS DON'T COME EQUAL

"Even the most analytical thinkers are predictably irrational; the really smart ones acknowledge and address their irrationalities."

DAN ARIELY, AUTHOR AND PROFESSOR OF
PSYCHOLOGY AND BEHAVIORAL ECONOMICS.

No matter how smooth your interface, no matter how versatile your monetization strategy, and no matter how effectively you get user buy-in, there's still an elephant in the room question before you:

What price to charge?

Well, that's a question that has befuddled entrepreneurs since the beginning of modern trade. Product pricing involves acute knowledge of your industry, competitive landscape, overall economy, customer willingness to pay, and yeah, some luck. Leigh Caldwell's *The Psychology of Price* and

Hermann Simon's *Confessions of the Pricing Man* are great reads on the nuances of business pricing.[174]

Simon astutely compares successful pricing to "an exotic cocktail, with equal parts psychology, economics, strategy, tools and incentives stirred up together."[175] In this chapter, we've pruned out the "cocktail ingredients" that are most relevant to mobile app entrepreneurs. We start with some fundamental pricing strategy before discussing at length the more zesty ingredients: psychological pricing tools that modern apps have perfected.

FIRST THINGS FIRST: WHAT'S YOUR PRODUCT WORTH?

The tricky thing about the concept of value is that it can be fairly arbitrary. Who's to say what the value of an app is or isn't?

That question isn't actually rhetorical—the *who* is extremely vital here because the value is a matter of perspective. And the prices you end up setting will reflect which of the following perspectives you prioritize.

1. **Cost.** This is probably the most straightforward perspective. Here, the price you set is an answer to questions such as: How much does it cost to build and scale your app?

---

174 Leigh Caldwell, *The Psychology of Price: How to Use Price to Increase Demand, Profit and Customer Satisfaction*, United Kingdom: Crimson, 2012; Hermann Simon, *Confessions of the Pricing Man: How Price Affects Everything*, Germany: Springer International Publishing, 2015.

175 Simon, *Confessions of the Pricing Man.*

What are your yearly expenses? And then what price tags will help you reach your profit targets?

The goal here is achieving what we can call *sustainable pricing*. If you can find the intersection between what users are willing to pay, what benefits your margins, and what maintains (or even enhances!) the quality of your service, then you're golden. This, very literally, is the core tenet of user-centric monetization.

2. **Competition**. In the app marketplace, you often have to look beyond covering costs. The high stakes of competitive pricing beg a new round of questions: Can you afford to charge more than your competitors? If so, how can you offer more value? Are you sure your rivals aren't doing more for less?

This is where having consistent industry awareness comes into play. You need to keep a pulse on market benchmarks and emerging trends in order to stay in the race. After all, it's not by coincidence that Spotify, Pandora, and Apple music are all similarly priced.

3. **Market perception**: If your product lies in a niche with minimal direct competition, pricing might instead be driven by perceived value. Amazon Prime, for example, charges users $119 per year because (a) their service feels worth it and (b) few companies can even compete with Prime.

Similarly, Uber and Lyft have relatively opaque prices based on distance, location, time of day, and driver demand. Users still pay up, though, thanks to a lack of alternatives and the vague variability of all these value factors.

Here, perception dictates reality. And the perception you want is that your price is reasonable—that the value obtained is worth more than the price spent. Understanding this perception allows you to confidently identify a price range that captures your customers' spending comfort zone. Over time, you can test various prices in this range to find the points with the highest returns.

More practically speaking, perception seeps into decisions such as which features to offer free versus paying users: Your premium version must be worth the upgrade, but your free version still needs to be worth the download. As we'll elaborate on in Chapter 11, the solutions to such arbitrary questions are best derived by continuous testing.

Naturally, the realities of cost, competition, and value differ from industry to industry, company to company, and even within a company over time. And here's the thing: You may even find that they differ from one user to the next.

SECOND: IS YOUR APP WORTH THE SAME TO DIFFERENT USERS?

The answer is probably not. Again, value is a matter of perspective; no two users are the same, and no two perspectives are either.

That's why segmented and dynamic pricing models have become the norm for apps—to capitalize on numerous perspectives in a way that a fixed model cannot. Here's what these strategies look like:

1. **Fixed**. Here, all users pay the same prices for the app and/ or in-app items. It's a model frequently seen with paid apps like certain games (i.e., Fruit Ninja Classic, Minecraft) and utility apps (i.e., That SkyView constellation finder mentioned in Chapter 7).

The fixed model's advantage is that it's extremely simple to implement and objectively fair. But it can also leave money on the table. For some users, the fixed price might be too expensive and drive them away. For others, the set in stone price tag may actually be undercharging what they're willing to pay up.

2. **Segmented**. This one is most common. Users are grouped based on certain characteristics such as demographics, location, behavior, newness to the app, and more. For instance, we see the likes of YouTube, Hulu, and Spotify segment their tiered subscription offerings. But segmentation wears many hats. Some apps even vary prices depending on whether a user has an iOS or Android device!

How do you decide, for instance, if you should charge US users more than you charge UK users? Simply put: Through extensive market research—it's a game in which all billion-dollar apps (and billion-dollar companies, for that matter) are perpetually engaged.

Note that you do have to be careful not to cross ethical lines here. One example: Tinder found that users over thirty were willing to pay more for subscriptions. Soon after a price hike, the state of California found Tinder to be violating anti-age discrimination laws and penalized them accordingly.

3. **Dynamic Price Model.** Let's take the concept of extensive market research one step further. With dynamic pricing, we have *constant* market research and constant recalculation of prices based on those findings.

In other words, this model calls for prices to be fluid as to account for the natural variability of countless market factors. What kinds of factors? Well, we have users (think: previous purchase history, engagement patterns), competition (think: rivals' price reductions, state of the national economy), and value (think: brand perception, cultural trends), to name a few. Not too dissimilar from the pricing factors just mentioned.

We've long seen ever-changing industries like airlines, hospitality, and the retail sector use this dynamic approach, and apps are quickly following suit. To come back to one of our favorite examples, ridesharing apps like Uber and Lyft use dynamic pricing to dictate surge prices during rush hours. Some new-age mobile games have even ditched the Fixed model in favor of dynamic by slyly offering discounts on IAP prices when a player most needs assistance. This way, frustrated users will spend a few discounted dollars instead of giving up on the app entirely.

This goes to show when used effectively, this model is the epitome of what market research can do for a company.

But this is just the tip of the iceberg. Depending on your product and industry, there could be any number of other pricing considerations worth taking: What type of language to use, how many options to offer, when and where to express discounts.

…And it also depends on your users. Determining which considerations do and don't matter brings us back to the topic of empathy—the better you understand your users' core drives, the more robust your pricing model can be.

THIRD: WHICH PRICES WILL MOST APPEAL TO USERS?

This is where modern apps have thrived—the *presentation* of their prices.

Discerning a product's value is an essential part of the pricing process, but as we said, there are a few more ingredients to this cocktail. Because, as logical as our discussion has been to this point, the reality is that consumers aren't purely motivated by sensible incentives.

In fact, there's still lots we don't understand when it comes to spending behaviors. For instance, most people can't tell an expensive bottle of wine from a cheap one, yet we still associate a beverage's cost with quality. Or how about the old restaurant trick of removing the dollar sign from a menu item—that alone has been shown to boost sales.

According to Dan Ariely, it all boils down to the complexities of human psychology:[176]

"We are all far less rational in our decision-making than standard economic theory assumes. Our irrational behaviors are neither random nor senseless: they are systematic and predictable. We all make the same types of mistakes over and over because of the basic wiring of our brains."

So, let's step inside the shoes of a billion-dollar app exec and try to find the optimal pricing strategy for our "irrational" audience:

1. LUCKY NUMBER NINE

Surely, you've wondered: Why does every price end in nine? Is it just a gimmick? Is there actually a difference in sales between $19.99 and $20?

William Poundstone's book *Priceless* sought to answer that very question, examining a number of studies on customer response to price values. One experiment confirmed that 9 prices brought in as much as 24 percent more revenue; another discovered that identical items sold more frequently at $39 than at $44 or even $34![177]

As for the exact psychology behind this mental loophole, it's still something of a mystery. But that hasn't stopped the

---

176 Dan Ariely, *Predictably Irrational: The Hidden Forces that Shape Our Decisions*, United Kingdom: Harper, 2009.

177 William Poundstone, *Priceless: The Myth of Fair Value (and how to Take Advantage of It)*, Australia: Scribe Publications Pty Limited, 2010.

biggest names in the app world from embracing 9 as their own. Spotify, Pandora, Duolingo - you name it. They've got nines everywhere.

Gaming apps, in particular, follow this blueprint to a tee with their in-app purchases. And hey, remember Apple's first stab at monetizing music? Each song cost ninety-nine cents, not one dollar. Because, for one reason or another, it just works.

2. THE SWEET SMELL OF *FREE!*-DOM

Something's either free or it isn't.

It seems simple, but the power of *free* cannot be overstated. Ariely proved as much in his book *Predictably Irrational*, in which he recounts Amazon's discovery that its European sales were drastically lower in France because all French orders had a twenty-cent shipping charge. The rest of Europe? Free shipping, of course.[178]

Our own homegrown research has found an even more remarkable statistic: Apps with *free* in the title are downloaded, on average, roughly *twice as often* as apps without it. Two times as many downloads! It's a truly staggering difference, one that, according to Ariely, is a direct reflection of human nature:

"Most transactions have an upside and a downside, but when something is FREE! we forget the downside. FREE! gives us such an emotional charge that we perceive what is being offered as immensely more valuable than it really is."[179]

This discussion of *FREE!* even extends beyond money to time itself. We're much more willing to wait for something if we know we're getting it at the ultimate discount. *FREE!* justifies how we spend our time - even if it's on a meal we don't love or some concert we wouldn't otherwise have an interest.

...Or, for that matter, if it's on an app.

Here's where the advantage of video advertising over the paid ad-free approach comes into focus. As discussed in Chapter 7, many free-to-play gaming apps incorporate advertising that users can watch to earn more coins, unlock characters, or level up. Furthermore, *FREE!* opens the door to in-app

---

178 Ariely, *Predictably Irrational.*
179 Ibid.

purchases; you use it to lure prospects in and then hit 'em with upgrades once they're hooked.

3. COINS. TOKENS. GOLD STARS...ANYTHING BUT REAL MONEY

Speaking of in-app purchases, they tend to be a lot more appealing when they don't actually feel like purchases at all.

Here's what we mean: Studies have shown that people are much more willing to spend $20 with their credit cards than by pulling out cold hard cash. It seems that on a subconscious level, we respond favorably to buffers between our expenditures and the feeling of financial loss. Swiping a card is much less psychologically intrusive than handing over a physical dollar bill.[180]

But what if we add another buffer? And then another?

That's the sly trick gaming apps everywhere are using: They're free to download, but they're built upon a foundation of fake currency. So, you end up in a position where you're buying new armor for your character with special in-game coins that you can purchase via your already-attached credit card.

The distance from your bank account is tremendous. The transaction is one-click easy. And, at the end of the day, you don't actually know the real value of what you're buying. That's because the exchange rate of real money to virtual currency is intentionally made to be abstract.

---

180 Drazen Prelec and Duncan Simester. "Always Leave Home Without It: A Further Investigation of the Credit-Card Effect on Willingness to Pay." Marketing Letters 12, no. 1 (2001): 5–12. Accessed November 22, 2020.

For example, let's say you play a game with an in-app coin currency. It's not uncommon for the coins to come in packages like *1000 BooCoins for $19.99* and *2500 BooCoins for $29.99*—which begs the question: How much is each coin even worth? Such packages deliberately don't lend themselves to intuitive mental arithmetic.

We see many games take it one step further by adding *another* level of currency. So, in our game here, let's say 250 *BooCoins* buy you three *GhostCoins*:

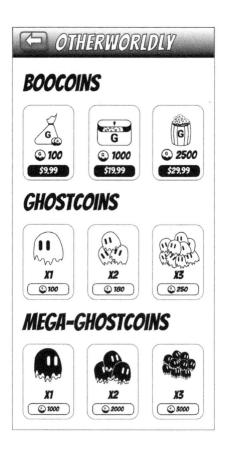

Now, the true value of *GhostCoins* is completely unclear, and you have no idea how much you're spending. And that's on top of the psychological buffer that the double layer of currency provides.

The math is unclear, which means the money you'll spend is also unclear. This is the same kind of trap tourists often fall into with unfamiliar foreign currency.

Even more sly is a strategy some apps implement of offering paid upgrades at pivotal points where you stand to lose well-earned progress. In other words, these games are literally designed to stress and frustrate you into making a payment.

Now, the extent to which you want to engage in such tricky tactics is up to you. Going overboard is likely to generate poor optics and leave a bad taste in some users' mouths. But that's not at all necessary; a happy middle ground between desirable in-app purchases and user-centric app design is absolutely possible.

4. ANCHORS, FOR COMPARISON'S SAKE

Next time you come across promotional sales, pay attention to exactly how retailers present their deals. In all likelihood, they're using one of several discrete methods proven to alter your price perception. Methods so ubiquitous that you probably never give them a second thought.

They work thanks to the almighty price anchor, an *original* value against which you compare the more appealing alternative price.

Here are the two most by-the-book forms of anchoring we have:

Strikethrough pricing—A straightforward technique where you display the sale price beside a crossed-out anchor price often used by travel apps like Expedia, Hotel.com, and Hotel Tonight.

The brilliance of such a simple detail is that it instantly captivates the parts of our brains that love discounts. You almost can't help but desire the best deal, regardless of what your price range would otherwise be.

Note, though, that some sellers are guilty of exploiting users by listing false strikethrough prices.

Price comparisons—Many subscription-based apps offer distinct prices that factor in an added time dynamic. Typically, this takes the form of cheaper rates with the caveat of longer contracts, as such:

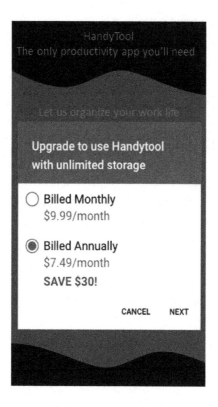

You can see this utilized in real life by brands like Pandora, ESPN, Evernote, and meditation app Headspace, whose $12.99/month anchor is presented alongside a much more alluring $5.83/month option. The catch, of course, is that the latter is billed annually at $69.99 upfront.[181]

To the buyer, the year-long plan feels like a steal. But the real winner is the Headspace exec, who enjoys the double whammy of a larger guaranteed payment and a long-term contract.

But the concept of anchoring doesn't end there.

5. THE GOLDILOCKS PRINCIPLE

Providing options isn't about giving customers a choice. It's about making that choice as easy as possible.

Because, if you think about it, the only way we determine the value of anything is through comparison. That's why we shop around, get several quotes, and talk to multiple vendors.

Something like strikethrough pricing is only effective if the product's worth is readily understood and accepted. But that's not usually the case, so for the rest of us, there's contextual pricing.

HandyTool's dual-subscription price comparison is certainly an example, but it lacks the most compelling option: The one in the middle.

---

181 Headspace: Meditation & Sleep, v. 4.21.0 (Headspace for Meditation, Mindfulness, and Sleep), Android 5.0 and up, updated November 17, 2020.

Back to William Poundstone's *Priceless*: One particular experiment found an eye-opening response to middle options. Provided two beer options priced at $2.50 and $1.80 respectively, 80 percent of customers rejected the *worst* choice and selected the former.

Once a third beer at $1.60 entered the mix, 80 percent now went with the $1.80 middle option and the remaining 20 percent took the premium beverage. Again, nobody settled for the bottom of the barrel.

One last iteration: Replacing the $1.60 beer with a high-quality $3.40 beer. As you can probably guess by now, sales for the $2.50 option, now in the middle, skyrocketed while the $1.80 one plummeted.[182]

The core lesson here is that by presenting different price points, the question becomes which plan customers should choose. Not whether they should buy your product in the first place.

It's the classic Goldilocks solution. In between two extremes lies the middle option, which is *just right.*

We often see ridesharing apps offer a trifecta of options, with the most reasonable "regular ride" smack in the middle as the clear winner:

---

182 Poundstone, *Priceless*.

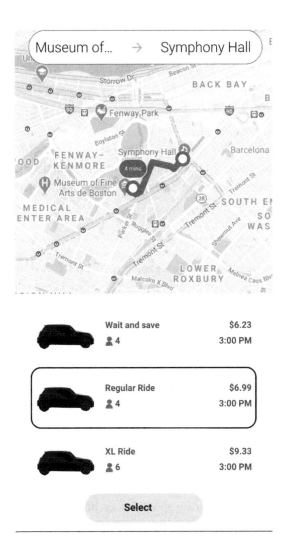

As a matter of fact, this common ridesharing tactic is actually a sneaky offshoot of the *Goldilocks* method of contextual pricing. We call it decoy pricing, in which one of the options only exists to push people toward the middle.

Do you see it? The decoy, of course, is the *wait and save* option; few are ever going to choose it just to save seventy-six cents.

Here's another example from Ariely:

The Economist offered a $59 Internet-only subscription next to two $125-priced subscriptions—one for paper and internet, one for paper only. Nobody signed up for just paper, obviously, while 84 percent took paper and the internet. But when they removed that decoy paper option, 84 percent fell to 32 percent!

Simply having the $125 paper option, even if it got no subscribers, helped create a decoy effect that more than doubled the highest offer's sales figures.[183]

Table 1. Actual Offer:

Offer		Distribution of Preferences
Internet	$59	16%
Paper	$125	0%
Paper + Internet	$125	84%

Table 2. Experiment:

Offer		Distribution of Preferences
Internet	$59	68%
Paper + Internet	$125	32%

---

183 Ariely, *Predictably Irrational.*

To understand the reason behind it, think of it this way: In the experiment, you're comparing the internet to paper plus internet and wondering if adding paper is worth a whole $66 extra. With the actual offer, though, you're more likely to compare paper to paper plus internet and see the latter as an obvious value choice.

If you've ever played big-name mobile games like *Candy Crush* or *Clash of Clans*, you've probably seen offers that mirror *The Economist*'s strategy. They might look something like:

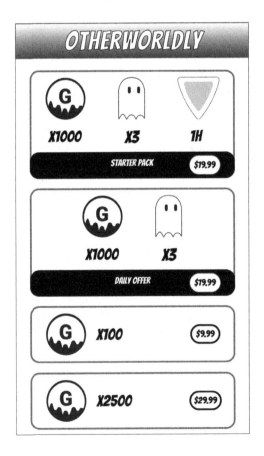

The daily offer is a decoy that makes the equally priced starter pack appear to be a no-brainer. But imagine the same screen without the daily offer. That starter pack doesn't look like such a bargain, now, does it? And that's the power of manufacturing a middle option.

FINAL WORD: DON'T FORGET THE BIG PICTURE
Let's circle back to Hermann Simon's pricing cocktail.

A good drink needs flavor and substance, right? This is what we can liken to the first two sections of this chapter, in which we sought to identify what a product is worth (and to whom).

But in order to sell, an exotic cocktail depends on its presentation. And that's really what apps are accomplishing with their psychological pricing: Presentation that appeals to users' subconscious and compels them to buy.

In other words, such pricing tactics are a part of implicit marketing. This means it's probably about time we talk about explicit marketing as well.

CHAPTER 10

MESSAGING | FIND YOUR VOICE; SPEAK THEIR LANGUAGE

"Kodak sells film, but they don't advertise film; they advertise memories."

THEODORE LEVITT, ECONOMIST, AND A PROFESSOR
AT THE HARVARD BUSINESS SCHOOL

So, you had a brilliant idea for an app.

You identified a user need and spent countless hours researching the market. Your engineers, designers, and product team have then worked vigorously to develop a seamless interface with exciting features. Now, your stakeholders are impressed, and you're sitting confident, ready to launch this thing into the stratosphere.

…But hold on a second. Your work is far from over.

It's time to face a harsh reality. Competition in the app market is brutal. With millions of apps out there, how do you ensure that yours is the one users download? Of course, you know your app is great, but how will your audience know?

The answer lies in strategic brand messaging—before, during, and after you launch your product. And no matter what industry you find yourself in, that journey starts with a unique value proposition.

BEFORE YOU LAUNCH: HONE DOWN YOUR MESSAGE

On the one hand, you have your company values. What does your company offer? What do you care about? What reputation do you want to build?

On the other, you're weighing your prospective users' values. What do they care about? And what makes them tick?

The challenge, though, isn't just to answer these questions. The challenge is to connect the two value systems with a single overarching message. And that starts with your unique value proposition (UVP), otherwise known as a unique selling proposition (USP).

WHAT EXACTLY *IS* A UNIQUE VALUE PROPOSITION?

According to Investopedia, it's a statement that expresses the essence of your product or service in a compelling manner.[184] To do so effectively, it should typically answer three core questions:

1. Who is your app's intended audience?
2. What benefits will your target audience get from using your app?
3. Why is your app better at delivering this value than alternatives?

The answers you reach will guide your brand image on a number of levels.

For instance: For your users, your UVP will draw them in and win over their lasting loyalty. More specifically, it's a way to entice quality leads—you know, those users who genuinely care about what you're offering.

In terms of competition, UVP is a powerful vehicle in differentiating yourself from the pack. It gives you control over how people see your app versus your competition's app.

Finally, this message can be a helpful fulcrum for your company's internal operations. Use it as a rallying cry—as the cohesive belief system that binds your teams together.

Overall, it can be seen as a focal point for your company's messaging. It's a statement or two, often in the form of a catchy tagline, that sells your primary benefit.

---

184 Alexandra Twin, "Value Proposition: Why Consumers Should Buy a Product or Use a Service," Investopedia, Updated July 5, 2020.

QUICK EXAMPLE: LET'S SAY YOU'RE A GYM OWNER

You could market your facility to a high-performing athlete, a time-strapped working mom, or just someone looking to get back in shape. The kind of gym you end up running depends as much as anything on the message you put out there. And if you're looking to attract a specific crowd, that message has to appeal to them.

For example, let's imagine a fitness chain called Platinum Gym that's open 24/7. A simple UVP for Platinum Gym could be something like *Get Stronger Around the Clock* to effectively tap into the core benefit of constant accessibility.

But what if you're running a gym with a class oriented format? Let's call this example Solstice Gym. Here you might want your UVP to highlight the idea of *Achieving Goals Together.* Because your gym isn't just any old facility, it's a safe space for gym-goers to shed their fears and follow through on their New Year's resolutions.

For Platinum and Solstice alike, the UVP serves as a central anchor that directs its brand marketing toward the desired audience. We see this type of targeting in ads all around us—from TV shows to retail stores to cafes. And yes, to mobile apps. You can't just hope it'll appeal to someone; the app needs to be designed with a prospective user base in mind.

SPEAKING YOUR AUDIENCE'S LANGUAGE

Your UVP can't just answer those questions above. It must answer them in the right way. This means keeping your message clear and concise. Rather than decorating your descriptions with lavish adjectives, simply let your benefits do the talking.

And that brings us to the main point: Great UVPs talk in benefits, not features.

Features are the tangible characteristics of your product. They're your gym's weight room, treadmills, and outdoor swimming pool. They're what you technically provide, but they're not what users truly desire.

That's where benefits come in, to address the deeper goals. What can your service allow them to accomplish? These are the healthy lifestyle, stress-free weight loss, or regimented muscle-building that your users covet.

Consider further how Steve Jobs famously presented the iPod. Not as a device that stores a gigabyte of data but as a device that fits 1,000 songs right in your pocket. And while a select few companies with loyal to the core users can focus more on the features (ironically, like Apple now), most growing brands strike gold by demonstrating benefits.

Here's a well-constructed example of such benefit-laden language from food delivery service Deliveroo:[185]

"Your favorite restaurants and takeaways, delivered straight to your door."

---

185 "Deliveroo - Food Delivery," Deliveroo, accessed October 1, 2020.

Just like that, in a brief ten-word sentence, Deliveroo speaks simultaneously to the craving for delicious food and the convenience of home. It presents a problem, combining those two desires, and immediately solves it.

Elsewhere on its site, we find equally compelling value propositions aimed at its partners:

- For delivery riders—"Flexible work, competitive fees" nails down the two most appealing value points of anyone looking to make an extra buck.[186]
- For participating restaurants—"Get a sales boost of up to 30 percent from takeaways" likewise conveys the advantages of partnering with Deliveroo. Not only will they handle food delivery (typically a headache for restaurants), but they'll also provide a modest sales boost.[187]

Targeting different, specific audiences with separate, benefit-focused value propositions has allowed Deliveroo to scale rapidly. If your app also needs to address multiple groups, this is the blueprint to follow.

On WhatsApp, we see an even shorter tagline:[188]

"Simple. Secure. Reliable messaging."

186 "Ride with Us - Apply Now!" Deliveroo, accessed September 30, 2020.
187 "Become a Deliveroo Partner," Deliveroo, accessed October 1, 2020.
188 "WhatsApp," WhatsApp, accessed September 30, 2020.

Followed by this blurb: "With WhatsApp, you'll get fast, simple, secure messaging and calling for free, available on phones all over the world."

Even without reading the subscript, we instantly get what they're about. And what more do we need? They've covered the principal pain points of messaging apps before we even have a moment to worry about them.

Investing tool Acorns is another interesting case. Their website header gets the job done with the tagline, "Acorns helps you grow your money."[189]

Notice how Acorns spins their message in a personal way by emphasizing the words *you* and *your*. They also use *grow* to hammer home their core value, rather than more impersonal alternatives like *gain, profit,* or *capitalize*.

Much like Deliveroo and WhatsApp, Acorns uses a relatable tone and benefit-driven language to cultivate a unique brand persona. And that's what your first marketing step needs to look like—whether you're opening a new gym or developing a brand-new app.

---

189 "Acorns—Invest, Earn, Grow, Spend, Later," Acorns, accessed September 30, 2020.

READY TO LAUNCH: SET YOURSELF UP FOR USER ACQUISITION

Now that you've figured out your UVP, it's time to yell it from the rooftops. It's no-good spending all that time on a carefully curated message if nobody even hears it.

First thing's first, though...

PINPOINT YOUR LAUNCH GOALS

What does success mean for your app?

Ultimately, it hinges on which metrics you covet. Is it the number of downloads? Five-star ratings? A high average revenue per user?

Whatever you choose, make sure that choice is established prior to takeoff. Design your launch strategy around the desired metric and create a framework for measuring your returns.

OPTIMIZE YOUR APP STORE PRESENCE

According to a survey by Google and Ipsos MediaCT, nearly 40 percent of all downloaded apps are discovered through app store search results.[190] No matter your industry—fitness, weather, at-home karaoke—the importance of ranking high in search results is unquestionable.

---

190 James Tiongson, "Mobile App Marketing Insights: How Consumers Really Find and Use Your Apps," Think With Google, May 2015.

To get a leg up here, you need your app store presence to mirror your UVP. This means continuing to reflect the language of your target audience and finding new ways to distinguish yourself strategically. Google and Apple even have app store resources to guide your use of keywords, graphics, titles, and descriptions. You can bet the most successful apps have covered their bases in terms of such optimization tactics.

So, when you search for *order food delivery*, it's no surprise that DoorDash and Postmates come up as some of the top options. Nor is it a shock that Tinder, Ok Cupid, and Plenty of Fish headline the list for *free dating apps*. These brands typically excel at generating visibility, and they've seamlessly extended that prowess to the app store.

Some companies even go the extra mile to come up when users search for similar alternatives. Facebook, for instance, has gamed the app store to secure a spot in the related suggestions for TikTok searches.

OPEN THE MANY DOORS OF APP DISCOVERY

The app store may be king, but it certainly doesn't sit atop the throne alone.

For starters, popping up in relevant Google searches is a tried-and-true method for a reason. If you can nail down your SEO, someone looking for a new gym membership might just happily stumble upon your fitness tracking app.

Beyond Google, consider partnering with similar apps and websites for a healthy dose of cross-promotion. Such an affiliation can let quality prospects find you without specifically searching for you.

And lastly, don't forget about direct marketing to stir up that word-of-mouth buzz. Put some effort into traditional avenues like social media advertising and podcast sponsorship. Utilize the reach of bloggers, influencers, and product-focused websites like Product Hunt and Crunchbase to get your name out there. Consider even creating an engaging teaser video to circulate around these numerous channels.

And at the end of the day, do your due diligence by tending to your user base so that their glowing testimonials end up doing the promotional work for you.

BEYOND THE LAUNCH: THE STORY DOESN'T END THERE

At this point, you've put your app out there and acquired some users. Well done!

But now, you're faced with pressing follow-up questions: How do you retain these users? And how do you evaluate your systems of acquisition and retention? You can't just leave these matters to chance.

Keep them coming back for more

First thing's first: Don't think of selling your app as a one-off transaction. Instead, think of it as a continuous relationship; as you continue to engage users and provide additional value, they'll return the favor with in-app purchases and positive reviews.

The thing is the onus is on *you* to keep it alive. You have to actively compel their engagement.

Typically, the way to do this is with push notifications and in-app messaging. So, don't be afraid to send users an occasional discount or alert. If it's useful, they'll appreciate it. But like all your customer-facing communication, frequency is a delicate balance. You don't want to frustrate them with a barrage of notifications.

That's without mentioning that the content of these notifications also matters tremendously. What do you think will boost engagement: a generic mass message or a personally tailored recommendation? No doubt, the answer is the latter! After all, the most successful campaigns don't just offer something users *might* want. They offer something this specific user has indicated an interest.

DON'T FORGET ABOUT EXISTING USERS: A CASE STUDY

There's a tug-of-war between acquisition and retention. Both are necessary, but you need to carefully assess the importance of each throughout your product lifecycle.

Oftentimes, apps get so hung up on bringing in new users that they lose sight of all the old users they're losing. Counteracting those statistics and building brand loyalty is a challenge—often, an expensive one at that. As a reminder,

Leanplum measures that an average app loses over 90 percent of its users over a ninety-day period after install.[191]

Pixowl, a world-building mobile game company, found out as much in the early days of its number one app: The Sandbox.

Despite impressive download numbers (currently over forty million), many of their users quickly became inactive.[192] So Pixowl partnered with Leanplum to send push notifications to these idle gamers at a time when they are most likely to play (before school, during lunch break, or on their commute home).

The results of the campaign were astounding: A 16 percent rise in users who returned to the app and a 2 percent increase in average revenue per purchase![193] All from simply inviting them to keep playing.

TRACK, MEASURE, ANALYZE, REPEAT

How did Pixowl arrive at these numbers? By monitoring key metrics and employing A/B tests.

Pixowl's A/B test divided users into two groups: A control group and a variant group called *Optimal Time Group*. This latter segment received the new notifications based on their individual history of using the app, whereas the control

191 "With Declining App Usage, Mobile Engagement Matters," *Leanplum* (blog), February 3, 2019.

192 Jordan Heal, "The Sandbox Gaming Platform Receives $2.5m Investment," *Yahoo Finance*, May 29, 2019.

193 "Pixowl Increases Retention & Revenue with Leanplum," Leanplum Case Studies, accessed October 1, 2020.

group continued receiving notifications at a fixed time during the day.[194]

This is just one example of how data is marketing gold. With the right tools, you can track website visits, length of time on a page, link clicks, purchasing habits, and more. Leveraging these analytics as Pixowl did is essential for assessing outreach strategies, predicting performance, and getting maximum bang for your buck.

Plus, the stats you gather can then be repurposed as marketing ammo. For example, look at the platform of the mobile marketplace OfferUp.[195]

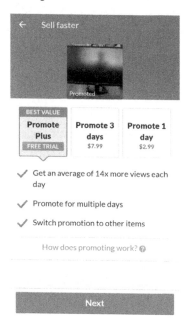

194 Pixowl case study, Leanplum.
195 OfferUp: Buy. Sell. Letgo. Mobile marketplace, v. 3.81.2 (OfferUp Inc.), Android v. 5.0 and above.

Their in-app purchase items guarantee an average of fourteen times more page views—a fact they found from tracking advertised items. Consider how much more convincing this specific detail is than a general promise to *improve your sales.* It's truly night and day.

FINAL WORD: MARKETING IS A MARATHON WITH NO FINISH LINE

When we think of a mobile app launch, we think of a single point in time—the aha moment when your app appears in the app stores and changes the world forever.

In reality, mobile app marketing is less a big epiphany than a long series of gradual breakthroughs. Pixowl and OfferUp didn't just magically conjure up these audience engagement tactics; they used extensive insights to refine their acquisition and retention strategies over time.

And that's what you want: A constant cycle of testing initiatives, collecting data, and using it to start all over again. In fact, as we're about to see, this mentality should apply well beyond marketing.

CHAPTER 11

INNOVATION | TRY, TEST, ADAPT, REPEAT

"If you have always done it that way, it is probably wrong."

CHARLES KETTERING, AMERICAN INVENTOR AND LONG-
TIME HEAD OF RESEARCH AT GENERAL MOTORS

When we talk about true innovation, we're talking about breaking through our proverbial ceilings, even when everyone around us is staying put in complacency.

It's what lies at the heart of our most valued goals: Growth, profitability, cost reduction, and, ultimately, gaining a competitive edge. And in the world of tech, this competitive edge comes in the form of disruption.

Let's examine that concept a bit closer. According to Investopedia, a disruptive technology "is an innovation that significantly alters the way that consumers, industries, or businesses operate. A disruptive technology sweeps away the systems or habits it replaces because it has attributes that are recognizably superior." [196]

Consider the internet, iPhone and Android, cloud computing, and wireless broadband (4G LTE)—disruptive technologies that transformed the cultural landscape and set the foundation for us to even discuss app development. It's the beautiful snowball effect of innovation: disruption breeds opportunities for further disruption.

But, of course, it's not that simple. There are millions of unremarkable products in the app store that nobody gives a second thought to. And you've likely encountered a number of them only to follow the same old script. Download it, use it a few times, and then delete it to make space for more photos.

Occasionally, though, an app comes along that transcends such mediocrity. That epitomizes the concept of disruption. It enters our lives and introduces a few quick swipes that dramatically alter the way we shop, travel, communicate, get the news, and more.

They're more than industry game-changers; they're humanity game changers. And they all have one thing in common: A highly efficient solution to a key user problem—often, a problem we haven't even realized we have yet.

But once we do realize it, those proverbial ceilings don't seem quite as rigid anymore.

---

196 Tim Smith, "Disruptive Technology Definition," Investopedia, updated October 2, 2020.

DISRUPTIVE INNOVATION AT BILLION DOLLAR APPS

There are no rules for disruptive innovation. That's kind of the point.

But the following five mentalities have been behind a whole lot of world-altering innovation in our recent history—helping define everything from WhatsApp messaging to NASA's moon landing.

1. SHOOT FOR THE MOON

When President John F. Kennedy famously declared, "We choose to go to the moon in this decade," he didn't just change the future of humanity's space exploration.[197] He inspired a revolutionary approach to problem-solving.

His *moonshot thinking* started with a drastic problem. And even though a realistic solution wasn't yet conceivable, his words lifted the ceiling of what we believed could be accomplished. Within seven years, that mindset transformed an impossible promise into Neil Armstrong's footprint.

Fifty years later, Google pioneered its Moonshot Factory called X for engineers and entrepreneurs to develop breakthrough technologies outside the realm of accepted possibility. Thinking bigger than big, the central goal of X is a "10x impact on the world's most intractable problems, not just 10 percent improvement."[198]

---

197 Jerry Woodwill, "JFK Rice Moon Speech," Space Movies Cinema, NASA, accessed October 2, 2020.
198 "X – The Moonshot Factory," Alphabet, accessed October 2, 2020.

These kinds of lofty aspirations lie at the core of most innovative app companies. Because they aren't in the business of making another file manager, music player, or picture editor, they're going after problems that can change the world.

Take Uber, for example. Right from the beginning, they sought to indulge a never before asked question: "What if you could request a ride from your phone?" In a market long dominated by taxis and public transportation, alternatives were unthinkable. Now, they're indispensable. We can't picture life without them, much like we can't imagine twentieth-century history without the moon landing.

Airbnb started out a little more haphazardly—as a means for their founders to pay the rent. But they quickly saw the potential they'd tapped into and started asking Moonshot questions of their own. "Is there a market for short-term sharing and renting of existing properties?" The answer has changed the world of travel accommodations forever.

2. TAKE IT STEP BY STEP...BY STEP

Rome wasn't built in one day. Your app won't be either. What was true thousands of years ago still holds true.

While Moonshot thinking is exciting–it stimulates our imaginations!–methodical iteration is what brings those ideas to fruition. Disruption doesn't happen on day one: It took years to get from JFK's proclamation to the moon.

The road is a long one, full of calculated risks and unforeseen obstacles. Whatever methodology your team abides by (be it Agile, Lean, Six Sigma, Design, or another), you want it to provide a constant loop of feedback that enables marginal improvements. Otherwise, your next iteration will just be different, not necessarily better.

With enough marginal improvements, though, you can eventually–perhaps, unexpectedly–find yourself at a goldmine, pickaxe in hand. This is true for some of the best-known apps, including one of our favorite recurring examples: WhatsApp.

Originally, Jan Koum and Brian Acton had an idea for an app that displayed status updates of phone contacts. It was a neat concept–a simple interface showing what your friends are up to–but it had some problems. Namely, it kept crashing. And it had few users.

Given the lack of traction, Koum nearly gave it all up.

But before he could, Apple introduced the world to push notifications, which seamlessly integrated into early WhatsApp. Every time you changed your status, you'd ping your friends with it. And then they'd reply with a ping of their own. Essentially, the notification feature spawned its own form of instant messaging.

And so, Koum and Acton pivoted to build the chat function that WhatsApp is now known for. From there, they kept pivoting and innovating to become one of the only available options for free messaging (this is back during Blackberry's BBM heyday). Eventually, they gained acclaim for a number of perks: Working internationally, being compatible across devices, and requiring only the internet and a phone number to sign in. Heeding users' wishes, they wasted no time releasing updated versions of the app that supported photo and video sharing.[199]

But they didn't start here, with over 2 billion users.[200] They started with a contact status board buried somewhere deep in the app store. And *that* is the power of iteration.

3. TAKE YOUR APP FOR A TEST DRIVE

The creative process behind products and prototypes is the fun part, right? For many, it's easy; you have a brilliant lightbulb idea, and, in your head, it all works perfectly.

But things get scary when you put it in front of real users: What if everything *doesn't* work smoothly? Hate to break it to you, but in all likelihood, it won't work smoothly. Koum and Acton can attest to that. So that's why we conduct tests— to course correct, fix assumptions, better understand users, and ultimately circle back around with a superior product.

Now, you don't actually need a fully fleshed-out app to test your vision: A working prototype will do just fine. There are even apps out there that let you turn hand-drawn sketches into quick prototypes. For instance, the app POP (Prototyping on Paper) is an awesome resource that doesn't require any coding; just draw out your ideas, upload some photos, and let POP create a basic prototype for you.

---

199 Parmy Olson, "Exclusive: The Rags-To-Riches Tale of How Jan Koum Built WhatsApp Into Facebook's New $19 Billion Baby," *Forbes*, February 19, 2014.

200 John Porter, "WhatsApp Now Has 2 Billion Users," *The Verge*, Feb 2, 2020.

Whether you end up using POP or performing A/B tests or going a different route, *this* is the part of the iterative process that provides the most crucial feedback. The insights you gain from testing can be your greatest asset, but they come with a caveat. Validation means nothing if it's coming from the wrong audience. Just think way back to Doug Evans and his Juicero disaster. Initial hype came exclusively from his Silicon Valley echo chamber, not from eventual prospects.

With all that in mind, dig deep and ask yourself: What sort of knowledge can transform my WhatsApp from an unknown to a cultural pillar? Then take the leap and implement what you have learned from your tests in your next iteration.

4. INJECT DATA INTO YOUR DECISIONS

When we talk about data-based decision-making, the name of the game is metrics. Harkening back to our marketing discussion a few chapters ago, gathering data is a fool's errand if you haven't identified which data matters most.

Here's where we introduce the concept of North Star Metrics, which are the metrics that you decide will best reflect both company success and customer-perceived value. Their purpose is pinpointing a specific goal. "X weekly five-star reviews" or "Y daily social shares" is easier to digest than a vague concept of success.

With a North Star Metric in mind, you can confidently experiment with A/B tests and monitor user behavior to hone down your features. And your programmers can plow forward with automated simulations that help them finetune the source code and stomp out pesky bugs.

Ultimately, good data translates into good decisions, and your successful experiments become lasting solutions.

But numbers don't always tell the whole story. So, when we talk about usability testing, the focus is on the individual consumer. Here, we dig below the analytics to perform one-on-one interviews, ask in-depth questions about user needs, and identify any gaps in usability. Other methods of getting qualitative feedback from users are rooted in surveys, focus groups, and testimonials.

In other words, we don't want to completely abandon the human element; we're not robots! Observing users' reactions, impressions, reviews, and behaviors can also help uncover trends that data-based testing might miss.

An interesting instance is WhatsApp's surge in status notifications. Undoubtedly, user engagement metrics revealed the growing popularity of this new feature. But when recalling the episode, Koum and early consultant Alex Fishman didn't mention data; they spoke of their friend group's change in app usage. Witnessing their network embrace chatting via status updates impacted their Moonshot thinking as much as anything else.

5. FAIL FAST, SUCCEED FASTER

So, you dreamed big and stayed diligent, iterating and updating your idea with the help of metric-driven testing, and you still failed.

No point in sugarcoating it. Failing sucks, but it's part of the game. Things rarely go as planned. Whether you're learning to ride a bike or bake a cake or design an app, make failure a constructive *part* of the process, not the end of it.

Gaming company Rovio Entertainment hit dozens of such dead ends and sniffed the edge of bankruptcy before finally getting a fish to bite. To be specific, they created fifty-one games you've never heard of. But then they made a fifty-second game. And they called it *Angry Birds*.[201]

Over a decade later, those fifty-one failures and one bird-launching success have garnered over four billion global downloads and $300+ million in yearly revenue.[202] And that's just the games; we're not even talking about all the merchandising or *The Angry Birds Movie* and its $350 million box office gross.[203] Or the 2019 sequel that raked in another $150 million![204]

---

201 Paul Kendall, "*Angry Birds*: The Story behind IPhone's Gaming Phenomenon," *The Telegraph*, February 07, 2011.

202 Matthew Forde, "Here's How Much Money Rovio's Mobile Games Are Making," PocketGamer.biz, March 12, 2019.

203 *The Angry Birds Movie*, Box Office Mojo, accessed October 2, 2020.

204 *The Angry Birds Movie 2*, Box Office Mojo, accessed October 2, 2020.

And if that's not enough of a testament to the power of perseverance, consider the app Burbn. Or, as you likely know it, Instagram.[205]

The initial name was arbitrary, simply prompted by co-founder Kevin Systrom's love of whiskey. The original interface was similarly aimless as it contained a bevy of scattered social features. Users were few; prospects for growth were fewer.

But Systrom and developer Mike Krieger looked into the data and found that one area of the app had some solid traction: Photo sharing. And, well...the rest is history.

"Burbn was a false start," Systrom admitted. "You always have to evolve into something else." [206]

That's the benefit of failure—there's rarely evolution without it—because evolution requires a growth mindset. As you iterate, test, fail, and repeat, you may just come to face a hard truth: The best version of your app isn't the one you initially envisioned. It's the one that evolved from your failures.

FINAL WORD: THAT'S WHY ADAPTABILITY IS SO IMPORTANT

Without it, we don't get WhatsApp or Instagram or any number of apps that have disrupted life for the better.

---

205 Megan Garber, "Instagram Was First Called 'Burbn,'" *The Atlantic*, July 2, 2014.
206 Ibid.

But that's what we need: The "Nth" version of your idea, which bakes in all the lessons from your prior failures. Maybe those lessons push you to change a few features, or maybe they force you to pivot your product entirely—regardless, those failings and frustrations are necessary to create something of value.

The problem, however, is that it's extremely easy to fall victim to the sunk cost fallacy, which is the tendency to continue investing in something because of all the time, money, or effort you've already put in. Unfortunately, we commonly see this cardinal sin of innovation: Founders get overly attached to their precious little brainchild, becoming so consumed with it that they fail to read the room.

So, heed this warning: Move past your failures and be willing to pivot on a dime with your subsequent iterations.

For further reading on innovation, you can hear directly from these masters: Eric Ries in *The Lean Startup* and Clayton Christensen in *The Innovator's Dilemma*.[207]

---

207 Eric Ries, *The Lean Startup: How Today's Entrepreneurs Use Continuous Innovation to Create Radically Successful Businesses*, United Kingdom: Crown Business, 2011; Clayton M Christensen, *The Innovator's Dilemma: The Revolutionary National Bestseller that Changed the Way We Do Business*, United States: Harper Business, 2000.

PART III

CHAPTER 12

DUOLINGO

———

"By playing games, you can artificially speed up your learning curve to develop the right kind of thought processes."

NATE SILVER, FOUNDER AND EDITOR-
IN-CHIEF OF *FIVETHIRTYEIGHT*

"I'd really love to learn to Chinese, but…"

Learning a new language is hard. Mastery takes commitment, and most of us give up after just a few lessons. After all, research has shown quite definitively that we humans simply aren't geared to prioritize long-term goals over instant gratification.[208]

What we're much better at, unfortunately, is picturing the glorious results. Just imagine impressing friends or coworkers at a party with your newfound knowledge of Italian! Or maybe taking a trip to Tokyo and connecting with locals through fluent Japanese. With these images in mind,

---

208 "Study: Brain Battles Itself over Short-Term Rewards, Long-Term Goals," Princeton, accessed October 13, 2020.

language learning seems great and simple, and so we promise to practice each and every day.

But, in reality, the process is an arduous one with minimal instant gratification and all sorts of barriers. For starters, language lessons require time, financial resources, and, on top of that, a special kind of persistent discipline to practice. Retaining any of your learnings is difficult without a practice buddy and, even then, progress comes at a snail's pace.

Sooner or later, the lack of substantial results will turn you away like a frustrated gym-goer unable to lose weight. Your patience and determination will wane, and you'll lose sight of that Barcelona daydream where you confidently order tapas in Spanish.

For most adults, then, language mastery—whether via in-person classes, online tutoring, or solo methods—seems mostly like a pipe dream.

"FOCUS ON THE USER AND ALL ELSE WILL FOLLOW"

That's one of Google's guiding mantras, and for the past decade, Duolingo has been a prime example of why it holds true.[209]

In 2010, co-creators Luis von Ahn and Severin Hacker set out to make language education free and accessible to everyone through technology. Not only did they want to solve the

---

209 "Ten Things We Know to Be True," Google, accessed October 13, 2020.

frustrations of language learning, but also to make people addicted to learning!

And the numbers of their success speak for themselves. As of October 2020, Duolingo offers ninety-seven different language courses in thirty-five plus languages.[210] The mobile app has become the world's most downloaded education app with a whopping 300 million learners worldwide and a valuation of over $1.5 billion.[211]

According to AngelList, there are about 800 companies in the language education space, from incumbents like Rosetta Stone to startups such as Memrise, Babbel, FluentU, and Colingo.[212] But none seem to have the scale, popularity, or success of Duolingo.

How did Duolingo attain such explosive growth? There are several reasons, but all seem to have one theme in common: Relentless focus on users. Let's take a closer look.

1. AN INSPIRING MISSION
Front and center on Duolingo's webpage is written:

"Learn a language for free. Forever."[213]

210 "Free Language Courses," Duolingo, accessed October 13, 2020.
211 "Duolingo: About," LinkedIn, accessed October 13, 2020; Paul Sawers, "Duolingo Raises $30 Million from Alphabet's CapitalG at $1.5 Billion Valuation," VentureBeat, December 4, 2019.
212 "Language Learning Startups," AngelList, accessed October 13, 2020.
213 "Duolingo - The World's Best Way to Learn a Language," Duolingo, accessed October 13, 2020.

There are no hidden costs, and, unlike Wikipedia, the company doesn't ask for donations. Truly, the company's mission is to give everyone "access to a private tutor experience through technology." Whether you're a Hollywood celebrity or a public school student in a developing country, they believe you should have access to language learning.[214]

Von Ahn's inspiration for Duolingo came from his upbringing in Guatemala, where he saw firsthand how poverty prevented people from the opportunities that his high-quality education allowed:

"In many countries, learning English can double your income potential," von Ahn explained, "but I saw that the people who most needed to learn English were also those who could least afford it. It didn't seem fair, and that inspired Duolingo's mission to make language education free and accessible to everyone."[215]

And therein lies the special core of the Duolingo mission: Making learning fun, easy, and most importantly, free.

"Staying true to our mission has helped us in two ways," von Ahn continued in a *GeekWire* interview. "One is being able to attract really good employees. Most of our employees have competing offers from very well-known companies, like Facebook or Google. They choose us usually because of the

---

214 "About Us," Duolingo, accessed October 13, 2020.

215 Luis von Ahn (@Vonahn), "I Am Luis von Ahn, Co-Inventor of CAPTCHA & ReCAPTCHA, Founder/CEO of Duolingo, MacArthur Fellow and Computer Science Professor. AMA!" Reddit, accessed October 13, 2020.

mission. Also, our users, a lot of them are big advocates for us because they see our mission and think Duolingo, they're the good guys. Nobody thinks Rosetta Stone is the good guy. It's not like they're bad people. They just didn't position themselves as being the good guys because their mission was ultimately to make money. For some people, that works, but that's not an inspiring mission."[216]

Now, Duolingo certainly could have set up a paywall and cashed in big time on paid lessons. But that would've sacrificed their *good-guy* persona, losing the attention of that user down in Guatemala. Instead, they've stayed true to accessibility, acting almost like a nonprofit despite being a for-profit company. The result has been international acclaim and a user base so large that their free, ad-based model delivers more revenue than any win-now paywall would have.

2. AN ADDICTIVE LEARNING APP

But apart from keeping the app free, how does Duolingo make language learning accessible to all kinds of users? After all, some users are dedicated enough to spend several hours learning each day while others only have ten minutes in passing. Duo manages to attract both groups.

Somehow, they've designed their entire platform to *trick you* into committing to your long-term goals. From the user perspective, here's why it works:

---

216   Taylor Soper, "Inside the Mind of Duolingo CEO Luis von Ahn as $700M Language Learning Startup Eyes IPO in 2020," *GeekWire*, February 23, 2018.

Less is more. It's the reason we never read the terms and conditions. When facing an overwhelming amount of information, we tend to shut down and stop paying attention. In his book, *The More of Less,* Joshua Becker aptly said, "You don't need more space. You need less stuff."[217]

Duolingo's minimalistic, step-by-step design has taken this *less stuff* approach to heart, helping their users avoid the anxiety and overwhelm that is so common for the complex process of language learning.

When designing new products, it is thus important to keep the following questions in mind:

How can we be as concise as possible? And how can we avoid information overload?

Gamification. This is the big one. This is how Duolingo overcomes the greatest obstacle that language learning programs face: Keeping people motivated.

If you've ever used Duolingo, you know it works because it doesn't feel like a lecture. Rather, it feels like a game—with scoring and checkpoints and the like. In fact, we can break this down into four components:

1. **Setting attainable goals**. Much like in all walks of life, the big picture can be daunting. But by breaking down

---

217 "Quote by Joshua Becker: 'You Don't Need More Space. You Need Less Stuff,'" Goodreads, accessed November 16, 2020.

that big picture into many small, reasonable tasks, the overwhelm slowly goes away.

On Duolingo, this is what the *daily goal* function does. Instead of worrying about mastering the entirety of the Spanish language, you only have to worry about completing an allotted amount of time spent. You get to choose your daily goal (ranging from five minutes of learning per day to twenty minutes)—none of which feel particularly difficult.

2. **Witnessing progress in real-time**. This is the beauty of having checkpoints that are clear, distinct, and numerous: There's no ambiguity about where you are in the learning process.

Duolingo is organized in a highly compartmentalized way. Each language is broken down into various themed sections. Within each section lie a dozen or more unique lesson categories. Within each category are a handful of levels that get harder as you complete them. And finally, each level contains a series of short, pertinent lessons.

On the app, it's much less convoluted than it sounds written out because of how the gamification utilizes this segmentation. When you finish a lesson, a gold bar moves to track your progress, and you receive *lingots*, their form of virtual coins. When you complete a level, you receive a crown. When you've done everything in a category, its icon turns to gold. And when you place out of a whole section, you're rewarded with a brand-new section unlocking for you.

In other words: These checkpoints tie every step of the process to an immediate visual incentive.

3. **Coming back for another round.** Keeping people engaged inside the app is one story; compelling them to reopen the app when not in use is another. The Duolingo team identified emails and push notifications as the most effective nudges to help users stay consistent. So, they send these out once every day (actually—once every 23.5 hours, as supported by their extensive testing).[218]

As we mentioned in Chapter 5, though, Duolingo gives users the reins when it comes to notification settings. If you don't like their defaults, you can customize them to whatever suits your goals or shut them off completely. Thus, despite being an active notification sender, the Duolingo app isn't intrusive, thanks to both their established best practices *and* their commitment to giving you full control.

4. **Making it a recurring habit.** One last key incentive that Duolingo uses is the *streak*. Simply put, the streak is a running count of consecutive days that you've fulfilled your daily goal.

Keeping a multi-day streak can increase the number of lingots you receive, but really, it's just a proven psychological tool to get you more invested. Nobody likes seeing a streak vanish. It is, after all, a visible piece of evidence of your accomplishment.

---

218 "The Tenets of A/B Testing from Duolingo's Master Growth Hacker," First Round Review, accessed November 16, 2020.

Elaborating on the effects of the streak, here's a list of other Duolingo rewards that encourage feedback and consistency:

a. XP (experience points)—You earn these points by completing a lesson and achieving preset daily goals; essentially, they're a measurable way to track progress.
b. Badges—Small tokens of reward, the former of which can be used to buy fun in-app bonuses.
c. Progress tree—Concepts are broken down into those bite-sized lessons called Skills and arranged in a progress tree, giving you a clear visual of your progress.
d. Social element—You can engage with friends or other learners on forums and discussion boards. The goal is to foster an online community that further incentives you to use the platform.
e. Leaderboard—It's a pretty simple competition mechanic: The more you study, the more points you get, and the higher you get on Duolingo's user-wide leaderboard. The desire to *beat* other users and gain some semblance of recognition can motivate some learners to take the extra step.

3. CONTENT BY THE PEOPLE, FOR THE PEOPLE

This is the meat of the app—the product wouldn't be successful if its content didn't deliver. Believe it or not, though, Duolingo gets most of its content created for free. They hire linguists and second-language-acquisition researchers, but they also get help from hundreds of volunteers to create this massive catalog of language courses.

The volunteers are thoroughly vetted, of course, and they do their due diligence, typically spending at least three or four months per course. Duolingo's in-house teams and beta testers then leave feedback and work back-and-forth to finetune the product as much as possible.

What you end up with for each language are approximately 400 expert-approved lessons containing thousands of comprehensive sentence examples.[219] So the content does deliver in both quality and quantity, despite Duolingo investing minimal capital into it!

And it's not just quality and quantity: Duolingo consistently delivers creatively as well with unusual languages (i.e., Klingon and High Valyrian) and unexpected sentences like "They are washing the holy potato" or "He is my wife" or even "Her marriage is a public scandal."[220] Such unconventional sentences always fire up Duolingo's discussion boards and give their lessons a little flare, keeping them memorable.

It's true that completing all the skill lessons on Duolingo isn't enough to acquire native speaker proficiency just yet. However, if you are consistent with Duolingo, you can safely expect to reach beginner-to-intermediate levels of proficiency. Not a bad starting point, given that the app is free!

219 Michael J. Coren, "Duolingo's Crowdsourced Language-Learning Model Is Letting Some Weird Things Slip through the Cracks," *Quartz*, May 20, 2018.

220 "'They Are Washing the Holy Potato,'" Duolingo Forum, October 17, 2015; "Duolingo Has Weird Sentences," Duolingo Forum, April 4, 2014; "'Her Marriage Is a Public Scandal,'" Duolingo Forum, September 3, 2013.

4. DIFFERENTIATION WITH DUO

Let's talk about the owl named Duo. Duolingo's green owl mascot/ logo/ cheerleader/ motivational coach guides you through the app experience with insider tips and heartfelt inspiration. And apart from being a cute gimmick, Duo actually serves a higher purpose for their brand:

- Duo effectively humanizes the language learning experience and gives you a sense of companionship. Compare that to many other self-taught learning apps that have come and gone where you feel alone in your journey. But on this app, Duo is your friend. He appears consistently at critical moments, can be dressed in a wacky outfit (for a modest payment of lingots), and brings a sense of levity to each lesson.
- Hand-in-hand with that point is Duo's role as a differentiator. Seriously, can you even picture the logos of Rosetta Stone or Babbel? Memrise? Pimsleur? But if you've ever seen Duo, the reaction now is instant recognition.

...And it's not just recognition; it's also association. You see the owl, and you don't think, "Ugh, language learning." No, you think of Duolingo's warm colors and fun graphics, and friendly interface. You think of the *fun* that they've injected into their app experience. All that plays into its differentiation, and is epitomized by the presence of Duo.

HOW DOES DUOLINGO MAKE MONEY?

When Duolingo first started out, the company's top priorities were growth and value—not profit. They gave everyone their premium experience without ads in the hopes of winning over new users and potential investors.

Back then, Duolingo's business model was unlike any other: On top of the free service, they turned their own users into translators for big, content-heavy publishers like CNN and BuzzFeed.[221] These users got to learn and practice through these translation exercises while Duo received revenue and the publishers enjoyed an increased international reach. Essentially, Duolingo's software would compare different users' translations and pick the best options to get entire documents translated.

Forbes praised this framework as "crowdsourcing capitalism" while MIT called it "the cleverest business model in Online Education."[222]

However, like most business models, this translating venture was by no means perfect.

First, it confused the company's mission. Duolingo strove to be a pioneer in free education, but it was being pushed by business partners into more and more translation work.

Second, this model wasn't scalable. There's only so much money to be made from a limited supply of documents

221 Luis von Ahn, "Why Did Duolingo Move from Translation to Certification for Monetizing?" Quora, January 12, 2016.

222 Parmy Olson, "Crowdsourcing Capitalists: How Duolingo's Founders Offered Free Education to Millions," *Forbes*, January 22, 2014; Tom Simonite, "The Cleverest Business Model in Online Education," MIT Technology Review, November 29, 2012.

needing translation. And by 2016, with nearly 150 million users in tow, Duolingo knew it could do better.[223]

In September of that year, Duolingo execs decided to pivot the app away from translation services to capitalize on their massive user base.

In 2017, they introduced advertising to the platform—specifically, full-page interstitial pop-ups are shown after each lesson. Each one of these ads has a message from Duolingo that says, "This ad helps us keep education free," essentially reinforcing their mission statement.

That same year, they also launched Duolingo Plus—a premium subscription model. Like other apps with premium plans, Duolingo's entails an ad-free experience with additional benefits like:

a. Offline access. Whether on a plane to Paris or in a low-internet zone in South Asia, Duolingo lets you download lessons for offline access.
b. Progress quizzes. These assess and score your grasp of the material to date—a helpful tool for understanding your progress.
c. Streak repair. It's a bit of a cheat feature to maintain your streak in case something comes up, and you accidentally miss a day.

---

223 Lyanne Alfaro, "How This 'genius' Grew the Language-Learning App Duolingo to 150 Million Daily Users," CNBC, December 14, 2016.

It's not a bad offer at $7/month, but as you might expect, the vast majority of users stick to the free version for which Duolingo is so famous. That said, the 3 percent of users who *do* pony up for Plus help bring in a staggering $180 million in net revenue. That's the power of having a massive user base!

Note: These numbers are accurate as of our publication, but they've been steadily on the rise. In 2018, 1.75 percent of users were paying, with *only* $36 million in revenue. In 2020, we've seen COVID-19 push Duolingo beyond its initial subscriber growth projections. It seems that global lockdowns are a popular time for premium language learning.[224]

So now we've covered Duolingo's ads and subscription offerings, but they have one more monetization trick up their sleeves. They've also created what they call the Duolingo English Test (DET). The purpose of the test is to help foreign students prove English proficiency when applying to American colleges and universities.

Prior to the DET, these students' only option was paying $215 to take the three-hour-long Test of English as a Foreign Language (TOEFL) from the Educational Testing Service. The DET presents a pretty enticing alternative. It's only $49, takes less than an hour's time, is recognized by over 180 academic institutions, and (unlike the TOEFL) can be completed remotely.

---

224 Susan Adams, "Game of Tongues: How Duolingo Built A $700 Million Business with Its Addictive Language-Learning App," *Forbes*, August 31, 2019; Natasha Mascarenhas, "Duolingo CEO explains language app's surge in bookings," *TechCrunch*, September 29, 2020.

Together with advertising and subscriptions, the DET has helped Duolingo grow its revenue from $1 million in 2016 to over $180 million in 2020.[225]

LISTEN, LAUNCH, TEST, AND REPEAT

To get to this point, the VP of Product Management Cem Kansu, and the Duolingo team listened carefully to users' frustrations to get a clear sense of their values. This is how they found out how many users take pride in maintaining their streak counts, even to the point where they'd pay to recover them. And voila! The repair feature was born.

The result? A neat 54 percent increase from their previous subscription conversion rate—all from simply embracing user feedback.[226]

Kansu also learned of the importance of creating targeted solutions; trying to please their entire, massive user base with any one feature was a lost cause. Take his approach to promoting Duolingo Plus:

Initially, purchase links were presented on in-app ads. It's a logical approach—run ads on the platform and offer a link just below the ad to subscribe to premium and be ad-free.

225 Frederic Lardinois, "Duolingo Hires Its First Chief Marketing Officer as Active User Numbers Stagnate but Revenue Grows," *TechCrunch*, Accessed November 30, 2020.

226 Cem Kansu, "MAU Vegas 2018—From Zero to Top Grossing: Duolingo's Lessons from Monetizing Free Education," Grow.Co, May 15, 2018.

The problem was that users became blind to all ads on the service—including the ones for Duolingo Plus. Once users saw the ad, they dismissed it immediately, leading to lower click-through rates (CTR), cost per click (CPC), and Plus subscriptions.

So, Kansu and Co. rebranded the Plus ad into a simple "Learn more" pop-up showcasing their famous owl mascot Duo in a spacesuit. When targeting the users who mostly ignored their ads, the result was a 90 percent increase from their previous subscription conversion rate.[227]

Through it all, Kansu's team ensured that their monetization strategies stay authentic to the Duolingo experience. This goes back to their mission of keeping the experience free and user-friendly. Even with new ads, features, and subscriptions, the app stays simple, clean, and popular.

According to Kansu, this unceasing popularity is "proof that it's possible to provide access to free language education and build a sustainable business at the same time."[228]

"What a ride this has been!" says Kansu. "And we are only getting started."[229]

227 Cem Kansu, "MAU Vegas 2018," Grow.Co.

228 Cem Kansu (@cemkansu) "'I'm Incredibly Proud of What We Have Achieved at @duolingo: 2 Years Ago We Had Zero Revenue, Today We Are the World's Top Grossing Education App. This Is Proof That It's Possible to Provide Access to Free Language Education and Build a Sustainable Business at the Same Time," Twitter, December 12, 2018.

229 "Cem Kansu," LinkedIn, accessed October 15, 2020.

CHAPTER 13

SPOTIFY

@MACHINEgg is run by Alex Richardson, a popular Esports commentator, host, and presenter.[230]

In the mid-2000s, the music industry had a glaring problem. And that problem was pirates.

They may not have looked like Blackbeard, but they still posed a serious threat to artists' treasured work. Mass anti-piracy ad campaigns came out, but the general public couldn't be bothered to give them much care. After all, we're speaking

---

230 MACHINE /// (@MACHINEgg), "'I Swear My @Spotify Discover Weekly Is Always 🔥," Twitter, October 26, 2018.

about the upper echelon—musicians, actors, production agencies, and TV execs. Much to their chagrin, nobody felt too guilty exploiting their content.

This struggle to guard digital channels was relatively new, though. Back in the 90s, the music industry was particularly thriving, having reached a peak revenue of $14.6 billion in 1999, and then Napster came along.[231] Shawn Fanning and Sean Parker's file-sharing creation introduced the masses to the concept of free media right at your fingertips.

Over the next decade, Napster and a generation of copycat services completely upended the music industry. Profits plummeted, and the piracy war waged on. But, as an unintended side effect, they also helped the industry evolve by demonstrating users' music preferences: Namely, extensive access to individual songs (rather than full albums).

Apple took note and tried selling legal song downloads at ninety-nine cents a pop, but this model failed to satisfy users' demand. Its value still wasn't worth the price.

But eventually, we *did* get a solution that was worth the price. And with it, music industry revenue finally swung back up:[232]

---

231 "US Sales Database," RIAA, accessed November 12, 2020.
232 Ibid.

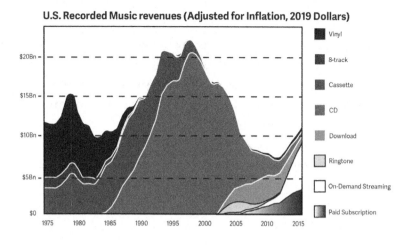

U.S. Recorded Music revenues (Adjusted for Inflation, 2019 Dollars)

Vinyl
8-track
Cassette
CD
Download
Ringtone
On-Demand Streaming
Paid Subscription

[Note that this graph exceeds our $14.6 billion figure due to inflation adjustment.]

Welcome to the land of on-demand music streaming! Tonight's headliner, coming all the way from Stockholm: It's none other than Spotify.

HOW SPOTIFY DEFEATED PIRACY...AND EVERYONE ELSE

"I realized that you can never legislate away from piracy," Spotify co-founder and CEO Daniel Ek told *The Telegraph* in 2010. "The only way to solve the problem was to create a service that was better than piracy and at the same time, compensates the music industry."[233]

---

233 Rupert Neate, "Daniel Ek Profile: 'Spotify Will Be Worth Tens of Billions,'" *Telegraph UK*, February 17, 2010.

In theory, it's simple: Superior product and fair compensation. This core solution currently resonates with over 320 million global users, including over 144 million paid subscribers or 30 percent of the global music subscription industry.[234] For reference, Apple Music has over sixty million customers, while Amazon Music checks in at fifty-five million at the time of this publication.[235]

But, of course, it's not all that simple. *How* do you create a service that so handily beats piracy? And then how do you monetize it to simultaneously compensate artists, entice users, and deliver profits?

These are the questions that form the foundation of Spotify's growing empire. Let's first examine the former:

STEP 1: BUILD A WINNING PRODUCT

"What is something people are willing to pay for?" asked Sean Parker, also an early Spotify board member. "I think that answer is convenience and accessibility."[236]

That, in an oversimplified nutshell, is how Spotify beat piracy at its own game. They took music and made it *more* convenient and *more* accessible. So much so that if you now

---

234 "Company Info," Spotify, accessed November 12, 2020; David Trainer, "It Sounds Like Spotify Is In Trouble," *Forbes*, October 13, 2020.

235 Stuart Dredge, "How Many Users Do Spotify, Apple Music and Streaming Services Have?" Music Ally, February 19, 2020.

236 Josh Constine, "Spotify Wants to Be Everything to Everyone," *TechCrunch*, August 10, 2013.

compare Spotify to even the best piracy service, the contrast is laughable.

No matter where you look, Spotify covered its bases. Every single thing they do, they do better:

AN ENDLESS CONTENT LIBRARY TO DISCOVER.
We're talking over sixty million tracks with some 40,000 added *daily.* Throw in another 700,000 podcasts (a number that's quickly growing), and you have enough audio to fill several lifetimes.[237] Press play now; you won't run out anytime soon.

Now, you don't just gain access to fifty million songs overnight. Ek's team spent years developing partnerships with major music label companies like Sony, Universal, Warner, and Merlin. Sony, for its part, got in the game early as a shareholder and investor, trading music rights for equity in a deal that continues to pay off in dividends.[238]

Spotify has also made things easier for individual artists looking to gain credibility, promote music, and build an audience. Its algorithmically fueled stations and suggested playlists facilitate new music discovery better than radio or piracy ever could.

---

237 "Company Info," Spotify; "Annual Report, 2019—Financials," Spotify, accessed November 12, 2020; Tim Ingham, "Nearly 40,000 Tracks Are Now Being Added to Spotify Every Single Day," Music Business Worldwide, April 29, 2019.

238 Micah Singleton, "This Was Sony Music's Contract with Spotify," *The Verge*, May 19, 2015.

And don't forget about their global initiatives to shine a spotlight on international artists that would otherwise be lost on the average listener.

INSTANT AVAILABILITY AT YOUR FINGERTIPS.

A deep catalog of audio content is just one part of the story. But it means nothing if you can't play it all in a fraction of a second. Ek said as much in a Quora post:

"We spent an insane amount of time focusing on latency when no one cared because we were hell-bent on making it feel like you had all the world's music on your hard drive."[239]

The key to this quick response time is multifaceted data retrieval. Your most popular songs sit on your device as encrypted, local copies while the rest rely on nearby Spotify servers or peer-to-peer sharing. So, if the app can't find a local copy, it fetches a small part of the song from the nearest server. And on top of this dynamic setup, Spotify's engineers have fixed a ton of small technical protocols that work to chip away at buffer times, millisecond by millisecond.

If you're familiar at all with the old framework of Napster, you'll realize that Spotify's file-sharing approach is extremely similar. Oh, except for the tiny detail that it's actually legal (which we'll discuss further in a bit).

239 Daniel Ek, "Daniel Ek's Answer to What Are Some Early Decisions That Were Key to Spotify's Success?" Quora, February 16, 2016.

AN INTERFACE WORTH WRITING HOME ABOUT.
Not only is the Spotify app extensive, fast, and legal, but it's also super user-friendly.

That seems like an obvious must-have now, but it's a huge leg up on those convoluted piracy programs. Remember the headache of searching through sketchy Limewire file lists, waiting for downloads, and hoping for passable sound quality? If not, consider yourself lucky.

Today, we get to enjoy a seamless, all-in-one app for making playlists, finding artists, viewing albums, setting up a song queue, discovering new hits, and...Well, you get the point.

But it's intuitive design only scratches the surface of the conversation. On a more macro level, Spotify managed to utilize the convenience factor of mobile data. Back in 2007, listening to music on your iPod required downloading and syncing individual files. Spotify trimmed all the fat off that process, using the increasingly present Internet to give us instant access without doing any legwork.

Lastly, if you have Spotify, you've likely noticed a steady stream of updates, enhancing its overall functionality. That's because, unlike competitors Apple, Amazon, or Google, Spotify's sole focus is audio streaming. And that dedication truly shows in the Premium version: No ads, no constraints, only high-quality audio, and an app you never want to close.

SPREAD THE LOVE WITH THE CLICK OF A BUTTON

"We believe that music is the most social thing there is, and that's why we've built the best social features into Spotify for easy sharing and the ultimate in music discovery."[240]

That's Ek again, harping on another one of Spotify's bigger selling points. Music isn't just the *you* experience of mid-2000s MP3 players; it's the *us* experience of an interactive platform. With it, we can access our friends' playlists, check whom they follow, see what they're listening to, and even share via social media.

The latter is largely thanks to a partnership with Facebook. In just a few taps of the thumb, you can post links from Spotify onto your news feed, friends' timelines, messenger, or WhatsApp chats. In 2020, this may not seem so groundbreaking, but in September 2011, it was such a dramatic stride forward that active users skyrocketed by one million *in one week!*[241]

"Even if you aren't a total music freak," Ek continued, "Chances are you have a friend who is and whose taste you admire." And now, you no longer have to admire from afar.[242]

---

240 Mike Butcher, "Spotify Reveals the Detail behind Its US Launch," *TechCrunch*, July 14, 2011.

241 Neil Patel, "Spotify's Secret to Adding 8,000 Paying Subscribers a Day," *GeekWire*, February 15, 2012.

242 Mike Butcher, "Spotify," *TechCrunch*.

STEP 2: MAKE IT PERSONAL...IN A GOOD WAY

Curating a library of over sixty million songs is challenging enough on its own. But as it turns out, making audio accessible is only half the battle. The next challenge for Spotify is making all this music *discoverable*.

Enabling us, the users, to easily find things we like is what keeps us engaged, but it's easier said than done. Because when it comes to our preferences with music, they're typically more unique and more fluid than with other content (like, say, TV streaming). Each individual's taste fluctuates depending on mood, time of day, cultural trends, present activity (i.e., driving, working), and so on.

And then we have to consider the sheer volume: Music is limitless in quantity. This means that while there should be no shortage of songs that satisfy our tastes, there's also no shortage of songs that don't. How, then, do we parse through all that noise to find new music that we like?

Before Spotify, doing so was a bit of a hassle. If you can remember those dark ages, people relied on word-of-mouth recommendations, radio or television broadcasts, and maybe the occasional social gathering.

ENTER: SPOTIFY'S PERSONALIZATION STRATEGY

This is what makes Spotify a Billion Dollar App—its relentless focus on personalized recommendations for each of their 320 million monthly active users. And while these algorithms aren't flawless, Spotify's recommendations represent a dramatic upgrade over those alternatives we long relied on.

We see this personalization all over the app: The "Uniquely yours" playlists compiling your most-listened-to songs—the various "For Fans Of _____" suggestions. The "Recently played" and "Continue listening" bookmarks for recent music and podcasts. The list goes on, and it culminates with the famous Discover Weekly playlist—a unique thirty-song mix of new songs that pops up each Monday morning as a jolt of auditory inspiration.

> "It makes me feel seen. It knows my musical tastes better than any person in my entire life ever has, and I'm consistently delighted by how satisfyingly just right it is every week, with tracks I probably would never have found myself or known I would like."[243]

SOPHIA CIOCCA, *THE NEW YORK TIMES*

These recommendations do more than garner praise; they support direct business goals. After all, when users enjoy new song discoveries, they're more likely to return to the app. That's why they put such a big focus on facilitating such discovery.

---

243 Sophia Ciocca, "How Does Spotify Know You So Well?" Medium, October 10, 2017.

And according to their stats, this customization *does* boost user engagement: Users who listen to Discovery Weekly stream music twice as long, on average, as those who don't.[244] In other words, personalization is the tool with which Spotify cultivates the impassioned brand loyalty that most companies can only dream of having.

Now that's all good and well, but the next question that emerges is how. How do they consistently generate such on-the-nose recommendations?

If there were only one type of listener in one distinct market, some kind of manual approach could maybe work. But Sophia Ciocca isn't the only one; hundreds of millions of active users are enamored with their Discover Weekly! It isn't magic—this is where artificial intelligence comes into play.

Under the hood, Spotify's recommendation engine utilizes three types of machine learning, each with its own particular benefit:

Collaborative filtering. As we saw in Chapter 6, this one feeds you suggestions based on the activity of similar users—essentially simulating a friend's rec. So as a simplified example: Let's say Spotify groups you with 10,000 other users who often listen to the same albums, "like" a bunch of the same songs, and generally have similar listening activity. If 9,500 of those listeners go on a huge Elton John kick this month, you'll be much more likely to come across 'Tiny Dancer' in the near future.

---

244 Sarah Perez, "Spotify Will Now Let Brands Sponsor Its Discover Weekly Playlist," *TechCrunch*, January 7, 2019

Natural language processing. This one's a bit techie. Here, the app creates a digital profile of sorts for each song. This profile consists of characteristic *tags* based on the internet discourse around each song. By factoring in the public reception to a song, Spotify stays a step ahead of emerging trends—always in a prime position to suggest the hot new thing.

Acoustic analysis. This one is more about the nuts and bolts of a song. By identifying and assessing auditory elements (i.e., pitch, tempo), Spotify can form suggestions independent of popularity or other people's listening habits. This means that acoustic analysis is the one responsible for that obscure Norwegian song you randomly came across and fell in love with last week!

Put together, these three methods create the sensation that the app *just gets you* on a deep, spiritual level. And while, for our purposes, we've narrowed this conversation to music, you can bet that Spotify's podcast algorithms are likewise utilizing collaborative filtering and natural language processing.

STEP 3: CREATE AN EVERYBODY WINS BUSINESS MODEL

Put yourself in Spotify's shoes for a moment. You've created an all-around superior service—great! But that's only one part of defeating piracy. You now need to draw people away from the free aspect of it.

Before you get ahead of yourself, remember that the piracy problem we're fixing is *illegal*. So, you have the impossible task of introducing both legality *and* payment into a transactional exchange that satisfies the music industry, your global audience, and the investors propping this whole thing up.

That's the twisted balancing act of monetization that early era Spotify faced. Here's how they tackled it:

HOW SPOTIFY PAYS ARTISTS AND STAYS LEGAL

The difficulty of their business model is that they don't control supply—the music itself. In fact, one of the biggest concerns for Ek and Co. was getting enough artists on board and then keeping them on board with a satisfactory payment agreement.

This process started with those aforementioned label companies and their licensing rights. "People thought we were crazy to work with the music industry," Ek recalled. "The general thinking was to just do whatever you wanted with music and then ask for forgiveness later."[245]

But they didn't just do whatever. Instead, they worked meticulously to build a music catalog that was sustainable for everyone. As a result, Spotify's partnerships with major record labels now provide over 80 percent of its music. In exchange, Spotify rewards these record labels with hundreds of millions of listeners and a large chunk of its revenue. Though, some artists have questioned whether it's a large enough cut.

---

245 Daniel Ek, "What Are Some Early Decisions That Were Key to Spotify's Success?" Quora.

And that's where we come to the tricky prospect of compensation. If you had asked Taylor Swift back in 2014, she would have criticized Spotify for "perpetuating the perception that music has no value" while removing her music from the platform.[246] In those days, Swift's concerns were not at all unique. When you hear that Spotify only pays out $0.0030 to $0.0044 per song stream on average, it's hard not to think someone's getting ripped off. [247]

But since then, as Spotify's industry disruption has turned into industry norm, the benefit to artists has become clear. Success for the app means success for the artists. As Ek has stated on numerous occasions, their monetization incentives are intrinsically intertwined: The revenue from ads and subscriptions can pay out greater than radio ever could, and these returns continuously escalate as songs rack up listens.

"We don't use music to drive sales of hardware or software. We use music to get people to pay for music. The more we grow, the more we'll pay you. We're going to be transparent about it all the way through."

DANIEL EK.[248]

Taylor Swift wasn't the last skeptic of this compensation model, but the overwhelming consensus among artists is that Spotify is friend, not foe. Since Spotify's launch, it has paid

---

246 Taylor Swift, "For Taylor Swift, the Future of Music Is a Love Story," *WSJ*, Updated July 7, 2014.

247 Dmitry Pastukhov, "Streaming Payouts [2020]: What Spotify, Apple, & Others Pay," Soundcharts Blog, June 26, 2019.

248 Daniel Ek, "$2 Billion and Counting (Archived)," Spotify Blog, November 11, 2014.

over $22.5 billion to labels, publishers, and artists (including Taylor Swift, who rejoined the platform in 2017).[249] Now, sure, that friendship is a default requirement—streaming *is* king, nowadays. But it sure beats piracy, doesn't it? More and more artists seem to think so—they've taken note and are reaping increasingly substantial benefits.

HOW SPOTIFY STIRS A RECIPE FOR REVENUE

So, you've created an awesome app stocked with music. How do you get listeners who haven't paid for music in over a decade to pull out their wallets? The answer lies with that little trick called freemium.

To reiterate, this business model starts with a free, stripped back version of the main, subscription-based service. And for Spotify, it accomplishes two monetization goals.

1. **It supports a wide range of ads**

First off, the free tier is ad-supported. In exchange for the content you receive, you have to sit through an audio advertisement every thirty minutes or so and come across the occasional interstitial and native ad.

Behind the scenes, Spotify's *Ad Studio* platform allows the promoted brands their own form of personalization: They can select ad format (audio, video, etc.), platforms (mobile, desktop), start/end dates, and target demographic information such as country, location, age, gender, and interests. On

---

249 "Company Info," Spotify.

a minimum budget of $250, these brands can reach as many as 26,000 people.[250] Pretty cost-effective, right?

The ad formats are quite diverse, mixing audio and video as well as mobile and desktop. Some ad experiences that Spotify offers advertisers are:[251]

- **Audio ads.** As previously described, it's thirty promotional seconds between songs before unlocking more free music—a small price to pay.
- **Video ads.** Some are similar to audio ads, running for thirty seconds between songs. Others pop up with a call-to-action banner while users browse the platform. One distinction: Video ads only run when the user has the app open—for all devices.
- **Sponsored playlists.** i.e., "Today's Top Hits" presented by KIA Motors, where KIA gets a desktop banner and brand logo on mobile versions of the playlist.
- **Other banners.** i.e., A prominent display atop the homepage, a temporary clickable message on desktop/web app, an overlay that pops up when the app is opened.

These ads aren't the only drawback of freemium, though. Nonpaying users are confined to limited releases and listening via shuffle play (meaning they can't set a queue or listen to a playlist/album in sequence). It's nice, especially for free, but eventually, the insufficiencies wear users down until they can't resist the full version and finally pull the trigger to upgrade.

---

250 "Spotify Advertising," accessed November 12, 2020.
251 "Ad Experiences," Spotify Advertising, accessed November 12, 2020.

2. It opens the door to Premium

As previously discussed, the power of the freemium model is that it can be an intermediary step in converting the audience to Premium. All it takes is a reasonable $9.99/month ($5.99/mo for students, $14.99/mo/six people for a family plan), and you have no ads or listening restrictions—the entire world of music, podcasts, and benefits listed above are yours.[252]

So, there's the kicker, not only are users slowly warmed up to the water but once they jump in, they'll have no hesitation paying relatively low prices for a high-end service that swims laps around the alternatives.

Premium sounds pretty enticing, right? That's what modern companies like Microsoft, Evernote, and Spotify are smartly counting on with their limited freemium options. "The ad-supported service is also a subsidy program that offsets the cost of new user acquisition," explained CFO Barry McCarthy, adding that "scale can be a great enabler."[253]

In 2019 alone, Spotify's growth mindset raked in over six billion purely from Premium payments. Compare that to roughly $680 million from ads.[254] It seems they've hoodwinked us all into converting…And yet, is anyone complaining?

Users aren't complaining and certainly not stakeholders. Spotify capitalized on the market inefficiencies of Apple's pay per song formula with a Netflix-esque subscription model that

---

252 "Premium," Spotify, accessed November 12, 2020.

253 Becky Peterson, "Spotify Loses Money on Free Subscribers," *Business Insider*, March 15, 2018.

254 "Annual Report, 2019—Financials," Spotify.

lends itself to greater customer acquisition. And sure, the Netflix parallel isn't absolute: Netflix doesn't pay royalties per view while Spotify doesn't control any of its supply. But the fact remains that these two streaming companies have similarly planted definitive flags in their respective media corners.

A FINAL WORD ON SPOTIFY: DELIVERING VALUE 101

Convenience and accessibility; massive profits are driven by reasonable prices. Clever acquisition enabling rapid scaling. Combine it all, and you get an app that has embedded itself as a cultural fixture.

That's the beauty of what Spotify has accomplished. They've framed their product as a true win-win. It wasn't just a matter of defeating piracy from an ethical standpoint…*Or* from a usability standpoint…*Or* from a monetization standpoint. It was a matter of *and*—for music creator, consumer, and especially to the middleman who brought them all together.

CHAPTER 14

TINDER

———

"Making the simple complicated is commonplace; making the complicated simple, awesomely simple, that's creativity."

CHARLES MINGUS, JAZZ BASSIST

On July 19, 1695, an unusual advertisement appeared in a London periodical:

"A gentleman about thirty years of age, that says he has a very good estate, would willingly match himself to some good young gentlewoman, that has a fortune of £3,000 or thereabout, and he will make settlement to content."[255]

We don't know who this thirty-year-old man with *very good estate* was. But we do know one thing: He had just placed one of the first personal ads ever. And the periodical's editor, John Houghton, immediately saw the potential for the world of dating (or, *courtship*, rather). He explains:

---

255 Clarence Moran, *The Business of Advertising*, United Kingdom: Methuen and Company, 1905.

"I have undertaken to advertise all sorts of things that are honourable and what follows is not otherwise, and I am well paid for it." Continuing, he notes, "tis probable such advertisements may prove very useful."[256]

Yes, even back in the 1600s, singles needed an easier way to meet one another.

Houghton capitalized off this reality but soon encountered a glaring issue. People were shying away from a fear of embarrassment. So he created a degree of anonymity: "Nobody shall know anything of the matter, but where I shall reasonably believe they are in good earnest," he promised.[257]

It's a relatable concern, no? Much may have changed over the last 400 years, but it seems we have some timeless constants. When it comes to love, no matter the century, people generally have:

- An innate need for intimacy and companionship
- A deep-rooted fear of rejection

And, as humans do, where there are problems, a market emerges to fix them.

Luckily for this market, its focal point is a powerful attention grabber: Sex! There's a reason we hear "Sex sells" everywhere—because it's true! Houghton was among the first to

---

256 Ibid.
257 Ibid.

tap into this goldmine, and now subliminal sexual messaging is an advertising staple.

Think about the sexually charged ads you see from clothing and hygiene retailers like Abercrombie & Fitch or Axe. Even automobile brands like Nissan often utilize the appeal of bikini clad women to promote their vehicles. The reason this all works is the same reason someone like Kim Kardashian can become an icon: Sexuality is a potent marketing tool.

Given this obvious allure of sex, you'd think a mobile app that connects people to date would be an instant killer.

And yet ...

EARLY ONLINE DATING: REALITY FALLING SHORT OF EXPECTATIONS

Let's take it back to the land of 2012. Hundreds of dating apps and websites are floating in an overcrowded sea. Each one is loudly promising to help you "meet hot singles now!" And nearly every one quickly sinks to the bottom, never to be heard from again.

So, what's the problem? Why can't anyone capitalize here?

Well, to be fair, websites like eHarmony and Match.com *do* capitalize and *do* enjoy considerable popularity. But still, they can't shake a certain social stigma associated with online dating. On some level, there's a perception that the people who use these sites are unattractive or lacking in social skills. Essentially, dating websites aren't cool.

Some of this stigma holds water, but it has less to do with coolness than credibility. The average dating website is littered with dubious bots, deceptive catfishers, and scheming con artists. You're just as likely to give away your bank account password as you are to find true love.

And the platforms' notorious flaws don't end there. Many websites claiming to use *scientific algorithms* to find your perfect match have nothing remotely scientific going on behind the scenes. Even the more legitimate sites have tremendous roadblocks, requiring users to fill out tedious forms and lengthy autobiographies. Believe it or not, a few platforms even hire employees to interact with users and pretend to like them with the goal of squeezing out more subscription fees!

That's what you're getting for about $20 a month in 2012: A fool's chance, at best. But with smartphones and user-centric design on the rise, the time is ripe for some industry disruption.

ENTER TINDER—A MODERN SOLUTION TO AGE-OLD PROBLEMS

Exactly how much of a need was there for a better dating app? Well, after a little over a year of launching, Tinder reported over two million matches a day.[258] In 2013, *TechCrunch* crowned it the "best new startup." A year later, it earned "breakout of the year" honors at the Webby Awards.[259]

---

258 Olga Khazan, "How to Date Online like a Social Scientist," *Quartz*, December 11, 2013.

259 Felicia Shivakumar, "Tinder Wins Best New Startup of 2013," Crunchies Awards 2013 – *TechCrunch*, February 11, 2013; "Webby Awards: Tinder,"

Today, it's one of the top-grossing apps ever, downloaded in over 190 countries and available in over forty languages.[260] Some estimates pin Tinder at around sixty million users; if it were a country, it would rival Italy and South Africa in terms of population.[261] In 2019, that popularity translated to $1.2 billion.[262]

That is how much need there was for an app that finally made dating easier. Former Tinder CEO Sean Rad had this to say in a Reddit AMA in 2015:

"We started Tinder years ago because we had this obsession with breaking down the barriers in meeting people around you…. We knew that if we could simply take the fear out of meeting someone, that we could bring the people closer together. And we've done just that…. We have created over six billion matches (twenty-six million new ones every day). That's six billion potential connections that would likely never have existed before Tinder; each one having the potential to change someone's life forever."[263]

WebbyAwards, accessed November 6, 2020.

260 "FORM S-1 | Match Group, Inc," United States Securities and Exchange Commission, October 16, 2015; "Match Group—Investor Relations," Tinder, accessed October 4, 2020.

261 Padraig Belton, "Love and Dating after the Tinder Revolution," *BBC News*, February 13, 2018; "SA Population Reaches 58.8 Million | Statistics South Africa," accessed November 6, 2020; "Indicatori Demografici," L'Istituto nazionale di statistica | Italy, accessed November 6, 2020.

262 "Match Group Reports Fourth Quarter 2019 Results," Match Group, February 4, 2020.

263 Sean Rad (sean_rad), "IAMA Sean Rad, Cofounder & CEO of Tinder. AMA!: IAmA," Reddit, accessed October 4, 2020.

Essentially, this philosophy sought to solve the glaring pain points of intimacy. But how exactly did Tinder succeed more than any other dating service in history? Two answers:

1. A smart user interface that optimizes human psychology and gamification (hello swiping!)
2. A monetization model that'll make you jealous (while still being free!)

So, don't brush off Tinder because it's a dating app. While the final product may appear somewhat superficial, there's a lot to be learned from how Tinder changed the dating game.

A DESIGN THAT PUSHES ALL THE RIGHT EMOTIONAL BUTTONS

The premise of Tinder is quite simple: You set up a minimalist profile with a few pictures, a brief description, and your sexual preference. The app then finds other users near you and presents each one as a card. Interested? Swipe right. Otherwise, swipe left. If both parties give the thumbs up, we have a match, and the option to chat pops up.

At a glance, that's all there is to it. So, let's give it a longer look.

STEP ONE: MAKE IT PAINLESS

A key takeaway we keep circling back to is the importance of solving users' pain points. All great apps do it, and, unsurprisingly, it's where those early dating programs came short.

On the one hand, these apps did nothing to reduce our innate fear of rejection. Therefore, by using one of these early dating apps, you were very likely subjecting yourself to your worst anxieties without any safety net. And a bleak spiral of rejection isn't exactly the recipe for a successful app.

On the other hand, these apps also often failed to provide any safeguards from unwelcome advances. As such, using them became synonymous with getting pestered and harassed— further cementing the hopelessness of online dating.

With a swift wave of their magic wand, Tinder swept away both issues. In retrospect, the mentality that led them there is actually fairly straightforward:

"No matter who you are," Rad continues, "you feel more comfortable approaching somebody if you know they want you to approach them."[264]

Enter: The double opt-in method. It only allows for a conversation if both people are up for it. That's Tinder's big idea.

Back to the fear of rejection—if you swipe right on someone, they won't find out unless they *also* swipe right on you. If they're not interested, no worries! They'll never know which way you swiped. This sort of anonymity creates a buffer between the user and any embarrassment.

---

264 "Tinder Co-Creator Sean Rad's Interview Fail," *BBC Newsbeat*, November 19, 2015.

If, instead, you're trying to avoid unwanted attention, here's your golden ticket: You and you alone now control who messages you. (Note: Bumble has gained mass popularity by going a step beyond Tinder with another buffer, only letting women in heterosexual matches send the first message).

No more can't take the hints. No more won't-take-no-for-an-answers. And the rejection buffer helps here as well: You won't face the awkwardness of directly turning anyone away.

Just like that, the two biggest pain points of dating aren't quite so painful. All thanks to the double opt-in.

STEP 2: GET USERS COMING BACK FOR MORE

Removing the negatives, though, is only the start of Tinder's winning formula. Next, they figure out a way to augment the most enjoyable aspects of online dating. The result isn't just painless; it's addicting.

How do they accomplish this? Primarily through their celebratory "It's a Match!" message and all the excitement that goes with it.

What that message does is fulfill users' desired outcomes. According to renowned growth marketer Lincoln Murphy, desired outcome comes down to two factors: *required outcome* and *appropriate experience*."[265]

---

265 Lincoln Murphy, "Desired Outcome Is a Transformative Concept," Sixteenventures.com, accessed November 6, 2020.

First comes the *required outcome* aspect. It's the cup of coffee from Starbucks. The ride to your destination from Lyft. The dating connection from Tinder.

But what really makes a brand special is how they frame the *appropriate experience* to stand out in their industries and satisfy customer expectations. Starbucks' chic decor and unique ambiance. Lyft's easy-to-use interface and quick pick up.

And with Tinder, that experience is all about capturing the thrill of a match. Even the app's color theme is geared around this climactic message, going unexpectedly dark to further shock your senses. That giddiness you get—that's Tinder communicating its value proposition directly to your senses.

Is this the most transformative innovation? Maybe not, but it's miles ahead of anything competitors were doing. And, more importantly, it cultivates that temporary reward we all crave. Much like Facebook's likes, Tinder's matches induce dopamine highs that keep bringing us back for more.

STEP 3: NOW KISS—KEEP IT SIMPLE AND STRAIGHTFORWARD

Indeed, Tinder took the complicated—the stressful, the nerve-racking—and made it *simple and straightforward*. And we see this on both a physical and psychological level.

Physically, we have the brilliance of the swipe. This incredibly natural hand motion "was born out of a desire to mimic real-life interactions with a card stack."[266] All you need to use the app is one hand on the phone and one thumb swiping.

This model has now become iconic. And it's set a precedent not just for dating apps, but for apps in general. Tinder has put the power of simplicity on full display.

In fact, one of the reasons it's so easy to use from a tactile standpoint is a complete lack of clutter. This brings us to the psychological element. Tinder keeps the information displayed to an absolute minimum.

This goes completely against the old standard for dating apps, what with their long-form user profiles. But Tinder went against the grain, instead prioritizing a handful of features based on how users actually interact. For each potential match, you initially only see a full-screen photo, their name and age, and, in smaller text, their school or job.

The truth is, we form most first impressions based on surface-level qualifiers anyway. And, for better or worse, we prefer simplicity to cognitive overload. Tinder realized this and leveraged it. They eliminated all the guesswork, streamlined our experience, and enabled us to make as many swipes as possible as easily as possible.

But they also revolutionized profile creation by cutting your choice of filters. With an old-school dating app, you'd have to fill out all sorts of surveys specifying your partner

266 Taylor Soper, "Tinder Founder Sean Rad Explains Why the Dating App Is So Popular," *GeekWire*, March 20, 2015.

preferences: Height, hair color, body type, religion, ethnicity, interests, and on and on.

With Tinder, you only need to enter three pieces of information: The gender you're interested in, an age range, and geographical distance radius. They've skipped all contemplation—the *hard work*, if you will.

It's not a shock that this works. Simply recall our Chapter 5 discussion on cognitive overload, in which buyers preferred supermarket displays with fewer varieties of jam. By limiting information and by abstaining from bells and whistles, Tinder has removed friction and given users more of what they actually want.

STEP 4: CONNECT SOCIALLY; FOSTER TRUST

When signing up for Tinder, you have the option to log in via Facebook to import your age, location, and profile pictures from there. Then, you can additionally link up your Instagram and even Spotify accounts. The entire Tinder experience incorporates the power of integrations.

For starters, these integrations play up the app's coolness factor. Intertwining its functionality with popular social media platforms gives Tinder a certain social utility. It connects your dating profile with other valued elements of your digital persona. And thus, it feels particularly relevant.

But it's also extremely practical. Automatically adding info via Facebook is what makes it simple and straightforward. And if you want to exceed the six photo limit, just press

"Connect Instagram." This convenience factor cannot be ignored, especially relative to its predecessors.

And speaking of, perhaps the biggest benefit of Tinder's integrations is added legitimacy. The presence of authentic social accounts means fewer scams, fake accounts, and catfishing attempts. Some nefarious frauds still exist, they probably always will, but gauging who's real is a lot easier now than it was in 2010.

Modernity, convenience, and trust—all of this comes back to the interaction design for Tinder. And with such excellent design, it becomes a lot easier to monetize.

A MONETIZATION MODEL THAT IS ABOUT MORE THAN MONEY

Companies litter the app store graveyard because they focused so much on dollar signs that they lost sight of user experience. Some even started viewing UX as a hindrance— as a cost to their business!

Obviously, such a mentality is shortsighted; quality UX is an investment you make with the goal of a high ROI down the road. A good monetization strategy depends on this.

But a *great* monetization strategy builds on top of your UX. That's the key to what Tinder has achieved: A monetization strategy that works in tandem with their interface. That's how Tinder got to be the #1 grossing app worldwide—not by prioritizing dollars alone, but by achieving this delicate balance between monetization and UX (specifically, Interaction Design).[267] Here's how they did it:

FIRST, THEY CREATED A FREEMIUM SERVICE WITH APPROPRIATE LIMITATIONS

If you're a free user, each day, you get one hundred right swipes and one Top Pick (a chance to match with a top profile curated for your preferences).

Tinder still monetizes off your app usage with native ads that seamlessly integrate with its simple design experience. As you swipe through potential dates, Tinder shows you ads from its partners. And like any individual's profile, you can swipe left or right on these ads; left takes you past the ad with no further interruption while right gives Tinder the green light to shoot your inbox a message from the advertiser.

The pros of Tinder's native ad setup are twofold. For one, their ads can be expertly targeted to match your preferences; after all, they typically have access to your social profiles. And two, brands receive undivided attention with these fullscreen promotions; no matter how quick a swiper you are, it's impossible to miss them.

THEN, THEY BROKE ALL THEIR OWN RULES

"My job as I walk into the office every day is to think of what rules we can break. And what features we can give to some

---

267 Julia Chan, "Top Grossing Dating Apps Worldwide for July 2020," Sensor Tower, August 20, 2020.

subset of the customers, but not everybody, because it would literally break the game of Tinder."[268]

That's from Jeff Morris, Jr., Tinder's renowned former Director of Product Management of Revenue. He came onto the scene back in 2015 when Tinder was still tiptoeing the line between a fleeting fad and cultural institution. And he was a big reason it swung the latter's way.

To Morris, breaking the rules isn't about utter madness. It's about examining the app and finding ways to go against its framework to give customers:[269]

1. More access
2. More exposure

Each app is built on certain rules, on certain things you can and can't do. Tinder, for example, doesn't allow you to reverse a swipe. What's done is done; that's part of the agreement.

But what if you could pay to break that rule? Or any number of other rules that Tinder is built upon?

These are the questions Morris asked as he dove into the app's data. His goal was to identify ways of providing exclusive access and exposure that would turn high-value prospects into repeat buyers.

---

268 Android Developers, "Tinder: Going Gold," YouTube, uploaded September 6, 2018.
269 Ibid.

And so, he broke Tinder's rules and created these paid features:[270]

a. Likes You: Lets you see who's liked you without having to swipe right on them.
b. Unlimited swipes: Lets you swipe right on as many profiles as you want (otherwise, the upper limit is one hundred per day).
c. Super Likes: Lets you break the anonymity of the double-opt-in by expressing interest in someone when they see your profile card. Both people still need to swipe right to chat.
d. Passport: Lets you browse profiles in a different geographical location.
e. Boost: Sends your profile to the top of nearby users' queues.
f. Unlimited Rewinds: Lets you go back and correct your swipe as needed.
g. Choose who sees you: Makes sure your profile only comes up for those you've liked
h. Turn off ads: removes all ads from the platform

By breaking some of Tinder's fundamental rules, each of these features adds legitimate, worth-the-money value for its power users. And, just as importantly, they do so without any negative impact on the core experience. But we'll get there.

---

270 "Tinder Subscriptions," Tinder, accessed October 5, 2020.

NEXT, THEY SET UP TIERS OF PRODUCTS

Morris structured these rule-breaking features primarily through a two-pronged freemium model with plans Tinder Plus and Tinder Gold.

The former consists of Unlimited Likes, Unlimited Rewinds, five daily Super likes, Passport swipes, the Choose Who Sees You, and one Boost every month. It's a reasonable package for anyone looking to improve their chances, with a price tag in the range of $10 to $20 per month.

For those all in on Tinder, the Gold plan throws in the Likes You feature and full access to daily "Top Picks" as well. Prices are a few dollars higher, but certainly not an obstacle for anyone truly interested.

Subscriptions aside, Tinder also sells Boosts and Super Likes as à la carte products—both strong options for users who want a quick leg up without the whole monthly plan platter.

The big takeaway from this monetization mishmash is that Tinder has something juicy for every level of customer. They have value-packed bundles for the enthusiasts, a natural method of converting users with low-commitment products, and a direct way to profit from free users.

And because free users make up most of their audience, they're the ones Morris had top-of-mind while deciding how to break those rules.

FINALLY, AS MORRIS WOULD SAY, "MONETIZE WITH STYLE"[271]
Morris knew exactly what game he was playing: The nature of mobile apps is that the majority of users will be free, and the bulk of revenue will come from a tiny subset.

Now, he could have done what many product managers in his shoes would have been tempted to do: Exploit Tinder's massive scale by hiding core features behind a paywall and calling it a day. Sure, they might have made more money right off the bat, but the app would have suffered in the long-term.

Instead, Morris sculpted a monetization strategy bent on keeping free users around.

"What we're trying to do is add value without negatively impacting the core experience," he explains in an interview on the podcast *This is Product Management* with Mike Fishbein. "And that's a very tricky thing to do, but it's always something we're very aware of."[272]

That awareness shows. None of the subscriptions, one-off items, or ads ever impede free users. If anything, they fit seamlessly with Tinder's aesthetically pleasing interface.

And that's the point. "My mantra within our team is we want to monetize with style," Morris adds.[273]

---

271 "Jeff Morris Jr," AngelList, accessed November 6, 2020.
272 "129 Revenue Is Product Management by This Is Product Management," SoundCloud, accessed November 6, 2020.
273 Ibid.

What you get is functionality and profitability existing in perfect harmony.

On the practical business side, what Tinder may lose from free customers, it gains back in advertising through its massive user base. And thus, wider global reach, increased opportunities for conversion, and a strong brand image.

Plus, shying away from any schemy monetization tactics is yet another badge of legitimacy for Tinder—already many badges ahead of any dating apps before it.

KEEP YOUR FOCUS; CHANGE THE GAME
"The Product Managers who succeed are those who stick with one idea for an unreasonable period of time."[274]

That's Morris again, summing up Tinder's entire big-picture approach to building the app and monetizing it. Since 2015, they've basically released just one major product per year. Instead of chasing different ideas all over the place, their aim is perfecting *one* idea.

They've found their corner, their niche, and put all their focus into conquering it. In fact, they may have *over-conquered* it. Tinder's design can be so addictive that ethical debates have sparked up around swiping and its effect on dopamine. But this is a rabbit hole for another time; if you're interested,

---

274 Jeff Morris Jr. (jeffmorrisjr), "Building Products & The Importance of Focus," LinkedIn, May 6, 2017.

check out Jaron Lanier's *Ten Arguments for Deleting Your Social Media Accounts Right Now.*[275]

For the most part, it's safe to say that Tinder developed an interface that blows its predecessors out of the water. The result isn't just an app that alleviated the pains of dating. Or just another app that rakes in substantial revenue. The result is a cultural phenomenon.

Tinder removed the stigma toward online dating—the "why would you use those apps?" dismissals—and transformed it into something widely accepted. Something commonplace. Something *cool.*

275 Jaron Lanier, *Ten Arguments for Deleting Your Social Media Accounts Right Now,* United Kingdom: Random House, 2018.

CHAPTER 15

POKÉMON GO

"Excuse me, officer? Could you help me get out? I'm stuck in a tree.... I was trying to catch a Pokémon."

It's a sentence that would've been completely ludicrous back in 2015. But come July of 2016, ridiculous Pokémon-related escapades became something of a common occurrence, in one iteration or another.

If it wasn't someone stuck in a tree, it was a group getting trapped in some abandoned mines.[276] Or a guy catching a Pidgey next to his wife who was in labor.[277] Or two Canadians carelessly crossing the border into Montana.[278]

The stories go on and on, and they even cross into the morbid. While following a Pokémon down to a nearby river, one

---

276 "Pokémon Go Teens Stuck in Caves 100ft Underground," *BBC News*, July 15, 2016.

277 Hugh Langley, "The Best and Weirdest Pokémon Go Stories so Far," *TechRadar*, July 11, 2016.

278 "Pokémon Go Players on the Hunt Illegally Cross Canada-US Border | Pokémon Go," *The Guardian*, July 23, 2016.

nineteen-year-old girl in Wyoming stumbled upon a dead body.[279] Another young man in Oregon actually kept playing *after getting stabbed* instead of seeking medical attention!

He told authorities: "It's important to me. I've basically got to catch 'em all."[280] And he was far from the only one. Because when Pokémon Go entered our lives, the world promptly lost its collective mind.

Backed by Nintendo and The Pokémon Company, the mobile game developers at Niantic Inc. created an app that instantly became a cultural sensation. Never before had a mobile game so seamlessly integrated augmented reality (AR)—an interactive feature in which game content interplays with the user's current physical environment.

Combine that cutting edge innovation with a dynamic gaming experience and decades of global Pokémon hype, and unintentional border crossings aren't all you get.

You also get mobile game world records, completely shattered. According to the folks at Guinness, Pokémon Go set a new benchmark for most revenue in its first month ($206 million) and the fastest game to $100 million (twenty days). It also received the most first-month downloads (130 million), topping the charts of a record seventy different countries![281]

279 Harry Cockburn, "Pokémon Go Leads Teenage Girl to Discover Dead Body in Wyoming," *The Independent*, accessed November 7, 2020.

280 Richard Thompson, "'Pokémon Go' Fan Stabbed While Playing Game, Continues Mission to 'Catch 'Em All' after Attack," *Boston 25 News*, updated July 13, 2016.

281 Rachel Swatman, "Pokémon Go Catches Five New World Records," Guinness World Records, August 10, 2016.

The Pokémon Go fever was so pronounced that some of our highest-usage apps like Facebook and Twitter actually saw a noticeable dip in their own traffic.[282]

Niantic's app hit an early peak that most app developers can only dream of reaching. But as impressive as those first few months were, what's really worth our attention is the story of Pokémon Go after that initial surge.

Because here's what happened: Predictably, engagement dipped significantly. By the end of 2016, daily user counts had dropped by twenty-three million. Most people, justifiably, figured the app had had its run as a fun summer fling and was now dropping off. After all, free games tend to have a substantial degree of user turnover; it's all to be expected.[283]

Except, that's not quite how Pokémon Go's story has gone. After pulling in $832 mil in user revenue through six months of 2016, residual traction only delivered another $589 mil through all of 2017. But here's where we encounter the massive plot twist. A second life with user spends back up to $816 mil in 2018 and a best-yet $894 mil in 2019![284] August of 2019 somehow proved to be the app's most profitable month since the initial launch, eclipsing $100 mil for the first time since the early days of players neglecting stab wounds in the

282 Sarah Perez, "Pokémon Go Tops Twitter's Daily Users, Sees More Engagement than Facebook," *TechCrunch*, July 13, 2016.

283 "Why Pokémon Go May Have Passed Its Peak," *BBC News*, August 24, 2016.

284 Craig Chapple, "Pokémon GO Has Best Year Ever in 2019, Catching Nearly $900 Million in Player Spending," Sensor Tower, January 9, 2020.

name of catching 'em all.[285] And even the shock of COVID-19 couldn't hinder Pokémon Go's resurgence. The game surpassed $1 billion in annual revenue by November of 2020![286]

As we write this in late 2020, user downloads are still climbing. Revenue is still pouring in. If you had any doubts about Pokémon Go's staying power, rest assured it is very much still *a thing*.

Which begs the question: How is any of this possible? How did Pokémon Go manage to reverse its 2017 downswing into the sustained commercial success of 2018 and beyond?

The answer is by building (and continuously developing) an innovative app with an equally user-centric monetization model on top of it. Let's break it down:

BE THE VERY BEST, LIKE NO APP EVER WAS
Remember Clayton Christensen's Jobs-to-be-done theory from Chapter 4? In which we look at the products we buy through the lens of what functions they fulfill?

Well, as we're about to see, the benefits of Pokémon Go extend way beyond the simple joys of playing a game. By combining the comfort of familiarity with the excitement of novelty and innovation, the app has continually fulfilled a wide array of valued *jobs* for a similarly wide array of users.

---

285 Tom Phillips, "Pokémon Go Active Player Count Highest since 2016 Summer Launch," *Eurogamer.Net*, updated June 27, 2018.
286 Craig Chapple, "Pokémon GO Hits $1 Billion in 2020 as Lifetime Revenue Surpasses $4 Billion," Sensor Tower, November 3, 2020.

1. TAPPING INTO NOSTALGIA

Admittedly, this point probably had more of an impact on the record-breaking 2016 numbers than on the second wave in 2018, but it's an important element, nonetheless.

Because there's no way Pokémon Go becomes the gold standard for AR gaming apps without its preexisting fandom. The folks at Niantic smartly capitalized on an already-loyal target audience; thanks to Pokémon's nostalgia factor, prospective users weren't starting from square one.

Instead, these users were pleasantly surprised with something that felt *new but* [still] *familiar.*"[287] In other words, the now-adult millennials and Gen Xers who may have once traded Pikachu cards or played Pokémon Gold on Game Boy were immediately predisposed to give this game a try, regardless of what the gameplay actually entailed.

(Sidenote: Nostalgia worked so well for Niantic that they doubled down in 2019 with the AR game *Harry Potter: Wizards Unite*—jury's still out on it, so we'll make sure to cover that story down the road in our inevitable sequel, *The Trillion Dollar App!*)

But Pokémon Go didn't just borrow the established creative infrastructure of its source material—it integrated into and built off it as well. For instance, we've seen new generations of Pokémon added alongside the classics. And game features

---

287 Lisa Eadicicco, "Pokémon Go Is Getting a Big Boost from Nostalgia," *Time*, July 12, 2016.

once seen on Gameboys have now been modernized to accommodate in-person play.

In such a way, Pokémon Go has combined its foundation of rich history with the possibility for endless world-building. So, what you get isn't just a game; it's a whole culture.

2. INSPIRING ACTIVITY AND INTERACTIVITY

One of the more curious elements of Pokémon Go is that it requires certain activities that video games tend not to. This really could've been a huge negative, going outside the parameters of customer expectations, but instead, users have responded favorably. These elements, it seems, have improved the realism and tangential benefits of the gaming experience.

Over the years, it's been one of the media's favorite points of praise. Pokémon Go bucks the trends of laziness and social isolation that we often attribute to gamers.[288]

From a physical standpoint, the app does indeed drag users off their couches to breathe some fresh air, soak in that Vitamin D, and get their daily steps in. There are even in-game rewards for walking set distances. According to one study, this has caused the number of Pokémon Go players who meet the recommended levels of daily physical activity to have doubled! [289]

---

288 Nick Vega, "'Pokémon Go' Could Make You Healthier, Study Suggests," *Business Insider*, March 13, 2017.

289 Victoria R. Wagner-Greene et al., "Pokémon GO: Healthy or Harmful?" *American Journal of Public Health, 107(1), 35–36.*

So, while it may not be a full-body workout, for many, it's become more than a game. It's become an incentive for healthier habits.

Even more pronounced are the game's social features, which start with friend connections and gift-giving capabilities. When Pokémon Go implemented these functions in September 2018, active users quickly jumped up by 35 percent.[290]

But Pokémon Go has gone way beyond that baseline; they've since created countless opportunities for teaming up in person for various challenges. Again in 2018, they doubled down on the social aspect with over thirty events worldwide, plus a dozen Community Days and four Special Raiding days. By 2019, those events were bringing in well over 2.5 million total attendees![291]

We don't need to get into the fine details of those events to see the point: Pokémon Go's unique gatherings have deeply resonated with users. So, what you get isn't just a video game; it's a tight-knit community. And a genuine, real-life experience.

3. AUGMENTING OUR SHARED REALITIES
Socializing and moving around is great, but what's generated the most buzz for Pokémon Go over the years has

---

290 "The Rise of AR, Summer Adventures and Updates for the Fall," Niantic, September 11, 2018

291 "Our Live Events are where it all comes together," Niantic, accessed November 10, 2020.

undoubtedly been its technology. From the very start, they incorporated features that games simply hadn't done before on a grand scale, and people took notice.

Namely, we're talking about AR. What a novelty it was to have Pokémon characters simulated on your phone screen as though they were standing right in front of you. But then they can run past you, *down your street* or *into the park*, forcing you to run after them to get them back in your screen's line of vision.

To make this sensation as realistic as possible, the app expertly utilizes both your phone's camera and GPS functionalities. This whole innovation made a huge splash back in 2016, and Niantic has since made tremendous strides in furthering developing its AR.

In 2018, for instance, they introduced *occlusion*, a feature that enables virtual characters to convincingly interact with their environments. So, you might now see a Pokémon disappear behind an obstacle and then reappear, or maybe it'll jump onto someone's lap![292]

They've also beefed up their multiplayer AR capabilities. Another big 2018 innovation made it possible for people to occupy and engage in the same virtual AR space across different devices.[293] A year later, this was installed into Pokémon

292 Nick Statt, "Niantic Is Opening Its AR Platform so Others Can Make Games like Pokémon Go," *The Verge*, June 28, 2018.
293 Ibid.

Go via the *Buddy Adventure* feature in which multiple players *and* Pokémon can interact on screen.[294]

The list goes on: Enhanced 3D graphics, Pokémon reactions to player movement, and even screenshots that account for your location's lighting. And we see these innovations spill over into other games as well—Wizards Unite included.

Niantic has fully plunged into this AR gaming niche, and as a result, they're making more than just games; they're creating cutting edge gadgets. In a way, they're tapping into the same drive that compels so many of us to get the newest iPhone or play with the latest drone.

And, as we're about to see, they're tapping into the same drive that compels so many of us to happily *pay for these gadgets* time and time again.

POKÉMON-CENTRIC MONETIZATION

But Pokémon Go's 2018 resurgence wasn't just a matter of innovative product design; it was also due to its multifaceted monetization model.

As it's a free app, the door is always open to new users. And once inside the app, users are enticed to buy over and over again—but not in a pushy way. In fact, the means of monetization actually add to the gameplay experience.

---

294 Matthew Reynolds, "Pokémon Go Buddy Adventure Explained - How to Get Hearts, Excited Buddies, and All Buddy Level Rewards Including Best Buddy Explained," Eurogamer.Net, updated April 15, 2020.

That's not all, though. Pokémon Go's monetization goes beyond user-centric to also be partner-friendly—also opening the door to eager sponsors and advertisers.

In other words, Pokémon Go's monetization model is a win-win for all stakeholders and their own bottom line. And this is most immediately visible with its in-app purchases.

HIGH-APPEAL, LOW-NECESSITY IN-APP PURCHASES

Once again, Pokémon Go hits a perfect balance for consumers.

On the one hand, its IAPs work naturally within the structure of the game, and the extensive options can appeal to users both casual and die-hard. With your PokéCoins currency, you can choose from a grab bag of neat upgrades and perks.

But, on the other hand, they aren't essential to the gameplay experience. This is in stark contrast to popular titles like *Candy Crush* or *Clash of Clans*, which make players pay up for extra lives or to bypass lengthy wait times.

Nor are Pokémon Go's microtransactions at all intrusive. Nintendo actually faced heat for exactly this with *Mario Kart Tour*'s in-your-face microtransactions and unreasonably expensive currency.[295] But here? No "gotcha!" pop-up boxes, no unexpected costs to keep playing, no shady business whatsoever—just an out-of-your-way item store.

---

295 Dave Their, "Bad News: 'Mario Kart Tour' On Mobile Has Nasty Microtransactions," *Forbes*, May 23, 2019.

And while players are happy with the IAP setup, so too are businesses.

Many of them have benefited from investing in some of Pokémon Go's lures, which are IAPs that attract Pokémon to a preset location for a thirty-minute window. Anyone can buy them—many players do, to catch more creatures, as do businesses looking to generate a little more in-person traffic.

Or a lot more in-person traffic if you're the Denver Zoo. They spent $380 on lures one summer weekend, which, in tandem with a special discount for Pokémon Go players, brought back $58,000 in profits and 5,000 more visitors![296]

Some businesses have gone a step higher by setting themselves up as *PokéStops*. These are special locations within the game where players must go to acquire provisions and set their own lures; naturally, these spots attract tons of users. And businesses can either request such a spot for free...or swing for the fences with a large-scale sponsorship agreement.

ADVERTISING FOR ALL

Much like Yelp brings traffic to restaurants for a per-customer commission, so too did Niantic originally receive revenue for each visitor they sent to a partner's location.[297] According to Niantic's CEO John Hanke, such sponsored locations

---

296 Danika Worthington, "Businesses Use Pokémon Go to Lure More Customers," *The Denver Post*, August 15, 2016.

297 Marty Swant, "Pokémon Go Has Now Driven 500 Million Visits to Sponsored Locations," *Adweek*, February 28, 2017; Nate Swanner, "The Unique Way Pokémon Go Makes Money," Dice Insights, June 2, 2017.

received some 500 million game-inspired visits within the game's first year. Exact numbers vary, but at max fifty cents per unique visitor, that's an opportunity for up to $250 million in extra revenue.

In 2019, Sensor Tower even estimated that Pokémon Go raked in nearly $900 million in location-based revenue. The next closest game, *Dragon Quest Walk*, barely scratched $200 million.[298]

Now, the revenue figures aren't entirely disclosed, so perhaps take these numbers as best-case scenarios. But what's unambiguous is that this sponsorship package has attracted some of the biggest brands out there: Starbucks, McDonald's, and Sprint have each ponied up to put thousands of their locations on the Pokémon Go map.[299]

More recently, the folks at Niantic have rolled out a more defined sponsorship subscription with a two-tiered setup that includes:[300]

- A $30/month standard plan for a single sponsored PokéStop
- A $60/month premium plan for a sponsored *Gym* (which is a more valuable in-game location) as well as a one-hour *Raid Battle* mini-game.

---

298 Craig Chapple, "Pokémon GO Has Best Year Ever in 2019," Sensor Tower.
299 Darrell Etherington, "Pokémon GO Is Officially Teaming with Starbucks for 7,800 New Gyms and PokéStops," *TechCrunch*, December 8, 2016.
300 Tre Lyerly, "Pokémon GO Offers Sponsored Gyms, PokéStops To Small Businesses," Gamerant, November 10, 2019.

Even without being well-versed in the Pokémon Go lingo, it's hard not to be enticed by Niantic's proud claim that these sponsorships have led 91 percent of players to visit a partner's location. Restaurants, cafes, grocery stores, retail outfitters, and bars have all drawn new patrons thanks to the promise of Pokémon.[301]

But not only do these sponsored plans work for a diverse crowd of business types, but they also benefit businesses of all sizes. In fact, 56 percent of players say they've visited more small businesses than big-name brands due to Pokémon Go.[302]

Thus, enticing McDonald's, the Denver Zoo, and your little local cafe around the corner. Everybody eats. Thanks to the integration of physical spaces in a user-centric way.

A FINAL WORD ON POKÉMON GO: ADAPTABILITY AND INNOVATION HAND IN HAND

Before tooting Niantic's horn one more time, let's elaborate on some disclaimers. Very few apps come into the marketplace with a built-in die-hard fan base spanning Japan, the United States, and all around the globe. To say "making an app is easy; just follow Pokémon Go's lead" is as ignorant of context as a statement like "becoming President is easy; just follow what George W. Bush did."

---

301 "Business–Niantic," Niantic, accessed November 12, 2020.
302 Larry Kim, "9 Need-to-Know Facts on How Pokémon Go Players Engage with Businesses," *Inc.Com*, August 19, 2016.

That said, very few apps have adapted and innovated as effectively and consistently as Pokémon Go has, and there's something in that. Specifically, it's worth pointing out that Niantic didn't just throw darts at a board and hope for a bullseye. No, they pivoted and developed features and experiences based on user interest.

So, while, yes, Pokémon Go may have built off an extensive fanbase, it's spent the four years since earning that acclaim. Users are captivated by virtual reality. Boom, Pokémon Go's introducing first-of-its-kind graphic interactions. Now users are gathering in droves for social conventions. Boom, Pokémon Go's creating more in-game events.

Time and time again, they listened to their audience. And only after they really heard users' desires did they figure out how to update their monetization model accordingly.

In other words, they embraced user-centric monetization.

CONCLUSION

———

First off, a quick thanks for joining us on this journey! Hopefully, you're coming out of this with a new perspective on the world of mobile apps and the secrets behind the ones that stand out.

But, you know, as much as we love apps, they certainly didn't make writing this book easy on us. As soon as we finished a chapter or made it through a round of edits…Bam! Some dramatic change whacked us in the face and made some of our content obsolete.

For instance, we could barely keep up with all the TikTok shenanigans that unfolded as we wrote and rewrote the first chapter. Mentions of White House drama and Indian bans were added as they made headlines, and we were constantly on the lookout for how anti-China rhetoric would impact TikTok around the US election season.

On a less dreary note, Spotify also kept us on our toes with its unbelievably sustained user growth. From the first draft to the final, their user base jumped from 190 million to 320 million. That's within two years!

And of course (back to dreary), COVID-19 also changed the fortunes and perceptions of many mobile apps during this time. We witnessed the likes of Duolingo, Pokémon Go, Spotify, and star-of-2020 Zoom ride the pandemic wave to increased engagement while the likes of Uber, Lyft, and Airbnb fell down a few pegs. Where necessary, we included a relevant comment or two.

This was our experience these past couple of years, and you know what? The rapid change isn't about to become any less rapid. Just consider what the next decade of developments might have in store for us:

- AI-fueled personalization algorithms so advanced they'll be able to accurately recommend which clothes best fit you
- Augmented and virtual reality becoming integral components of not just games, but all sorts of industry experiences
- A revolution in monetization models and pricing frameworks that are built around the rise of cryptocurrency
- And on that note, blockchain's effect on data security for apps in the banking and insurance sectors
- 5G possibly making supersonic data transfer the norm

And so on. The immediate future of apps is certainly going to be exciting to witness. Though, to be fair, it also might be a little terrifying. It's entirely reasonable to worry about how invasive those AI-fueled personalization algorithms might

get. Or whether new findings will come out about nefarious ways our data has been harvested. Or even about how the addictive nature of apps has hurt younger generations. This list, too, unfortunately, can go on and on.

With this in mind, it's safe to say that our work has only just begun. That said, regardless of where new technologies and socio-political advancements take us, it's also safe to say that some principles will stay with us no matter what.

Anuj Mahajan

Twitter: @AnujMahajan90
LinkedIn: www.linkedIn.com/in/anujpm
Email: am3740@georgetown.edu

ACKNOWLEDGMENTS

———

This book wouldn't have been possible without the guidance, help, and keen eye of my dear friend and colleague Daniel Rozenblum. Dan's story-telling skills helped me hone this book to be something that is not only informative but also fun to read. While I had the vision, it would have all been for naught without his editing, writing, and presentation skills.

I look forward to teaming up with Dan on future projects.

It has also been a privilege to work with UX/ UI Designer Peter Strenge Torre, who drew beautiful app graphics and helped bring the lessons to life.

I'd also like to thank my friends Faizan Qureshi, Sandeep Mulagapati, Rhea Mahato, and Aditya Sawadh for helping me stay on course and reach the finish line.

It takes a village to write a book. And my village was the team at Creator Institute and New Degree Press, especially Eric Koester and Brian Bies. Also, a special shout out to Cynthia Tucker for keeping me on track for over a year.

Other thanks to Clement Kao as well as the numerous beta-readers for offering their valuable feedback throughout this journey, including:

Abhilasha Vyas	Meghana Devaraja
Alfred Chua	Mick Soumphonphakdy
Aman Sethi	Min Xiao
Amir Pilehvar	Mohit Ahuja
Ammro H	Mohit Gupta
Anant Shrivastava	Namit Shivaram
Andrea Chial	Nikhil Issar
Andrew Marzo	Nishant Shetty
Anirudh Venkatesh	Prajwal Kapinadka
Aziza Salomova	Rajan Mohan
Bhargava Vadlamani	Rajesh Kumar Verma
Brian Lee	Rama Chaitanya Samanchi
Charles Roels	Richa Shah
Chris Martiniak	Sahil Sharma
Chris Warren	Saloni Pokharna
Dhairyya Agarwal	Samankit Gupta
Dhrupad Bezboruah	Sarvesh Baveja
Doug Grant	Satya Pavan
Eric Koester	Saurabh Rais
Harshad Mali	Shanu Kalra
Jamie Russo	Shiraz J. Cupala
Jyn Bharadwaj	S Rajasekaran
Laurie Marks	Summi Sinha
Leneesh Pokala	Stuart Powell
Liana Presser	Tanvir Aziz
Marian Yamoah	Taras Stefyuk
Mark DeSimone	Tricia Mulcahy
Matt Stone	Vincent Yu

Additionally, I'd like to express my deepest gratitude to these incredible people and organizations for their inspiration:

People

Alex Richardson (Esports commentator, host, and presenter)

Cem Kansu (VP of Product, Duolingo)

Dong Nguyen (Founder, .GEARS)

Herman Saksono (Postdoctoral Fellow at Harvard University)

Kohta Wajima (General Manager, Dots)

Shawn Dunnaway (President at Explorations Media Group, LLC)

Steven Hoober (President - Design, 4ourth Mobile)

Organizations

PlayDots

App Annie

Bank of America

Comscore

Duolingo

eMarketer

Lifesum Inc.

Lyft, Inc.

NortonLifeLock Inc.

OfferUp, Inc.

Pew Research Center

Sensor Tower

YouTube (Google LLC)

And I want to gratefully acknowledge my mentors, Alex Mitchell and Brian Wang, for showing me the ropes of Product Management and instilling a lifelong passion for the craft.

Lastly, lots of love to my parents for their moral support on this ambitious project.

APPENDIX

———

CHAPTER 1–A TIKTOK STORY | THE POTENTIAL OF MOBILE APPS

"A Look Back at the Top Apps and Games of the Decade." AppAnnie. December 16, 2019. https://www.appannie.com/en/insights/market-data/a-look-back-at-the-top-apps-games-of-the-decade/.

Allyn, Bobby. "TikTok Tightens Crackdown on QAnon, Will Ban Accounts That Promote Disinformation." NPR. October 18, 2020. https://www.npr.org/2020/10/18/925144034/tiktok-tightens-crackdown-on-qanon-will-ban-accounts-that-promote-disinformation.

Arch. "How Do TikTok Gifts Work." Techjunkie. October 14, 2020. https://social.techjunkie.com/how-do-tiktok-gifts-work/.

"Auto-Renewable Subscriptions – App Store." Apple Developer. Accessed October 8, 2020. https://developer.apple.com/app-store/subscriptions/.

Briskman, Jonathan. "Top Apps Worldwide for Q1 2019 by Downloads." Sensor Tower. May 15, 2019. https://sensortower.com/blog/top-apps-worldwide-q1-2019-downloads.

Cellan-Jones, Rory. "Tech Tent: TikTok and the Uighur Muslims." *BBC News*. November 29, 2019. https://www.bbc.com/news/technology-50601906.

Chapple, Craig. "TikTok Crosses 2 Billion Downloads After Best Quarter for Any App Ever." SensorTower. April 29, 2020.

"CodeBroker 2017 Shopper Loyalty Survey Results." Codebroker. Accessed November 4, 2020. https://codebroker.com/landing-page/codebroker-2017-shopper-loyalty-survey-results/.

"Google Play vs. the IOS App Store | Store Stats for Mobile Apps." 42matters. Updated November 4, 2020. https://42matters.com/stats.

Gross, Doug. "Apple Trademarks 'There's an App for That.'" CNN. October 12, 2010. https://www.cnn.com/2010/TECH/mobile/10/12/app.for.that/index.html.

He, Amy. "US Adults Are Spending More Time on Mobile Than They Do Watching TV— EMarketer Trends, Forecasts & Statistics." eMarketer. Jun 4, 2019. https://www.emarketer.com/content/average-us-time-spent-with-mobile-in-2019-has-increased.

Hern, Alex. "Revealed: how TikTok censors videos that do not please Beijing." *The Guardian*. September 25, 2019. https://www.

theguardian.com/technology/2019/sep/25/revealed-how-tik-tok-censors-videos-that-do-not-please-beijing.

Iyengar, Rishi. "This Is What It's Like When a Country Actually Bans TikTok." CNN. August 13, 2020. https://www.cnn.com/2020/08/13/tech/tiktok-ban-trump-india/index.html.

Marszałek, Wiktoria. "How to Use Short-Video App, Douyin, For Your China Marketing." Nanjing Marketing Group. June 13, 2018. https://www.nanjingmarketinggroup.com/blog/How-To-Use-Douyin-For-China-Marketing.

"Mustafa Jabbar: TikTok Shut down." *Dhaka Tribune*. February 18, 2019. https://www.dhakatribune.com/showtime/2019/02/18/mustafa-jabbar-tik-tok-shut-down.

Nelson, Randy. "5-Year Market Forecast: App Spending Will Double to $171 Billion by 2024 Despite COVID-19." Sensor Tower. April 1, 2020. https://sensortower.com/blog/sensor-tower-app-market-forecast-2024.

Newton, Casey. "How TikTok Could Fail." *The Verge*. August 7, 2019. https://www.theverge.com/interface/2019/8/7/20757855/tiktok-growth-monetization-influencers-regulation.

"Pakistan bans TikTok over 'immoral' content." CNBC. October 9, 2020. https://www.cnbc.com/2020/10/09/pakistan-bans-tik-tok-over-immoral-content.html.

Perez, Sarah. "It's time to pay serious attention to TikTok." *TechCrunch*. January 29, 2019. https://techcrunch.com/2019/01/29/its-time-to-pay-serious-attention-to-tiktok/.

Perez, Sarah. "The Majority of Today's App Businesses Are Not Sustainable." *TechCrunch.* July 21, 2014. https://techcrunch.com/2014/07/21/the-majority-of-todays-app-businesses-are-not-sustainable/.

Purwaningsih, Ayu. "Indonesia Blocks 'pornographic' TikTok App." *DW Akademie.* July 5, 2020. https://www.dw.com/en/indonesia-blocks-pornographic-tik-tok-app/a-44537230.

Roose, Kevin. "TikTok, a Chinese Video App, Brings Fun Back to Social Media." *The New York Times.* December 3, 2018. https://www.nytimes.com/2018/12/03/technology/tiktok-a-chinese-video-app-brings-fun-back-to-social-media.html.

Saponara, Michael. "Cardi B Challenges Offset to a Rap Battle, Loser Buys Christmas Decorations for Their Homes." *Billboard.* November 28, 2020. https://www.billboard.com/articles/columns/hip-hop/8486981/cardi-b-challenges-offset-rap-battle-video.

"Service Fees." Play Console Help. Accessed October 8, 2020. https://support.google.com/googleplay/android-developer/answer/112622?hl=en

Sherman, Alex. "TikTok Reveals US, Global User Growth Numbers for First Time." CNBC. August 24, 2020. https://www.cnbc.com/2020/08/24/tiktok-reveals-us-global-user-growth-numbers-for-first-time.html.

Silva, Marco. "Video App TikTok Fails to Remove Online Predators." *BBC News.* April 5, 2019. https://www.bbc.com/news/blogs-trending-47813350.

"So Many Apps, So Much More Time for Entertainment." Nielsen. June 11, 2015. https://www.nielsen.com/us/en/insights/article/2015/so-many-apps-so-much-more-time-for-entertainment/.

Spangler, Todd. "TikTok App Nears 80 Million US Downloads, Lands Jimmy Fallon as Fan." *Variety*. November 20, 2018. https://variety.com/2018/digital/news/tiktok-jimmy-fallon-musically-app-downloads-1203032629/.

Stowers, Joshua. "A Guide to Developing a Mobile App for Business." *Business News Daily* (business.com). December 23, 2019. https://www.businessnewsdaily.com/9049-small-business-app-benefits.html.

Swanson, Ana and Mike Isaac. "Trump Says Microsoft Can Bid for TikTok." *The New York Times*. Updated August 26, 2020. https://www.nytimes.com/2020/08/03/technology/trump-tiktok-microsoft.html.

Sydow, Lexi. "The State of Mobile in 2020: The Key Stats You Need to Know." AppAnnie. January 15, 2020. https://www.appannie.com/en/insights/market-data/state-of-mobile-2020-infographic/.

"The App Store Turns 10." Apple. July 5, 2018. https://www.apple.com/newsroom/2018/07/app-store-turns-10/.

"The Average Smartphone User Accessed Close to 40 Apps per Month in 2017." AppAnnie. February 2, 2020. https://www.appannie.com/en/insights/market-data/apps-used-2017/.

"TikTok Fails Operating in Armenia." *Armenpress.* October 1, 2020. https://armenpress.am/eng/news/1029718.html.

Tolentino, Jia. "How TikTok Holds Our Attention." *The New Yorker.* September 23, 2019. https://www.newyorker.com/magazine/2019/09/30/how-tiktok-holds-our-attention.

"Video Social Networking App Musical.Ly Agrees to Settle FTC Allegations That It Violated Children's Privacy Law." Federal Trade Commission. February 27, 2019. https://www.ftc.gov/news-events/press-releases/2019/02/video-social-networking-app-musically-agrees-settle-ftc.

Wakabayashi, Daisuke. "Google Demands 30% Cut from App Developers in Its Play Store." *The New York Times.* Updated October 9, 2020. https://www.nytimes.com/2020/09/28/technology/google-play-store-30-percent.html.

Wang, Echo and Jonathan Stempel. "TikTok Sues Trump Administration over US Ban, Calls It an Election Ploy." *Reuters.* August 24, 2020. https://www.reuters.com/article/us-usa-china-tiktok-lawsuit/tiktok-sues-trump-administration-over-u-s-ban-calls-it-an-election-ploy-idUSKBN25K1SH.

Wang, Echo, Kane Wu, and Julie Zhu. "Exclusive: ByteDance Investors Value TikTok at $50 Billion in Takeover Bid – Sources." Reuters. July 29, 2020. https://www.reuters.com/article/us-bytedance-tiktok-exclusive/exclusive-bytedance-investors-value-tiktok-at-50-billion-in-takeover-bid-sources-idUSKCN24U1M9.

Wilhelm, Alex. "TikTok's revenue said to skyrocket over 300% in Q4." *TechCrunch.* January 3, 2020. https://techcrunch.com/2020/01/03/tiktoks-revenue-said-to-skyrocket-over-300-in-q4/?guccounter=1.

"Worldometer—Real Time World Statistics." Worldometers. Accessed November 4, 2020. https://www.worldometers.info/.

Zhang, Karen. "Hong Kong Children Expose Their Identities, Thoughts and Flesh to Millions of Strangers on Popular iPhone App TikTok, Post Finds." *South China Morning Post.* May 19, 2018.

CHAPTER 2—USER-CENTRIC MONETIZATION | THE CURE FOR APP FAILURE

Andrews, Marcus. "42% of Companies Don't Listen to Their Customers. Yikes. [New Service Data]." HubSpot. Updated June 05, 2019. https://blog.hubspot.com/service/state-of-service-2019-customer-first.

"Company Info." Spotify. Accessed November 12, 2020. https://newsroom.spotify.com/company-info/

"COVIDSafe App." Australian Government Department of Health. Updated October 28, 2020. https://www.health.gov.au/resources/apps-and-tools/covidsafe-app.

Dredge, Stuart. "How Many Users Do Spotify, Apple Music and Streaming Services Have?" Music Ally. February 19, 2020. https://musically.com/2020/02/19/spotify-apple-how-many-users-big-music-streaming-services/.

Etzioni, Eli. "App of the Week: Evernote Food Helps You Remember the Meals That Made an Impression." *GeekWire.* July 23, 2015. https://www.geekwire.com/2015/app-of-the-week-evernote-food-helps-you-remember-the-meals-that-made-an-impression/.

Graham, Paul. "How to Get Startup Ideas." PaulGraham.com. November 2012. http://paulgraham.com/startupideas.html?viewfullsite=1.

Grubb, Ben. "Coronavirus Australia: COVIDSafe Hasn't Detected One COVID-19 Case despite 6 Million Downloads." *The Sydney Morning Herald.* June 28, 2020. https://www.smh.com.au/politics/federal/dishonest-covidsafe-app-has-not-detected-a-case-despite-6-million-downloads-20200627-p556s7.html.

LaMonica, Martin. "How Safe Is COVIDSafe? What You Should Know about the App's Issues, and Bluetooth-Related Risks." *The Conversation US.* May 7, 2020. https://theconversation.com/how-safe-is-covidsafe-what-you-should-know-about-the-apps-issues-and-bluetooth-related-risks-137894.

Lardinois, Frederic. "Duolingo Hires Its First Chief Marketing Officer as Active User Numbers Stagnate but Revenue Grows." *TechCrunch.* August 1, 2018. https://techcrunch.com/2018/08/01/duolingo-hires-its-first-chief-marketing-officer-as-active-user-numbers-stagnate/.

Mangalindan, JP. "Why Google's Social Network Was a Spectacular Failure." *Yahoo! Finance.* October 9, 2018. https://finance.yahoo.com/news/googles-social-network-spectacular-failure-183906984.html.

Reed, Jim. "BBC - Newsbeat - Technology - Virtual Beer War Hits the iphone." *BBC*. October 17, 2008. http://news.bbc.co.uk/newsbeat/low/technology/newsid_7676000/7676081.stm.

Russell, Jon. "Evernote Is Killing Off Its Dedicated Food App." *TechCrunch*. August 27, 2015. https://techcrunch.com/2015/08/26/the-feast-is-over/.

Russell, Kyle. "Evernote Market Has Sold $12M in Products Since Launch." *TechCrunch*. October 2, 2014. https://techcrunch.com/2014/10/02/evernote-market-has-sold-12m-in-products-since-launch/.

Solomon, Brian. "Is Uber Trying to Kill Lyft with a Price War?" *Forbes*. January 25, 2016. https://www.forbes.com/sites/briansolomon/2016/01/25/is-uber-trying-to-kill-lyft-with-a-price-war/?sh=15efeb836573.

Staff Reporter, IBT. "Top 20 Most Expensive iPad Apps." *International Business Times (IBTimes)*. July 1, 2011. https://www.ibtimes.com/top-20-most-expensive-ipad-apps-552018.

Statt, Nick. "Evernote Is Shutting down Its Lifestyle Product Store." *The Verge*. February 1, 2016. https://www.theverge.com/2016/2/1/10890562/evernote-market-shut-down-moleskine-notebook-2016.

Stilgherrian. "COVIDSafe's Problems Aren't Google or Apple's Fault despite Government Claims." *ZDNet*. July 21, 2020. https://www.zdnet.com/article/covidsafes-problems-arent-google-or-apples-fault-despite-government-claims/.

Taylor, Colleen. "Everpix, The Cloud-Based Photo Startup, Is Shutting Down." *TechCrunch*. November 5, 2013. https://techcrunch.com/2013/11/05/everpix-shutting-down/.

"What Is User-Centered Design?" Interaction Design Foundation. Accessed November 5, 2020. https://www.interaction-design.org/literature/topics/user-centered-design.

CHAPTER 3–PURPOSE | THE ART OF PROBLEM-FINDING

"Doug Evans." People. Crunchbase. Accessed October 13, 2020. https://www.crunchbase.com/person/doug-evans.

Dunn, Jeff. "A Note from Juicero's New CEO." Medium. April 20, 2017. https://medium.com/@Juicero/a-note-from-juiceros-new-ceo-cb23a1462b03.

Gibbons, Sarah "User Need Statements." Nielsen Norman Group. March 24, 2019. https://www.nngroup.com/articles/user-need-statements/.

Huet, Ellen and Olivia Zaleski. "Silicon Valley's $400 Juicer May Be Feeling the Squeeze." Bloomberg. April 19, 2017. https://www.bloomberg.com/news/features/2017-04-19/silicon-valley-s-400-juicer-may-be-feeling-the-squeeze.

Johnson, Eric. "Full Transcript: Juicero CEO Doug Evans on Too Embarrassed to Ask." *Vox*. September 12, 2016. https://www.vox.com/2016/9/12/12893026/doug-evans-juicero-too-embarrassed-to-ask-podcast-transcript.

"Juicero—Funding, Financials, Valuation & Investors." Crunchbase. Accessed October 13, 2020. https://www.crunchbase.com/organization/juicero/company_financials.

"Juicero: Juicing Boss Defends $400 Machine." *BBC News*. April 21, 2017. https://www.bbc.com/news/business-39664483.

Koester, Eric. "The Startup Holy Grail: Product-Market Fit (Startup Factory Live Stream)." Facebook. March 12, 2020. https://www.facebook.com/erickoester/videos/2559176724350706.

Perry, Katy (@katyperry). "Was a good 🐈at my recovery party for @katyperrycollections having my carrot juice aka Beta Glow from @juicero with my bud and founder @dougevans 🧃🧃🧃 HIGHLY recommend … " Instagram. April 18, 2017. https://www.instagram.com/p/BTCvGUtjv-F/?hl=en.

"Quote by Albert Einstein: 'If I Had an Hour to Solve a Problem I'd Spend 5 … '" Goodreads. Accessed October 13, 2020. https://www.goodreads.com/quotes/60780-if-i-had-an-hour-to-solve-a-problem-i-d.

Rosman, Katherine. "How Organic Avenue Lost All Its Juice." *The New York Times*. November 4, 2015. https://www.nytimes.com/2015/11/05/fashion/organic-avenue-close.html.

CHAPTER 4—EMPATHY | IT'S PERSONAL AND IT'S BUSINESS

Arellano, Kristi. "Best Buy's Plan: Cater to 'Buzz,' 'Jill.'" *The Denver Post*. Updated May 8, 2016. https://www.denverpost.com/2005/08/21/best-buys-plan-cater-to-buzz-jill/.

"Business Books - Aiming High | Books & Arts." *The Economist.* June 30, 2011. https://www.economist.com/books-and-arts/2011/06/30/aiming-high.

Christensen, Clayton, Taddy Hall, David S. Duncan, Karen Dillon. *Competing Against Luck: The Story of Innovation and Customer Choice.* New York: Harper Business, 2016.

"Design Kit." Design Kit. Accessed October 12, 2020. https://www.designkit.org/resources/1.

Rogers, Ben. "Customer Segmentation to Increase Revenue: 3 Real Examples." Qualtrics. August 27, 2018. https://www.qualtrics.com/blog/how-best-buy-mercedes-benz-and-amex-used-segmentation-to-increase-revenue/.

Statt, Nick. "Yik Yak, Once Valued at $400 Million, Shuts down and Sells off Engineers for $1 Million." *The Verge.* April 28, 2017. https://www.theverge.com/2017/4/28/15480052/yik-yak-shut-down-anonymous-messaging-app-square.

CHAPTER 5—INTERACTION DESIGN | GIVE POWER TO THE PEOPLE

Bank of America Corporation. Bank of America Mobile Banking. V. 20.09. iOS 11.0 and watchOS 3.0 or later. Updated October 5, 2020.

Bumble Holding Limited. "Bumble–Dating, Make New Friends & Business." V. 5.193.1. Android 5.0 and up. Updated October 27, 2020.

Cellan-Jones, Rory. "Apple iPhone Faces Serious Rivals." *BBC News.* June 28, 2007. http://news.bbc.co.uk/2/hi/technology/6253704. stm.

Cherney, Max A. "Snap Earnings: Spectacles Were Big Money Losers, but More Are Coming." MarketWatch. May 1, 2018. https://www.marketwatch.com/story/snap-earnings-spectacles-were-big-money-losers-but-more-are-coming-2018-04-30.

Cho, Anjie. "The Basic Principles of Feng Shui." The Spruce. September 17, 2020. https://www.thespruce.com/what-is-feng-shui-1275060.

Dave, Paresh and Munsif Vengattil. "CORRECTED-Snap Loses Users for the First Time, Beats on Revenue." Reuters. Updated August 7, 2018. https://br.reuters.com/article/snap-results-idUSL1N1UX1KD.

Duolingo, Inc. Duolingo—Language Lessons. V. 6.90.0. iOS 12.0 or later. Updated October 26, 2020.

Gove, Jenny. "What Makes a Good Mobile Site? | Web Fundamentals." Google Developers. Accessed October 28, 2020. https://developers.google.com/web/fundamentals/design-and-ux/principles.

Greenburg, Zack O'Malley. "Spotify's Purchase of the Ringer Won't Be Cheap, But the Payoff Could Be Huge." *Forbes.* February 7, 2020. https://www.forbes.com/sites/zackomalleygreenburg/2020/02/07/the-musical-motivation-behind-spotifys-500m-podcast-spree/#577bd36f72de.

Heath, Alex. "Timeline of Facebook Copying Snapchat in Instagram, Messenger, Other Apps." *Business Insider.* May 27, 2017. https://www.businessinsider.com/all-the-times-facebook-copied-snapchat-2017-5#instagram-has-been-the-most-blatant-copycat-of-snapchat-and-its-stories-competitor-has-already-reached-200-million-daily-users-8.

Hernandez, Will. "Cure for Banking App Fatigue: Make Things Simpler." *American Banker.* August 01, 2019. https://search-proquest-com.databases.library.georgetown.edu/pqrlalumni/docview/2267229546/609BCAC8EBC04746PQ/47?accountid=142883.

Higgins, Tucker. "Supreme Court Hands Victory to Blind Man Who Sued Domino's over Site Accessibility." CNBC. October 7, 2019. https://www.cnbc.com/2019/10/07/dominos-supreme-court.html.

Hoober, Steven, and Eric Berkman. *Designing Mobile Interfaces: Patterns for Interaction Design.* O'Reilly Media. November 1, 2011.

Hoober, Steven. "1, 2, 3 For Better Mobile Design—4ourth Mobile." February 2, 2020. https://www.4ourthmobile.com/publications/1-2-3-for-better-mobile-design.

Intuit Inc. TurboTax Tax Return App – Max Refund Guaranteed. V. 6.12.0. iOS 6.0 and up. Updated October 9, 2020.

Iyengar, Sheena S. and Mark R. Lepper. "When choice is demotivating: Can one desire too much of a good thing?" *Journal of Personality and Social Psychology.* 79(6), 995–1006.

Kosoff, Maya. "'It Was Cataclysmic': Can Snapchat Survive Its Redesign?" *Vanity Fair.* Last modified May 10, 2018. https://www.vanityfair.com/news/2018/05/snapchat-publishers-discover-redesign.

Krug, Steve. *Don't Make Me Think: A Common Sense Approach to Web Usability.* Pearson Education, 2009.

Lyft Inc. Lyft - Rideshare, Bikes, Scooters & Transit. V. 6.55.3. iOS 11.0 or later. Updated October 26, 2020.

Norman, Don and Jakob Nielsen. "The Definition of User Experience (UX)." Accessed October 7, 2020. https://www.nngroup.com/articles/definition-user-experience/.

PayPal Inc. Venmo. V. 8.8.0. Android 5.0 and up. Updated October 13, 2020.

Pu, Guo (276-324). "The *Zangshu,* or Book of Burial." Translated by Stephen L Field, PhD. Accessed October 12, 2020. https://fengshuigate.com/zangshu.html.

Rumsey, Nic. "Petition · Snap Inc.: Remove the New Snapchat Update." Change.Org. Accessed October 12, 2020. https://www.change.org/p/snap-inc-remove-the-new-snapchat-update.

"Spotify's 'Your Library' Refresh: What You Need to Know." Spotify Newsroom. June 13, 2019. https://newsroom.spotify.com/2019-06-13/spotifys-your-library-refresh-what-you-need-to-know/.

"The World's Worst Website Ever!" Explorations Media Group LLC. Accessed October 12, 2020. https://www.theworldsworstwebsiteever.com/.

"What's New With Spotify Premium." Spotify Newsroom. October 18, 2018. https://newsroom.spotify.com/2018-10-18/whats-new-with-spotify-premium/.

WhatsApp Inc. WhatsApp Messenger. V. 2.20.201.23. Android 4.1 and up. Updated October 27, 2020.

Yelp Inc. Yelp: Find Food, Delivery & Services Nearby. V. 12.72.0. iOS 12.0 and watchOS 6.0 or later. Updated October 19, 2020.

Yurieff, Kaya. "Snapchat Stock Loses $1.3 Billion after Kylie Jenner Tweet." CNN. February 23, 2018. https://money.cnn.com/2018/02/22/technology/snapchat-update-kylie-jenner/index.html.

CHAPTER 6—PERSONALIZATION | BE UNIQUE... FOR EVERYONE

"2019 Form 10-K Annual Report" (PDF). SiriusXM Holdings. Retrieved July 21, 2020. https://www.sec.gov/Archives/edgar/data/908937/000090893720000011/siri-20191231x10k.htm

Boudet, Julien, Brian Gregg, Kathryn Rathje, Eli Stein, and Kai Vollhardt. "The Future of Personalization—and How to Get Ready for It." McKinsey. June 18, 2019. https://www.mckinsey.com/business-functions/marketing-and-sales/our-insights/the-future-of-personalization-and-how-to-get-ready-for-it.

Bright, Laura Frances. "Consumer Control and Customization in Online Environments: An Investigation into the Psychology of Consumer Choice and Its Impact on Media Enjoyment, Attitude, and Behavioral Intention." UT Electronic Theses and Dissertations, Texas ScholarWorks (TSW). December 2012. https://repositories.lib.utexas.edu/handle/2152/18054.

Chavez, Nicole and Mochammad Andri. "Indonesia Tsunami and Earthquake Death Toll Tops 400, Hundreds More Injured." CNN. Updated September 30, 2018. https://www.cnn.com/2018/09/29/asia/indonesia-earthquake/index.html.

Comscore Mobile Metrix. Share of Time Spent on Apps by Rank, Custom Defined List, Age 18+. June 2017. US. https://www.comscore.com/Insights/Presentations-and-Whitepapers/2017/The-2017-US-Mobile-App-Report.

Google LLC. YouTube. V. Varies with device. Updated October 28, 2020.

Gregg, Brian, Hussein Kalaoui, Joel Maynes, and Gustavo Schuler. "Marketing's Holy Grail: Digital Personalization at Scale." McKinsey. November 18, 2016. https://www.mckinsey.com/business-functions/mckinsey-digital/our-insights/marketings-holy-grail-digital-personalization-at-scale.

Griswold, Alison. "Pinterest Congratulates All the Single Ladies on Their Weddings." September 04, 2014. https://slate.com/business/2014/09/pinterest-accidentally-congratulates-single-women-on-their-wedding-plans.html.

Jannach, Dietmar, Markus Zanker, Alexander Felfernig, and Gerhard Friedrich. *Recommender Systems: An Introduction.* Cambridge: Cambridge University Press, 2010. doi:10.1017/ CBO9780511763113.

Lifesum AB. Lifesum: Diet & Macro Tracker. V. 11.2.1. iOS 11.2 and watchOS 3.0 or later. Updated October 19, 2020.

Oliver, John. "Facebook: Last Week Tonight with John Oliver (HBO)." Uploaded on September 23, 2018. YouTube Video. 00:02:30. https://www.youtube.com/watch?v=OjPYmEZxACM.

"Pandora Radio - Listen to Free Internet Radio, Find New Music." Pandora. Accessed October 28, 2020. https://www.pandora. com/corporate/mgp.shtml.

PlayDots Inc. Two Dots. V. 6.10.1. Android 4.1 and up. Updated October 26, 2020.

Saksono, Herman (@hermansaksono). "'Congrats' in Indonesian Is "Selamat." Selamat Also Means "to Survive." After the 6.9 Magnitude Earthquake in Lombok, Facebook Users Wrote "I Hope People Will Survive." Then Facebook Highlighted the Word "Selamat" and Throw Some Balloons and Confetti." Twitter. August 5, 2018. Https://T.Co/DEhYLqHWUz' / Twitter." Accessed October 28, 2020. https://twitter.com/herman-saksono/status/1026277395391807488.

Schrage, Michael. *Recommendation Engines.* The MIT Press. September 20, 2020. https://mitpress.mit.edu/books/recommen-dation-engines.

"With Declining App Usage, Mobile Engagement Matters." Leanplum. February 3, 2019. https://www.leanplum.com/blog/mobile-engagement/.

CHAPTER 7—MONETIZATION | STRATEGIES FOR STRIKING GOLD

ADVA Soft. TouchRetouch. V. 4.4.12. Android 5.0 and up. Updated September 17, 2020.

Ariely, Dan. *Predictably Irrational, Revised and Expanded Edition: The Hidden Forces That Shape Our Decisions.* HarperCollins. June 6, 2009.

"Auto-Renewable Subscriptions." Apple Developer (App Store). Accessed October 8, 2020. https://developer.apple.com/appstore/subscriptions/.

Chadha, Rahul. "Mobile Video Advertising 2019." eMarketer. January 7, 2019. https://www.emarketer.com/content/mobile-video-advertising-2019.

Coughlin, Tom. "175 Zettabytes By 2025." *Forbes.* November 27, 2018. https://www.forbes.com/sites/tomcoughlin/2018/11/27/175-zettabytes-by-2025/#23627b775459.

Frederick, Ben. "60% Of All Mobile Banner Ad Clicks Are Accidents." *MediaPost.* February 4, 2016. https://www.mediapost.com/publications/article/268266/60-of-all-mobile-banner-ad-clicks-are-accidents.html.

Fuscaldo, Donna. "PayPal All in with Venmo in 2020." *Forbes.*
January 30, 2020. https://www.forbes.com/sites/donnafus-
caldo/2020/01/30/PayPal-all-in-with-venmo-in-2020/#4e-
6caf1c3599.

"Google Play vs. the IOS App Store | Store Stats for Mobile Apps."
42matters. Updated October 7, 2020. https://42matters.com/
stats.

Hamburger, Ellis. "Indie Smash Hit 'Flappy Bird' Racks up $50K
per Day in Ad Revenue." *The Verge.* February 5, 2014. https://
www.theverge.com/2014/2/5/5383708/flappy-bird-revenue-50-
k-per-day-dong-nguyen-interview.

"In-App Advertising Formats." MoPub. Accessed October 26, 2020.
https://www.mopub.com/en/publishers/ad-formats.

Kumar, Vineet. "Making 'Freemium' Work." *Harvard Business
Review.* Accessed October 8, 2020. https://hbr.org/2014/05/
making-freemium-work?cm_sp=Article-_-Links-_-Comment.

Kushner, David. "The Flight of the Birdman: Flappy Bird Creator Dong Nguyen Speaks Out." *Rolling Stone.* March 11, 2014.
https://www.rollingstone.com/culture/culture-news/the-flight-
of-the-birdman-flappy-bird-creator-dong-nguyen-speaks-
out-112457/.

Lee, Dave. "YouTube Takes on Cable with New TV Service." *BBC
News.* Updated March 1, 2017. https://www.bbc.com/news/
technology-39124092.

Leskin, Paige. "YouTube History: How the Video-Sharing Website Became So Popular." *Business Insider.* May 30, 2020. https://www.businessinsider.com/history-of-youtube-in-photos-2015-10#december-2007-youtube-rolls-out-its-partner-program-to-select-creators-allowing-them-to-earn-money-from-their-content-based-on-ad-revenue-it-allows-youtubers-to-turn-their-hobby-into-a-career-not-even-a-year-later-the-most-successful-creators-were-earning-six-figure-incomes-18.

Miller, Matt. "Monetization Insights from App Professionals." AppAnnie. Accessed October 8, 2020. https://www.appannie.com/en/insights/app-monetization/app-marketers-developers-survey-2/.

Mint Software, Inc. Mint: Personal Finance & Money. V. 7.20.0. iOS 11.0 and watchOS 5.1 or later. Updated October 21, 2020.

Newton, Casey. "Why Rdio Died." *The Verge.* November 17, 2015. https://www.theverge.com/2015/11/17/9750890/rdio-shutdown-pandora.

Newton, Casey. "Why Vine Died." *The Verge.* October 28, 2016. https://www.theverge.com/2016/10/28/13456208/why-vine-died-twitter-shutdown.

Perez, Sarah. "YouTube to Invest $100M in Kids' Content That Showcases Character Strengths, like Compassion and Curiosity." *TechCrunch.* February 5, 2020. https://techcrunch.com/2020/02/05/youtube-to-invest-100m-in-kids-content-that-showcases-character-strengths-like-compassion-and-curiosity/.

Pernice, Kara. "Banner Blindness Revisited: Users Dodge Ads on Mobile and Desktop." NN/g. April 22, 2018. https://www.nngroup.com/articles/banner-blindness-old-and-new-findings/.

Perrin, Nicole. "US Native Advertising 2019 - EMarketer Trends, Forecasts & Statistics." eMarketer. March 20, 2019. https://www.emarketer.com/content/us-native-advertising-2019.

"Resources - Our Fees." Venmo. Accessed October 8, 2020. https://venmo.com/resources/our-fees/.

"Service Fees." Play Console Help (Google Play). Accessed October 8, 2020. https://support.google.com/googleplay/android-developer/answer/112622?hl=en.

"Snapchat Ads for Business | Mobile Advertising." Snap Inc. Accessed October 8, 2020. https://forbusiness.snapchat.com/lenses.

Terminal Eleven. SkyView® Explore the Universe. V. 3.6.3. Android 5.0 and up. Updated December 3, 2019.

"The State of Mobile in 2020: The Key Stats You Need to Know." AppAnnie. Accessed October 26, 2020. https://www.appannie.com/en/insights/market-data/state-of-mobile-2020-infographic/.

Ustwo games. Monument Valley. V. 2.7.17. Android 4.1 and up. Updated January 23, 2020.

"Venmo Now Accepted at More Than Two Million US Merchants."
Business Wire. October 17, 2017. https://www.businesswire.com/
news/home/20171017005629/en/Venmo-Now-Accepted-At-
More-Than-Two-Million-U.S.-Merchants.

Vito Technology Inc. Star Walk 2 - Night Sky Map. V. 2.11.2. iOS
10.0 and watchOS 2.0 or later. Updated September 29, 2020.

Waikar, Sachin. "Disguised 'Native' Ads Don't Fool Us Anymore."
Stanford Graduate School of Business. January 8, 2018. https://
www.gsb.stanford.edu/insights/disguised-native-ads-dont-
fool-us-anymore.

Williams, Katie. "US Subscription App Revenue Grew 21% in 2019
to $4.6 Billion." Sensor Tower. January 23, 2020. https://sensor-
tower.com/blog/subscription-apps-revenue-2019.

CHAPTER 8–DATA PRIVACY | IN APPS WE TRUST

Anderson, Monica. "Mobile Apps, Privacy and Permissions: 5 Key
Takeaways." Pew Research Center. November 10, 2015. https://
www.pewresearch.org/fact-tank/2015/11/10/key-takeaways-
mobile-apps/.

Ariely, Dan. "Why Trust Is So Important and How We Can
Get More of It?" TEDxJaffa. Uploaded on October 20,
2017. YouTube video. 00:01:35. https://www.youtube.com/
watch?v=WHyApqVjddQ.

Bowles, Cennydd. "A Techie's Rough Guide to GDPR." Cennydd
Bowles. October 12, 2018. https://cennydd.com/blog/a-techies-
rough-guide-to-gdpr.

Conger, Kate. "Uber Begins Background Collection of Rider Location Data." *TechCrunch*. November 28, 2016. https://techcrunch.com/2016/11/28/uber-background-location-data-collection/.

"FTC Imposes $5 Billion Penalty and Sweeping New Privacy Restrictions on Facebook." Federal Trade Commission. July 24, 2019. https://www.ftc.gov/news-events/press-releases/2019/07/ftc-imposes-5-billion-penalty-sweeping-new-privacy-restrictions.

"General Data Protection Regulation (GDPR) – Official Legal Text." gdpr-info.eu. Accessed October 2, 2020. https://gdpr-info.eu/.

Issac, Mike. "WhatsApp Introduces End-to-End Encryption." *The New York Times*. April 5, 2016. https://www.nytimes.com/2016/04/06/technology/whatsapp-messaging-service-introduces-full-encryption.html.

Koebler, Jason. "Stop Using Third-Party Weather Apps." *Vice*. January 4, 2019. https://www.vice.com/en/article/gy77wy/stop-using-third-party-weather-apps.

NortonMobile, 2020. LifeLock for Norton 360. V. 1.23. Android 6.0 or later.

Panzarino, Matthew. "AI Photo Editor FaceApp Goes Viral Again on IOS, Raises Questions about Photo Library Access." *TechCrunch*. July 16, 2019. https://techcrunch.com/2019/07/16/ai-photo-editor-faceapp-goes-viral-again-on-ios-raises-questions-about-photo-library-access-and-clo/.

Reeve, Adam (@adamreeve). "Pokémon Go Is a Huge Security Risk." Tumblr. July 8, 2016. https://adamreeve.tumblr.com/post/147120922009/pokemon-go-is-a-huge-security-risk.

Rosenberg, Matthew, Nicholas Confessore, and Carole Cadwalladr. "How Trump Consultants Exploited the Facebook Data of Millions." *The New York Times*. March 17, 2018. https://www.nytimes.com/2018/03/17/us/politics/cambridge-analytica-trump-campaign.html.

Wamsley, Laurel. "Uber Ends Its Controversial Post-Ride Tracking of Users' Location." *NPR (The Two-Way Blog)*. August 29, 2017. https://www.npr.org/sections/thetwo-way/2017/08/29/547113818/uber-ends-its-controversial-post-ride-tracking-of-users-location.

CHAPTER 9–PRICING | ALL NUMBERS DON'T COME EQUAL

Ariely, Dan. *Predictably Irrational: The Hidden Forces that Shape Our Decisions*. United Kingdom: Harper, 2009.

Caldwell, Leigh. *The Psychology of Price: How to Use Price to Increase Demand, Profit and Customer Satisfaction*. United Kingdom: Crimson, 2012.

Headspace for Meditation, Mindfulness and Sleep. Headspace: Meditation & Sleep. V. 4.21.0. Android 5.0 and up. Updated November 17, 2020.

Poundstone, William. *Priceless: The Myth of Fair Value (and how to Take Advantage of It)*. Australia: Scribe Publications Pty Limited, 2010.

Prelec, Drazen and Duncan Simester. "Always Leave Home Without It: A Further Investigation of the Credit-Card Effect on Willingness to Pay." Marketing Letters 12, no. 1 (2001): 5–12. Accessed November 26, 2020. http://www.jstor.org/stable/40216581.

Simon, Hermann. *Confessions of the Pricing Man: How Price Affects Everything*. Germany: Springer International Publishing, 2015.

CHAPTER 10–MESSAGING | FIND YOUR VOICE; SPEAK THEIR LANGUAGE

"Acorns—Invest, Earn, Grow, Spend, Later." Acorns. Accessed September 30, 2020. https://www.acorns.com.

"Become a Deliveroo Partner." Deliveroo. Accessed October 1, 2020. https://restaurants.deliveroo.com/en-gb/?utm-campaign=workwithus&utm-medium=organic&utm-source=landingpage.

"Deliveroo—Food Delivery." Deliveroo. Accessed October 1, 2020. https://deliveroo.co.uk/.

Heal, Jordan. "The Sandbox Gaming Platform Receives $2.5m Investment." *Yahoo Finance*. May 29, 2019. https://finance.yahoo.com/news/sandbox-gaming-platform-receives-2-120031549.html.

OfferUp Inc. OfferUp: Buy. Sell. Letgo. Mobile marketplace. V. 3.81.2. Android v. 5.0 and above.

"Pixowl Increases Retention & Revenue with Leanplum." Leanplum Case Studies. Accessed October 1, 2020. https://go.leanplum.com/rs/959-TQV-890/images/Case_Study_Pixowl_FINAL_08.20.pdf.

"Ride with Us—Apply Now!" Deliveroo. Accessed September 30, 2020. https://deliveroo.co.uk/apply?utm-campaign=ridewithus&utm-medium=organic&utm-source=landingpage.

Tiongson, James. "Mobile App Marketing Insights: How Consumers Really Find and Use Your Apps." Think with Google. May 2015. https://www.thinkwithgoogle.com/marketing-strategies/app-and-mobile/mobile-app-marketing-insights/.

Twin, Alexandra. "Value Proposition: Why Consumers Should Buy a Product or Use a Service." Investopedia. July 5, 2020. https://www.investopedia.com/terms/v/valueproposition.asp.

"WhatsApp." WhatsApp. Accessed September 30, 2020. https://www.whatsapp.com/.

"With Declining App Usage, Mobile Engagement Matters." Leanplum (blog). February 3, 2019. https://www.leanplum.com/blog/mobile-engagement/.

CHAPTER 11–INNOVATION | TRY, TEST, ADAPT, REPEAT

Christensen, Clayton M. *The Innovator's Dilemma: The Revolutionary National Bestseller that Changed the Way We Do Business.* United States: Harper Business, 2000.

Forde, Matthew. "Here's How Much Money Rovio's Mobile Games Are Making." PocketGamer.biz. March 12, 2019. https://www.pocketgamer.biz/feature/70217/heres-how-much-money-rovios-mobile-games-are-making/.

Garber, Megan. "Instagram Was First Called 'Burbn.'" *The Atlantic.* July 2, 2014. https://www.theatlantic.com/technology/archive/2014/07/instagram-used-to-be-called-brbn/373815/.

Kendall, Paul. "Angry Birds: The Story behind IPhone's Gaming Phenomenon." *The Telegraph.* February 07, 2011. https://www.telegraph.co.uk/technology/video-games/8303173/Angry-Birds-the-story-behind-iPhones-gaming-phenomenon.html.

Olson, Parmy. "Exclusive: The Rags-To-Riches Tale of How Jan Koum Built WhatsApp Into Facebook's New $19 Billion Baby." *Forbes.* February 19, 2014. https://www.forbes.com/sites/parmyolson/2014/02/19/exclusive-inside-story-how-jan-koum-built-whatsapp-into-facebooks-new-19-billion-baby/#34306952fa19.

Porter, John. "WhatsApp Now Has 2 Billion Users." *The Verge.* February 2, 2020. https://www.theverge.com/2020/2/12/21134652/whatsapp-2-billion-monthly-active-users-encryption-facebook.

Ries, Eric. *The Lean Startup: How Today's Entrepreneurs Use Continuous Innovation to Create Radically Successful Businesses.* United Kingdom: Crown Business, 2011.

Smith, Tim. "Disruptive Technology Definition." Investopedia. Updated October 2, 2020. https://www.investopedia.com/terms/d/disruptive-technology.asp.

"The Angry Birds Movie 2." Box Office Mojo. Accessed October 2, 2020. https://www.boxofficemojo.com/release/rl1006863873/.

"The Angry Birds Movie." Box Office Mojo. Accessed October 2, 2020. https://www.boxofficemojo.com/release/rl3343091201/.

Woodwill, Jerry. "JFK Rice Moon Speech." Space Movies Cinema, NASA. Accessed October 2, 2020. https://er.jsc.nasa.gov/seh/ricetalk.htm.

"X – The Moonshot Factory." Alphabet. Accessed October 2, 2020. https://x.company/.

CHAPTER 12—DUOLINGO

"About Us—Duolingo." Accessed October 13, 2020. https://www.duolingo.com/info.

Adams, Susan. "Game of Tongues: How Duolingo Built A $700 Million Business with Its Addictive Language-Learning App." *Forbes.* August 31, 2019. https://www.forbes.com/sites/susanadams/2019/07/16/game-of-tongues-how-duolingo-built-a-700-million-business-with-its-addictive-language-learning-app/?sh=790e711f3463.

Alfaro, Lyanne. "How This 'genius' Grew the Language-Learning App Duolingo to 150 Million Daily Users." CNBC. December 14, 2016. https://www.cnbc.com/2016/12/14/how-this-genius-grew-the-language-learning-app-duolingo-to-150-million-daily-users.html.

"Cem Kansu." LinkedIn. Accessed October 15, 2020. https://www.linkedin.com/in/cemkansu/.

Coren, Michael J. "Duolingo's Crowdsourced Language-Learning Model Is Letting Some Weird Things Slip through the Cracks." *Quartz*. May 20, 2018. https://qz.com/1255133/duolingos-crowdsourced-language-learning-model-is-letting-some-weird-things-slip-through-the-cracks/.

"Duolingo - The World's Best Way to Learn a Language." Duolingo. Accessed October 13, 2020. https://www.duolingo.com/.

"Duolingo Has Weird Sentences." Duolingo Forum. April 4, 2014. https://forum.duolingo.com/comment/2490084/Duolingo-has-weird-sentences.

"Duolingo: About." LinkedIn. Accessed October 13, 2020. https://www.linkedin.com/company/duolingo/about/.

"Free Language Courses." Duolingo. Accessed October 13, 2020. https://www.duolingo.com/courses/all.

"'Her Marriage Is a Public Scandal.'" Duolingo Forum. September 3, 2013. https://forum.duolingo.com/comment/780186/Her-marriage-is-a-public-scandal.

Kansu, Cem (@cemkansu). "'I'm Incredibly Proud of What We Have Achieved at @duolingo: 2 Years Ago We Had Zero Revenue, Today We Are the World's Top Grossing Education App. This Is Proof That It's Possible to Provide Access to Free Language Education and Build a Sustainable Business at the Same Time." Twitter. December 12, 2018. https://twitter.com/cemkansu/status/1072859932159029248.

Kansu, Cem. "MAU Vegas 2018—From Zero to Top Grossing: Duolingo's Lessons from Monetizing Free Education." Grow. Co. May 15, 2018. https://grow.co/mau-vegas-2018-from-zero-to-top-grossing-duolingos-lessons-from-monetizing-free-education/.

"Language Learning Startups." AngelList. Accessed October 13, 2020. https://angel.co/language-learning.

Lardinois, Frederic. "Duolingo Hires Its First Chief Marketing Officer as Active User Numbers Stagnate but Revenue Grows." *TechCrunch*. Accessed November 30, 2020. https://techcrunch.com/2018/08/01/duolingo-hires-its-first-chief-marketing-officer-as-active-user-numbers-stagnate/.

Mascarenhas, Natasha. "Duolingo CEO explains language app's surge in bookings." *TechCrunch*. September 29, 2020. https://techcrunch.com/2020/09/29/duolingo-ceo-explains-language-apps-surge-in-bookings/.

Olson, Parmy. "Crowdsourcing Capitalists: How Duolingo's Founders Offered Free Education to Millions." *Forbes*. January 22, 2014. https://www.forbes.com/sites/parmyolson/2014/01/22/

crowdsourcing-capitalists-how-duolingos-founders-of-fered-free-education-to-millions/#119ecbeea725.

"Quote by Joshua Becker: 'You Don't Need More Space. You Need Less Stuff.'" Goodreads. Accessed November 16, 2020. https://www.goodreads.com/quotes/8240853-you-don-t-need-more-space-you-need-less-stuff.

Sawers, Paul. "Duolingo Raises $30 Million from Alphabet's CapitalG at $1.5 Billion Valuation." VentureBeat. December 4, 2019. https://venturebeat.com/2019/12/04/duolingo-raises-30-million-from-alphabets-capitalg-at-1-5-billion-valuation/.

Simonite, Tom. "The Cleverest Business Model in Online Education." MIT Technology Review. November 29, 2012. https://www.technologyreview.com/2012/11/29/181418/the-cleverest-business-model-in-online-education/.

Soper, Taylor. "Inside the Mind of Duolingo CEO Luis von Ahn as $700M Language Learning Startup Eyes IPO in 2020." GeekWire. February 23, 2018. https://www.geekwire.com/2018/inside-mind-duolingo-ceo-luis-von-ahn-700m-language-learning-startup-preps-ipo/.

"Study: Brain Battles Itself over Short-Term Rewards, Long-Term Goals." Princeton. Accessed October 13, 2020. https://pr.princeton.edu/news/04/q4/1014-brain.htm.

"Ten Things We Know to Be True." Google. Accessed October 13, 2020. https://www.google.com/about/philosophy.html.

"The Tenets of A/B Testing from Duolingo's Master Growth Hacker." First Round Review. Accessed November 16, 2020. https://firstround.com/review/the-tenets-of-a-b-testing-from-duolingos-master-growth-hacker/.

"'They Are Washing the Holy Potato.'" Duolingo Forum. October 17, 2015. https://forum.duolingo.com/comment/11118281/They-are-washing-the-holy-potato.

Von Ahn, Luis (@Vonahn). "I Am Luis von Ahn, Co-Inventor of CAPTCHA & ReCAPTCHA, Founder/CEO of Duolingo, MacArthur Fellow and Computer Science Professor. AMA!" Reddit. Accessed October 13, 2020. https://www.reddit.com/r/IAmA/comments/6bxr2v/i_am_luis_von_ahn_coinventor_of_captcha_recaptcha/dhqcqol/.

Von Ahn, Luis. "Why Did Duolingo Move from Translation to Certification for Monetizing?" Quora. January 12, 2016. https://www.quora.com/Why-did-Duolingo-move-from-translation-to-certification-for-monetizing.

CHAPTER 13–SPOTIFY

"Ad Experiences." Spotify Advertising. Accessed November 12, 2020. https://ads.spotify.com/en-US/ad-experiences/.

"Annual Report, 2019—Financials." Spotify. Accessed November 12, 2020. https://investors.spotify.com/financials/default.aspx.

Butcher, Mike. "Spotify Reveals the Detail Behind Its US Launch." *TechCrunch*. July 14, 2011. https://techcrunch.com/2011/07/14/spotify-reveals-the-detail-behind-its-us-launch/.

Ciocca, Sophia. "How Does Spotify Know You So Well?" Medium. October 10, 2017. https://medium.com/s/story/spotifys-discover-weekly-how-machine-learning-finds-your-new-music-19a41ab76efe.

"Company Info." Spotify. Accessed November 12, 2020. Accessed November 12, 2020. https://newsroom.spotify.com/company-info/.

Constine, Josh. "Spotify Wants to Be Everything to Everyone." *TechCrunch*. August 10, 2013. https://techcrunch.com/2013/08/10/the-quest-to-be-your-omni-jukebox/.

Dredge, Stuart. "How Many Users Do Spotify, Apple Music and Streaming Services Have?" Music Ally. February 19, 2020. https://musically.com/2020/02/19/spotify-apple-how-many-users-big-music-streaming-services/.

Ek, Daniel. "$2 Billion and Counting (Archived)." *Spotify Blog*. November 11, 2014. https://web.archive.org/web/20141111151000/https://news.spotify.com/us/2014/11/11/2-billion-and-counting/.

Ek, Daniel. "Daniel Ek's Answer to What Are Some Early Decisions That Were Key to Spotify's Success?" Quora. February 16, 2016. https://www.quora.com/What-are-some-early-decisions-that-were-key-to-Spotifys-success/answer/Daniel-Ek?ch=10&share=c520bc2e&srid=tNsh.

Ingham, Tim. "Nearly 40,000 Tracks Are Now Being Added to Spotify Every Single Day." Music Business Worldwide. April 29, 2019. https://www.musicbusinessworldwide.com/nearly-

40000-tracks-are-now-being-added-to-spotify-every-single-day/.

MACHINE /// (@MACHINEgg). "'I Swear My @Spotify Discover Weekly Is Always ☾." Twitter. October 26, 2018. https://twitter.com/MACHINEgg/status/1055874273376657410.

Neate, Rupert. "Daniel Ek Profile: 'Spotify Will Be Worth Tens of Billions.'" *Telegraph UK.* February 17, 2010. https://www.telegraph.co.uk/finance/newsbysector/mediatechnologyand-telecoms/media/7259509/Daniel-Ek-profile-Spotify-will-be-worth-tens-of-billions.html.

Pastukhov, Dmitry. "Streaming Payouts [2020]: What Spotify, Apple, & Others Pay." *Soundcharts Blog.* June 26, 2019. https://soundcharts.com/blog/music-streaming-rates-payouts.

Patel, Neil. "Spotify's Secret to Adding 8,000 Paying Subscribers a Day." *GeekWire.* February 15, 2012. https://www.geekwire.com/2012/spotifys-secret-adding-8000-paying-subscribers-day/.

Perez, Sarah. "Spotify Will Now Let Brands Sponsor Its Discover Weekly Playlist." *TechCrunch.* January 7, 2019. https://techcrunch.com/2019/01/07/spotify-will-let-now-brands-sponsor-its-discover-weekly-weekly-playlist/.

Peterson, Becky. "Spotify Loses Money on Free Subscribers." *Business Insider.* March 15, 2018. https://www.businessinsider.com/spotify-loses-money-on-free-subscribers-2018-3.

"Premium." Spotify. Accessed November 12, 2020. https://www.spotify.com/us/premium/.

Singleton, Micah. "This Was Sony Music's Contract with Spotify." *The Verge.* May 19, 2015. https://www.theverge.com/2015/5/19/8621581/sony-music-spotify-contract.

"Spotify Advertising." Accessed November 12, 2020. https://ads.spotify.com/en-US/.

Swift, Taylor. "For Taylor Swift, the Future of Music Is a Love Story." *WSJ.* Updated July 7, 2014. https://www.wsj.com/articles/for-taylor-swift-the-future-of-music-is-a-love-story-1404763219.

Trainer, David. "It Sounds Like Spotify Is in Trouble." *Forbes.* October 13, 2020. https://www.forbes.com/sites/greatspeculations/2020/10/13/it-sounds-like-spotify-is-in-trouble/?sh=79f-4bcee813b.

"US Sales Database." RIAA. Accessed November 12, 2020. https://www.riaa.com/u-s-sales-database/.

CHAPTER 14–TINDER

"129 Revenue Is Product Management by This Is Product Management." SoundCloud. Accessed November 6, 2020. https://soundcloud.com/tipm/129-revenue-is-product-management.

"Belton, Padraig. "Love and Dating after the Tinder Revolution." *BBC News.* Accessed February 13, 2018. https://www.bbc.com/news/business-42988025.

Chan, Julia. "Top Grossing Dating Apps Worldwide for July 2020."
Sensor Tower. August 20, 2020. https://sensortower.
com/blog/
top-grossing-dating-apps-worldwide-july-2020.

Developers, Android. "Tinder: Going Gold." YouTube. Uploaded
September 6, 2018. https://www.youtube.com/watch?v=Ob8p-
B9JdQNA&ab_channel=AndroidDevelopers.

"FORM S-1 | Match Group, Inc." United States Securities and
Exchange Commission. October 16, 2015. https://www.sec.
gov/Archives/edgar/data/1575189/000104746915007908/
a2226226zs-1.htm.

"Indicatori Demografici." L'Istituto nazionale di statistica |
Italy. Accessed November 6, 2020. https://www.istat.it/it/
archivio/238447.

"Jeff Morris Jr." AngelList. Accessed November 6, 2020. https://
angel.co/p/jmj.

Khazan, Olga. "How to Date Online like a Social Scientist." *Quartz.*
December 11, 2013. https://qz.com/156507/how-to-date-online-
like-a-social-scientist/.

Lanier, Jaron. *Ten Arguments for Deleting Your Social Media
Accounts Right Now.* United Kingdom: Random House, 2018.

"Match Group - Investor Relations." Tinder. Accessed October 4,
2020. https://ir.mtch.com/overview/default.aspx.

"Match Group Reports Fourth Quarter 2019 Results." Match Group.
February 4, 2020. https://ir.mtch.com/news-and-events/

press-releases/press-release-details/2020/Match-Group-Reports-Fourth-Quarter-2019-Results/default.aspx.

Moran, Clarence. *The Business of Advertising*. United Kingdom: Methuen and Company. 1905.

Morris Jr, Jeff. (jeffmorrisjr). "Building Products & The Importance of Focus." LinkedIn. May 6, 2017. https://www.linkedin.com/pulse/building-products-importance-focus-jeff-morris-jr-/.

Murphy, Lincoln. "Desired Outcome Is a Transformative Concept." Sixteenventures.com. Accessed November 6, 2020. https://sixteenventures.com/desired-outcome.

Rad, Sean (sean_rad). "IAMA Sean Rad, Cofounder & CEO of Tinder. AMA!: IAmA." Reddit. Accessed October 4, 2020. https://www.reddit.com/r/IAmA/comments/2zmms5/iama_sean_rad_cofounder_ceo_of_tinder_ama/.

"SA Population Reaches 58,8 Million." Statistics South Africa. Accessed November 6, 2020. http://www.statssa.gov.za/?p=12362.

Shivakumar, Felicia. "Tinder Wins Best New Startup of 2013." Crunchies Awards 2013 – *TechCrunch*. February 11, 2013. https://techcrunch.com/video/tinder-wins-best-new-startup-of-2013-crunchies-awards-2013/.

Soper, Taylor. "Tinder Founder Sean Rad Explains Why the Dating App Is So Popular." *GeekWire*. March 20, 2015. https://www.geekwire.com/2015/tinder-founder-sean-rad-explains-why-the-dating-app-is-so-popular/.

"Tinder Co-Creator Sean Rad's Interview Fail." *BBC Newsbeat.* November 19, 2015. http://www.bbc.co.uk/newsbeat/article/34865289/tinder-co-creator-sean-rads-interview-fail.

"Tinder Subscriptions." Tinder. Accessed October 5, 2020. https://www.help.tinder.com/hc/en-us/articles/115004487406-Tinder-Subscriptions.

"Webby Awards: Tinder." Webby Awards. Accessed November 6, 2020. https://winners.webbyawards.com/2015/specialachievement/247/tinder.

CHAPTER 15—POKÉMON GO

"Business–Niantic." Niantic. Accessed November 12, 2020. https://nianticlabs.com/en/business/.

Chapple, Craig. "Pokémon GO Has Best Year Ever in 2019, Catching Nearly $900 Million in Player Spending." Sensor Tower. January 9, 2020. https://sensortower.com/blog/pokemon-go-has-best-year-ever-in-2019-catching-nearly-900m-usd-in-player-spending.

Chapple, Craig. "Pokémon GO Hits $1 Billion in 2020 as Lifetime Revenue Surpasses $4 Billion." Sensor Tower. November 3, 2020. https://sensortower.com/blog/pokemon-go-one-billion-revenue-2020.

Cockburn, Harry. "Pokémon GO Leads Teenage Girl to Discover Dead Body in Wyoming." *The Independent.* Accessed November 7, 2020. https://www.independent.co.uk/news/world/

americas/pokemon-go-uk-release-date-teenager-finds-dead-body-playing-game-a7128441.html.

Eadicicco, Lisa. "Pokémon Go Is Getting a Big Boost from Nostalgia." *Time.* July 12, 2016. https://time.com/4402123/pokemon-go-nostalgia/.

Etherington, Darrell. "Pokémon GO Is Officially Teaming with Starbucks for 7,800 New Gyms and PokéStops." *TechCrunch.* December 8, 2016. https://techcrunch.com/2016/12/08/pokemon-go-is-officially-teaming-with-starbucks-for-7800-new-gyms-and-pokestops/.

Kim, Larry. "9 Need-to-Know Facts on How Pokémon Go Players Engage with Businesses." *Inc.Com.* August 19, 2016. https://www.inc.com/larry-kim/9-need-to-know-facts-on-how-pokemon-go-players-engage-with-businesses.html.

Langley, Hugh. "The Best and Weirdest Pokémon Go Stories so Far." *TechRadar.* July 11, 2016. https://www.techradar.com/news/gaming/the-best-and-weirdest-pokemon-go-stories-so-far-1324692.

Lyerly, Tre. "Pokémon GO Offers Sponsored Gyms, PokéStops To Small Businesses." *Gamerant.* November 10, 2019. https://gamerant.com/pokemon-go-sponsored-gyms-pokestops/.

"Our Live Events are where it all comes together." *Niantic.* Accessed November 10, 2020. https://nianticlabs.com/niantic-live/.

Perez, Sarah. "Pokémon Go Tops Twitter's Daily Users, Sees More Engagement than Facebook." *TechCrunch.* July 13, 2016. https://

techcrunch.com/2016/07/13/pokemon-go-tops-twitters-daily-users-sees-more-engagement-than-facebook/.

Phillips, Tom. "Pokémon Go Active Player Count Highest Since 2016 Summer Launch." Eurogamer.Net. Updated June 27, 2018. https://www.eurogamer.net/articles/2018-06-27-pokemon-go-player-count-at-highest-since-2016-summer-launch.

"Pokémon Go Players on the Hunt Illegally Cross Canada-US Border | Pokémon Go." *The Guardian*. July 23, 2016. https://www.theguardian.com/technology/2016/jul/23/pokemon-go-players-illegally-cross-canada-us-border.

"Pokémon Go Teens Stuck in Caves 100 ft Underground." *BBC News*. July 15, 2016. https://www.bbc.com/news/uk-england-wiltshire-36805615.

Reynolds, Matthew. "Pokémon Go Buddy Adventure Explained - How to Get Hearts, Excited Buddies, and All Buddy Level Rewards Including Best Buddy Explained." Eurogamer. Net. Updated April 15, 2020. https://www.eurogamer.net/articles/2019-12-19-pokemon-go-buddy-adventure-play-excited-6002.

Statt, Nick. "Niantic Is Opening Its AR Platform so Others Can Make Games like Pokémon Go." *The Verge*. June 28, 2018. https://www.theverge.com/2018/6/28/17511606/niantic-labs-pokemon-go-real-world-platform-ar.

Swanner, Nate. "The Unique Way Pokémon Go Makes Money." Dice Insights. June 2, 2017. https://insights.dice.com/2017/06/02/pokemon-go-money-sponsor/.

Swant, Marty. "Pokémon Go Has Now Driven 500 Million Visits to Sponsored Locations." *Adweek*. February 28, 2017. https://www.adweek.com/digital/pokemon-go-has-now-driven-500-million-visits-to-sponsored-locations/.

Swatman, Rachel. "Pokémon Go Catches Five New World Records." Guinness World Records. August 10, 2016. https://www.guinnessworldrecords.com/news/2016/8/pokemon-go-catches-five-world-records-439327.

"The Rise of AR, Summer Adventures and Updates for the Fall." Niantic. September 11, 2018. https://nianticlabs.com/blog/summer2018recap/.

Their, Dave. "Bad News: 'Mario Kart Tour' On Mobile Has Nasty Microtransactions." *Forbes*. May 23, 2019. https://www.forbes.com/sites/davidthier/2019/05/23/bad-news-mario-kart-tour-on-mobile-has-nasty-microtransactions/?sh=1bfab1dd69e6.

Thompson, Richard. "'Pokémon Go' Fan Stabbed While Playing Game, Continues Mission to 'Catch 'Em All' after Attack." *Boston 25 News*. Updated July 13, 2016. https://www.boston25news.com/news/pokemon-go-fan-stabbed-while-playing-game-continues-mission-to-catch-em-all-after-attack/398897054/.

Vega, Nick. "'Pokémon Go' Could Make You Healthier, Study Suggests." *Business Insider*. March 13, 2017. https://www.businessinsider.com/pokmon-go-health-exercise-study-2017-3.

Wagner-Greene, V. R., A. J. Wotring, T. Castor, J. Kruger, S.Mortemore, & J. A. Dake, (2017). "Pokémon GO: Healthy or Harmful?" *American Journal of Public Health.* 107(1), 35–36. https://doi.org/10.2105/AJPH.2016.303548.

"Why Pokémon Go May Have Passed Its Peak." *BBC News.* August 24, 2016. https://www.bbc.com/news/technology-37176782.

Worthington, Danika. "Businesses Use Pokémon Go to Lure More Customers." *The Denver Post.* August 15, 2016. https://www.denverpost.com/2016/08/03/pokemon-go-business-customers/.

Made in the USA
Middletown, DE
04 February 2021